Praise for *Beyond Literary Analysis*

English teachers have been waiting for this book sir̶
chetti and Rebekah O'Dell breathe new life into thaᴛ semicomatose assignment—the analytic essay. They ask us to totally reimagine it, to examine how analysis works "in the wild"—on blogs, websites, internet reviews, and to expand the range of "texts" students can analyze (music, video games, sports teams, movies). Then drawing on their own classroom work, they show how students can use the lessons from mentor texts in their own writing. A groundbreaking and absolutely essential book.

—Thomas Newkirk, author of *Embarrassment* and *Minds Made for Stories*

Are you ready for a mind-bending journey into analytical writing? This book holds a new vision for student engagement grounded in current, authentic, and relevant texts. I guarantee it will upend your understanding of analysis. Full of sentence and passage studies that ignite student voice, minilessons that clarify the intent of organizational structures, and a deep understanding of how best to learn from a mentor text, this book will make you a better writing teacher. It's simply brilliant.

—Penny Kittle, author of *Book Love* and coauthor of *180 Days*

Allison Marchetti and Rebekah O'Dell take the dusty skeleton of literary analysis and transform it into a responsive, sophisticated, magical genre of writing that we can teach our students to develop and adore. Using this book will produce the writing that you and your students will cherish most. These are the writings they will keep—the pieces they will publish. Marchetti and O'Dell's work brings relevance, voice, and life to a form that feels crusty and brittle with directions, templates, and redundancy. This book will not only make your students better writers but it will also help them to enter into the world they encounter with greater passion and insight than ever before.

—Kate Roberts, author of *A Novel Approach* and coauthor of *Falling in Love with Close Reading*

As tour guides to a brave new world, Rebekah O'Dell and Allison Marchetti reject the well-worn path of literary analysis and guide teachers to a vibrant new analytical landscape. By reframing the idea of text as anything that has a beginning, middle, and end, O'Dell and Marchetti entertain a "bigger vision for analysis" that helps students find their passion, explore their ideas, assert authority, and build solid structures for writing. Divided into three sections, the book offers an inquiry into traditional analysis, a compendium of practical lessons, and an exploration of subgenres, such as writing about movies, music, sports, and video games. In addition, this book is chock-full of dynamic mentor texts and classroom-ready techniques that will free your students to explore the vistas vital to their lives.

—Liz Prather, author of *Project-Based Writing*

beyond
literary
analysis

beyond
literary
analysis

Teaching Students to Write
with Passion and Authority
About Any Text

ALLISON MARCHETTI · REBEKAH O'DELL

HEINEMANN • Portsmouth, NH

Heinemann

361 Hanover Street

Portsmouth, NH 03801–3912

www.heinemann.com

Offices and agents throughout the world

Library of Congress Cataloging-in-Publication Data

Names: Marchetti, Allison, author. | O'Dell, Rebekah, author.
Title: Beyond literary analysis : teaching students to write with passion and authority about any text / Allison Marchetti and Rebekah O'Dell.
Description: Portsmouth, NH : Heinemann, [2018] | Includes bibliographical references.
Identifiers: LCCN 2017043235 | ISBN 9780325092492
Subjects: LCSH: English language—Composition and exercises—Study and teaching (Secondary) | Criticism—Study and teaching (Secondary)
Classification: LCC LB1631 .M38547 2018 | DDC 808/.0420712—dc23

LC record available at https://lccn.loc.gov/2017043235

Acquisitions Editor: Katie Wood Ray
Production Editor: Sean Moreau
Cover and Interior Designs: Suzanne Heiser
Typesetter: Kim Arney
Manufacturing: Steve Bernier

Printed in the United States of America on acid-free paper
22 21 20 19   RPW   3 4 5

For Andrew,
the most passionate person I know.

—AHM

For Grandmama,
the author of *The Magic Rock Garden
and Other Stories* and
Over Adventurous Trails.

—REO

For one another,
without whom this book, this dream,
this new world of teaching and
writing and thinking together,
wouldn't exist.

—AHM & REO

Contents

A downloadable Study Guide for *Beyond Literary Analysis*
is available at hein.pub/BeyondLitAnalysis.

Acknowledgments

Together, We Thank . . .

Katie Wood Ray, for fairy-godmothering us through these surreal moments in our careers, for answering our crazy emails with eleventh-hour ideas, for complete honesty, for giving the best and most thorough feedback two writers could ask for, for believing we were capable of writing this book.

Tom Newkirk, the seeming catalyst for all of our writing, for setting us down this path in the first place, and for his time and the piece of his brain that he gave us at the Heinemann cocktail party two Novembers ago.

Katherine Bomer, whose name was on our lips and whose book was in our hands almost daily as we wrote. And Roz Linder, whose book inspired us as we dug our way out of a very deep writing hole.

Kim Arney, Vicki Boyd, Kim Cahill, Sarah Fournier, Lisa Fowler, Suzanne Heiser, Pamela Hunt, Edie Davis Quinn, Sean Moreau, Jane Orr, and Brett Whitmarsh—your tireless enthusiasm and work on our behalf makes us look so good. We are grateful for all you do for us and all you have done for this book.

Amy Krouse Rosenthal, whose creative, joy-filled spirit inspires us (and our students every year) and carried us over this finish line.

The Moving Writers staff (that's you, Karla, Hattie, Megan, Matt, Mike, Tricia, Jay, and Stefanie!) who cheered us on and shepherded our beloved blog while we were feverishly writing.

Maria and Betsy for being the very best #moms we know.

Our students, the reason we do any of this, without whose work this book would not be possible.

The teachers we meet who inspire us with enthusiasm, questions, queries, and a never-say-die spirit.

The real writers whose names fill our bibliography, whose Twitter feeds we stalk daily for new mentor text inspiration—for reminding us that the world is ripe with amazing texts (that don't always fit on bookshelves) waiting to be broken down and studied and understood; for showing us there's so much more than a five-paragraph essay and a thesis statement in your last paragraph; for inspiring us to bring real-world analysis to our students who deserve so, so much more.

Allison Thanks . . .

Joe, my partner, my rock. For rising with me at the crack of dawn (and only falling back to sleep a few times) so I could write. For keeping me level-headed and helping me make a plan. For steering my ship back on course when I lost my way.

Peter, who fueled me with inspiration in the form of countless kisses and extra-long hugs and sweet giggles.

My mom, who has been gluing all my writing into a homemade chapbook since I was little.

Rebekah Thanks . . .

Allison—"and now whatever way our stories end, I know you have rewritten mine by being my friend."

Evan, for endless, saint-like patience and sacrifice as I gave up innumerable evenings and weekends of "us time" to write . . . and vent about writing. Thank you for holding all four of us together, for cheering me on, for insisting I take breaks, and for encouraging me to press forward.

Georgia and Will, for not caring at all that I needed to write and demanding that I pay attention to what's actually important—both of you. You keep me grounded in the most wonderful way.

> We shall not cease from exploration, and the end of all our exploring will be to arrive where we started and know the place for the first time.
>
> —*T. S. Eliot,* Four Quartets

Introduction

LIKE MOST OF OUR CRAZY IDEAS, THIS BOOK WAS BORN OVER A TEXT MESSAGE CONVERSATION.

And like most of our crazy ideas, we became obsessed with it and wanted to figure it out right away.

So we pushed the stacks of literary analysis essays to the side and started reading.

We read everything. We read more Linda Holmes. And Ken Tucker. Vince Cunningham. Danny Chau. Chloi Rad. Rachel Verona Cote.

And as we read, we had a few aha moments:

- No one is writing a boring essay about *The Catcher in the Rye.*
- Analysis is everywhere—but it's about video games and athletes' seasons and the latest album and the new Netflix series.
- The writing that truly held our attention oozed with enthusiasm and expertise and was seriously fun to read.

So that meant: If our students were ever going to be able to write insightful, funny, fresh analysis like Linda, we would have to chart a new course for teaching analytical writing.

Have you finished grading the essays?

No. Read this instead: "Captain America on the Potomac."

Hang on.

Ahhh Linda Holmes. She's so super smart.

Oh, wait! Listen to this first since you're watching Orphan Black right now: "Pop Culture Happy Hour: 'Orphan Black' and Dream Sequences."

I wish I could read ALL Linda Holmes all day.

I wish our students could write like Linda Holmes.

I wish I could throw these Catcher essays away (hellppppp).

Maybe we should.

Ha.

Well.

What about next year? I say No More Catcher Essays!

Bold move.

No, I'm serious!

Well, what would that look like?

Figure 0.1: The Text Conversation That Started It All

This is the book we wish we'd had on that night of the epiphany-inducing text conversation. A book to help us map the route for our young writers who deserve so much more than the same boring literary analysis assignment that we wrote in high school and our parents wrote before us. A book that offers our students the tools that real writers use to engagingly explore a text.

Fast-forward two years. Today we sit at our desks, looking at these student titles:

- HBO's Gospel: *Game of Thrones*
- What the Cover of *To Pimp a Butterfly* Says About the American Justice System
- Sarah Kay's Way To Success: The Balance Maintained in the Poem "If I Should Have a Daughter"
- How *Sgt. Pepper's Lonely Hearts Club Band* Reflects the Beatles' Longing for Their Old Touring Days of 1963
- How to Break Up Like Beyonce: How *Lemonade* Teaches Women Empowerment and Vulnerability
- How Eric Thames Proved Little Changes Lead to Big Results in Baseball

We're so excited to share the tools that will help *your* students explore and analyze the texts they love.

What You Will Find in This Book

This book is written to help you plan instruction that supports the development of writers, specifically writers who are analyzing texts.

The book is organized into three parts. Part 1 is an immersion into analytical writing that is current, authentic, and relevant to the students we teach today. We'll use the language of exploration to frame a new way of thinking about analysis. This process of analyzing a text is not unlike an explorer setting sail in search of a new land—a metaphor we'll draw on throughout this book to emphasize the discovery that is possible when students analyze texts of their own choosing.

In the first few pages of Chapter 1, we introduce you to a favorite analytical mentor text and show you how it does everything we want our students to be able to do, and so much more. Our goal in this part of the book is to free up *your* thinking about analytical writing so you can see it for what it truly is—an opportunity to explore a text with passion and authority.

We explore how analysis has been understood and taught in classrooms of the past and imagine what analytical writing can be in classrooms today (Chapter 2). In Chapter 3, we introduce you to the essential tools of authentic analysis—passion, ideas, structure, and authority—through another full mentor text (music analysis you can use in your classroom tomorrow!).

Sections 2 and 3 each begin with their own introduction. Section 2 is your lesson book—your guide to helping students find and explore and write about the texts they love. In "Exploring Passion," we show you how to nurture students' real-life passions. Like a bellows that blows oxygen-rich air into a fire, passion is a tool that can ignite your students' engagement with all sorts of texts, from traditional literature to the most esoteric of video games. In "Exploring Ideas," we show you how to help students identify texts within their passions, find writing topics, and develop fresh ideas that can be supported with evidence. In the next chapter, "Exploring Structure," we examine different ways to organize ideas using structures borrowed from the brightest and most engaging analytical writers. From the one-sentence paragraph to the last-paragraph claim, this chapter will encourage you to think outside traditional analytical frameworks in favor of new structures that add voice and interest to your students' writing. Finally, in "Exploring Authority," we offer tools to help students charge their writing with authority. Students with a lot of passion but little knowledge of their topic will learn how to gather information and infuse their writing with genre-specific vocabulary while staying true to their own voice.

Section 3 promises to be dog-eared and worn by the time you're finished with it. Organized into six mini chapters that explore different subgenres of analytical writing, it's your analysis almanac. Each chapter is jam-packed with our absolute favorite mentors, mentor texts, and "cheat sheets" for supporting students who are analyzing texts you've never heard of (Playdead's *INSIDE*, anyone? Clue: It's a video game our students are wild about).

The first three mini chapters explore the subgenres most of our students choose to write about: movie and television, music, and sports. Then, we enter the world of video game writing—some of the smartest, deepest analysis we've ever encountered. Finally, we walk you through a study of literary analysis A) because this is what we live for as English teachers; B) because you *will* have students who *choose* to write about literature (we were these students); and C) the literary analysis we've curated will change the way you think about literary analysis (goodbye five-paragraph essays) and the way you view your students' engagement with literature as readers and writers (they *do* have interesting, never-been-heard-before ideas to share!).

And because we don't know the students sitting in your classrooms like you do, and we don't know what fills their hearts and makes them who they are, Section 3 closes with a make-your-own-analysis-resources chapter. Here we walk you through our process for gathering resources to guide and inspire students and make it possible to teach through small-group instruction and writing conferences.

With samples throughout the book, you will see what students of all levels and experiences can do when they're invited into the world of authentic analysis and supported with mentor texts, targeted writing instruction, and the opportunity to write about their passions.

This book is for teachers who want to revive the art of analytical writing in their classrooms—from teachers of middle-grade writers who are making their first foray into analytical writing to teachers of experienced twelfth-grade writers who are looking ahead to college where their professors will expect much, much more.

In this book, we invite you to explore your teaching of analytical writing from a new perspective. To open your mind to the real world of analytical writing and challenge traditional notions about what students should be analyzing and how they should write. In short, we invite you to arrive where you started and know it for the first time—and to share this journey with your students and celebrate the writing that is born where passion and analysis meet.

CHAPTER ONE

analysis in the wild

A world of exciting, authentic analytical writing is at your fingertips if you just look for it. It's waiting for you on your Twitter feed and in your in-box. You listen to it on the drive home as NPR plays in the background. It's on the podcast you savor in quiet evening hours after a day's work. It's in the writing around the sports stats your students track as often as they breathe. Even literary analysis—the kind you thought lived only in dusty library books in the reference section or inside students' binders in the form of five-paragraph essays—exists if you look for it.

When you open your eyes and ears to the real world of analysis, you will discover powerful writing full of voice and passion. You will discover the smartest writing about your favorite players and your favorite movies and your favorite books. Writing that makes you think. Writing that inspires. Writing that is a far cry from the formulaic analysis you knew as a student.

Right here at the beginning, we want to show you a piece of *this kind* of analysis. The kind of analysis that exists in the wild. Authentic analysis.

Passionate, Authentic Analysis: A Mentor Text

In "By Heart," a semimonthly column series in *The Atlantic*, Joe Fassler interviews famous authors and then crafts their responses into exciting, authentic literary analysis. These pieces do not have five paragraphs or three-part thesis statements. No, the writing in this column bears few marks of classroom literary analysis. Instead, it has heart.

Based on a conversation with Anna North, a "By Heart" essay about *The Odyssey* is an example of all that analytical writing can be—compelling and thoughtful, cohesive and fresh. The essay does the thinking we want our students to do; it makes an argument about a text and supports it with evidence.

But it does so much more than that, too. It sings. It has highlighter-worthy passages. We have bookmarked and Evernoted and annotated it many times over. It contains life lessons. It does all the things that a fabulous, worthwhile piece of writing should and can do. And it's analysis.

As teachers, whenever we read, we wear our writing teacher hat. We consider how we could use this piece of writing with our students—how it could inspire and guide them in their own writing studies. So as you read, consider:

- What makes this piece of analysis compelling?
- How is this piece *similar to* writing your students are doing about literature?
- How is this piece *different from* what your students are writing about literature?

Writing Is the Process of Abandoning the Familiar

By Joe Fassler, "By Heart," *The Atlantic*

[. . .]

> North begins her exploration of *The Odyssey* with a personal anecdote about her grandfather.

Anna North: My grandfather first recommended *The Odyssey* to me. When he died a few years ago, I went looking for my original copy because I wanted to read from it at the funeral. I found it in my parents' house, with the original receipt still inside. So I could date exactly when I first got the book: I was eleven years old.

> The beginning of her exploration considers her very first encounters with this text— what she loved, what she was drawn to, what surprised her.

I have strong memories of reading it for the first time. *The Odyssey*'s a great book for kids. A lot happens. There's strangeness, magic, excitement. Of course, the names are very weird to a modern person, and I remember getting tripped up over that. But still, I loved it.

> In Chapter 4, we'll look at how childhood passions can become fodder for analytical writing years later!

It's an obsession that's stayed with me into adult life. I've always been interested in Greek and Latin literature. I'm excited by the ways those traditions show how old our concerns are. If you read Livy, for

Figure 1.1: Anna North discusses *The Odyssey* in *The Atlantic*'s "By Heart" Column

instance, you find that almost everything that's said in American politics had probably said by the Romans, too: everything from concerns about men not being manly enough anymore to debates about the kinds of things the founding fathers cared about. With *The Odyssey*, it's possible to see how many of the stories we still tell exist in ancient texts—they're archetypal. There are things that human beings like to talk about, and always have, and a quest is one of them.

For me, *The Odyssey* is more appealing than *The Iliad* and other war narratives. Compared to *The Iliad*, which may be more widely read, I think of *The Odyssey* as a book that's much more feminist. There are almost no women in *The Iliad* at all, because it's about a war in which basically no women were allowed to fight. *The Odyssey*, by contrast, has female characters, and they're much more interesting. They're ancient Greek, so they're not generally in positions of power, and yet some of them are very powerful. They are witches. They can turn you into a pig—things like that. There's lots of interesting thinking, too, on the ways in which Odysseus himself might be feminine or embody feminine qualities. As a character, his whole thing is less about his prowess and battle and more about his wits. The first line talks about how he's a man of twists and turns, which is one of his epithets—and though it's stereotypical to say that a woman couldn't be good at war and would only be good at twists and turns, it does feel like he has a gender-bending aspect as a character.

Obviously, *The Odyssey* is a hero-quest story, and that's one reason I became so fixated on it. I'm really interested in how someone becomes a hero or an icon. In what ways do you have to give up part of your humanity, your human life, when you're a hero? Odysseus obviously gives up a huge chunk of his life—time with his family, his ability to do normal things. But, by contrast, what does he gain? What are the ways that you become larger than life when you're a hero? In what ways can you become superhuman?

For a long time, I've been obsessed with this particular part of *The Odyssey* where Tiresias, the seer, explains to Odysseus what he has to do before he can really go home for good. The whole drama of the book has been Odysseus' getting home to Penelope and all her suitors. You'd think he'd be done after he returns, kills all those men, and

North zooms out and starts to hint at why these ideas matter beyond the text itself.

North uses comparison as a kind of evidence—a great option for our student writers, too!

North shares an idea about female characters in *The Odyssey* and supports it with specific examples— including the nuanced example of Odysseus himself!

North uses casual, colloquial language (like "his whole thing") throughout her very smart analysis.

North uses first person a lot, and yet her thinking about the text is smart and authoritative. Might our students be able to try this move in their writing?

Her use of rhetorical questions prompts the reader to get involved (and also want to keep reading!).

Figure 1.1: *continued*

continues

reclaims his family. Instead, Tiresias tells him that he has to do one more thing:

Look! Textual evidence! We English teachers know what this is!

> But after you have dealt out death—in open
>
> combat or by stealth—to all the suitors,
>
> go overland on foot, and take an oar,
>
> until one day you come where men have lived
>
> with meat unsalted, never known the sea
>
> nor seen seagoing ships, with crimson bows
>
> and oars that fledge light hulls for dipping flight.
>
> The spot will soon be plain to you, and I
>
> can tell you how: some passerby will say,
>
> 'What winnowing fan is that upon your shoulder?'
>
> Halt, and implant your smooth oar in the turf
>
> and make fair sacrifice to Lord Poseidon:
>
> a ram, a bull, a great buck boar: turn back,
>
> and carry out pure hekatombs at home
>
> to all wide heaven's lords, the undying gods,
>
> to each in order. Then a seaborne death
>
> soft as this hand of mist will come upon you
>
> when you are wearied out with rich old age,
>
> your country folk in blessed peace around you.
>
> And all this shall be just as I foretell.

Here, North paraphrases the text and then uses "in other words" to help her discuss exactly what that evidence means.

Tiresias instructs Odysseus that, before he can go home, he must take his oar and walk inland until someone mistakes it for a winnowing fan—a tool for winnowing grain—and asks him what it is. In other words, as soon as he's gone to a place where people don't know what an oar is, then he's gone far enough. If he plants the oar in the earth and makes an offering there, then he can go home. But he has to make this symbolic gesture of going so far away that his

Figure 1.1: *continued*

BEYOND LITERARY ANALYSIS

North
acknowledges what
is strange and
complicated in the
text. Our students
usually don't have
confidence to do this
because they think
they need to know
it all before they can
even begin writing.

North shows
vulnerability and
voice by continually
connecting her
interpretation of
the text to her own
feelings about and
reactions to the text.

North zooms
in on one personal
anecdote as
further evidence.

North is unafraid
to look at other
perspectives. This
brings nuance to
her ideas.

We love North's
turn of phrase
here—"But there's
a way of thinking
about this particular
passage . . ."—as
a means to discuss
the evidence from a
new angle.

A personal
experience as
supporting evidence!
Our students could
do this, too!

oar—the thing he's based his life on—becomes unrecognizable. Only then can he return home safely.

As advice, it doesn't make a whole lot of sense. There are a lot of instructions like this in *The Odyssey*: strange, inexplicable things you must do to avoid incurring the wrath of gods. But there's a way of thinking about this particular passage that *does* make sense to me: If the point of this book is to go on a journey, then to finish it you have to go away as far as possible before you can truly return and be done.

In a funny way, this takes Odysseus down a peg. He's a known hero to the Greeks, and he's been the hero of this story. I love the idea that, before he can go home, he has to go to this place where he's totally humbled. Not only do they not know who he is, they don't even know what his *oar* is. He's meaningless to them—and that's an interesting thing to force him to do.

I think a lot about home and away, and that's one reason this passage feels resonant to me. I've felt very conflicted about where my home is ever since I left Los Angeles, which is where I'm from. In all the places where I've lived, I've asked myself: Am I home now? It's a hard question for me to answer. But I like having this passage, which helps me define what *not* home is. This is how you know when you're really not home—when something precious to you becomes unrecognizable to everyone else—and that feels helpful to me.

An example is when I moved to New York after getting my MFA in Iowa City. I'd lived here not that long—maybe a month. And one day I walked into this coffee shop wearing these bright green pants. The guy behind the counter said, "Nice pants! Where did you get those?"

I told him I got them in Iowa City. He was like, "Where's that?"

And I said, "Um, it's in eastern Iowa."

"Oh," he said, "I thought it was a *store*."

That was the oar moment.

But there's an opposite of that type of moment, too: If you're far from home, but then you meet someone from your home, or see something you also have at home, and you have this enormous sense of recognition.

Another aspect of this comes up for me related to the fact that Odysseus basically has to do something for no reason. There's no clear reason why he should take this long journey Tiresias asks him to go on, and that's a lot like writing. Writing is this strange impulse, not a

Figure 1.1: *continued*

continues

very practical impulse, and it doesn't make sense to everyone. But for some reason—if you have the impulse—you have to do it anyway. You have to go on this long journey and do something that's really hard, and all of it *for no real reason*. I don't entirely mean that. I love reading, and I think books are so important, and both writing and reading give me a lot of pleasure. I think they have real meaning. And yet, it's not like you've built something when you write a novel. You're not producing anything physical. You're putting symbols together. Just the way that what Odysseus is asked to do is symbolic—planting his oar in the ground is a symbolic gesture.

> North uses "just the way" as another phrase to help her clearly tie personal experience (writing) to the text (Odysseus' journey).

On a different level, though, Odysseus' act has actual meaning: Presumably, the gods would be angry if he didn't do it. There could be real-life consequences if he fails to perform this action. Similarly, if you're someone who really loves writing, it can be really hard if you don't listen to that impulse. There could be real-life consequences, at least in terms of you feeling sad.

> North uses the dreaded "I think," but this piece feels far from wishy-washy or weak.

It might sound cheesy, but I think writing is a kind of a journey. For me, especially if I'm working on a novel, it takes at least a year of fumbling around before I really get anywhere. As you try to imagine yourself into this world, it's a process of writing stuff, throwing it out, writing, throwing it out. You're trying to create this place for yourself inside your head; it's very hard to get to that place, and it takes a long time to get there. But then, finally, there is the sense that maybe you've arrived, though you've had to discard a ton of stuff along the way.

> North zooms out again—connecting her experience and the text to a bigger idea about all human experience.

Sometimes I wish someone could tell me: *Just go to this specific place, and then you'll be there.* I think that's why I like that passage so much. It's almost a fantasy to imagine that someone would tell exactly how to get somewhere creatively, and you could just go there, and then you would know. "The spot will become plain to you," Tiresias says. And yet it's true with writing that, every now and then, you do get a feeling of total rightness. Suddenly, you can say: *Yes, now I'm in the right place with this piece of work*. That's when you can plant your oar in the turf.

> It's powerful when North directly tells us that she likes this passage—we can tell her analysis comes from a place of passion.

That feeling is the only thing I can use as a guide for when things are going well. There's so much wandering. But every now and then you have this clarity, and—ding!—the sudden sense that things are where they're supposed to be.

Figure 1.1: *continued*

The *How* of Analysis That Does So Much More

This compelling piece of writing is literary analysis, but it doesn't feel like it. At least not the kind we are used to reading in our classrooms. Unlike the dry, formulaic writing our students often produce about literature, this essay has a pulse. But how is that achieved? As teachers of writing, we need to be able to articulate the *how* of a writer's craft in order to teach students *how*. Over the next few paragraphs, we will explore the *how* in this piece as we might explain it to our students, and since we know the voice behind the analysis is North's, we'll refer to her as the writer.

Makes Personal Connections

North's writing is deeply personal: She invokes her grandfather in the first paragraph, sharing a private memory about searching for her first copy of *The Odyssey*, the "original receipt still inside," so she could read from it at his funeral. Through this anecdote, North invites the reader into her life while sharing an important lesson about books: They are timeless, and readers can return to them again and again throughout their lives, seeking something different each time.

In the next paragraph, she expands this anecdote, sharing a bit about her experiences reading it as a child. She remembers stumbling through the "weird" character names but acknowledging that she loved it nonetheless. She then transitions into her experience with *The Odyssey* as an adult, zooming out to remark on the timelessness of Greek and Latin literature—the first iterations of "the stories we still tell" today.

Communicates Voice

As we read these first few paragraphs, we are transported to a coffee shop in our minds. It's as if North is sitting across from us at a small square table telling us about her literary predilections. "It's an obsession that's stayed with me into my adult life," she whispers, taking a sip of steamed milk. Casual phrases like "I've always been interested in" and "There's a lot of interesting thinking" pull us into North's world as if we were flipping through the pages of her writer's notebook.

North uses her personal connection to *The Odyssey* to explain why she prefers it to other war narratives—because it's "a book that's much more feminist." To support this argument, she cites the power of female characters (for example, they are witches and can turn humans into animals) and Odysseus' feminine qualities.

The next paragraph is one of our favorites because you can see North's thinking unfolding right in front of you. She uses rhetorical questions about heroism to transition to her main argument about Odysseus and the hero's quest.

Offers Text Evidence

In order to present her claim about quests, she hones in on a single passage from *The Odyssey*. First, she contextualizes the passage by explaining what is happening in the book: Odysseus has just returned home and killed all of Penelope's suitors, but he is not finished yet. Then she introduces the twenty-line passage. Following the excerpt, North provides a brief summary of the passage: Tiresias instructs Odysseus to take his oar and walk far enough away from home that people do not recognize the oar for what it is.

States a Claim

In the eighth paragraph, North presents her claim. Marked by a colon and the wonderfully casual phrase, "But there's a way of thinking about this passage . . . ," she presents a thematic analysis of the epic as a whole: "If the point of this book is to go on a journey, then to finish it you have to go away as far as possible before you can truly return and be done."

North riffs on this idea in two ways. First, she discusses the impact of Tiresias' instruction on Odysseus, noting that Odysseus, a great hero, becomes "meaningless" to the people who don't recognize the oar. Then, she zooms out again, thinking about the hero's journey in the context of her own life. To support her claim about journeys, North shares the green pants anecdote about when she moved to New York City and refers to it as an "oar moment"—one of the things we love most about this essay for its clever language.

Finally, North links the oar, a symbol of Odysseus' identity, to its larger significance in the world.

Brings Closure

Finally, North zooms out at the conclusion, drawing a connection between her claim about *The Odyssey* and the writing life. When she shares her wish in the penultimate paragraph, it's as if she's leaning toward us, across the table, sharing a passionate, relatable secret: "Sometimes I wish someone could tell me: Just go to this specific place, and then you'll be there."

* * *

Isn't it refreshing to read a piece of analysis that's as cozy as a coffee date with an old friend and as smart as something you'd read in *The Atlantic*? In this powerful essay, we find all the things we want our students to be able to do—make a fresh claim, support it with evidence, choose a meaningful structure—and so much more. Honestly, reading this essay is one of the most pleasant and satisfying experiences we've ever had with literary analysis.

A Bigger Vision for Analysis

What would it take to get our students to write more like this? A bigger vision for analysis.

Taking our cues from North's piece and the thousands of others we've read to inform our instruction, we would like to broaden the definition of analysis for the twenty-first-century classroom, so that it is, at once, deeper and richer but also incredibly simple: *Authentic analysis is a piece of writing that explores a text.*

The word *analysis* comes from the Greeks, and a close look at its etymology reveals an original meaning that seems to convey the exact opposite of the drilled-down literary forms of the past. Analysis is "a breaking up, a loosening, releasing," a noun form of the Greek word *analyein*—"unloose, release, set free; to loose a ship from its moorings."

Let's break down this new definition of analysis:

"A Piece of Writing . . ."

Analytical writing isn't just one thing. Sometimes writers analyze a text in what Katherine Bomer (2016) calls a "journey of thought" essay, starting in one place, meandering through a maze of different but related ideas, and reaching a sense of conclusion by the end. Sometimes writers break apart a text through argument. Readers also encounter compelling analysis in reviews of a text. While the close kind of analysis we value in the classroom isn't the primary task of a review, critics do make a claim ("This movie is great!" or "This is the worst film of the year.") and support it with evidence. Often, reviews dip in and out of moments of close reading and analysis of the text at hand.

As we immersed ourselves in analytical writing, we noticed patterns in the kind of work writers were doing, and we named these patterns using student-friendly language. The chart below (Figure 1.2) highlights these diverse types of analysis that live in the wild.

Type	Definition
Impact	• Impact analysis looks at the effect a text has on something larger than itself. *Example claim:* Kendrick Lamar has revolutionized hip-hop.
Personal Connection	• Personal Connection analysis looks at how a text affects the person analyzing the text. *Example claim:* John Lewis' *March* made me a civil rights activist.
Themes, Lessons, and Deeper Meanings	• The biggest category of analysis, Themes, Lessons, and Deeper Meanings analysis tries to determine the message beneath the surface of a text. *Example claim:* In "River of Tears," Alessia Cara's use of opposites contributes to emotional tension.
Review	• Reviews make a judgment about the overall success of a text by evaluating the effectiveness of the elements that constitute it. *Example claim:* The Patriot's Super Bowl win came down to one simple play.
Trends and Patterns	• Trends and Patterns analysis looks at why a text is "in style" or how it has evolved over time. *Example claim:* Today's true crime podcasts and documentaries are America's new monster stories.
Footprints and Connections	• Footprints and Connections analysis considers how a text is related to or influenced by other texts. *Example claim:* Reading Obiama's *The Fisherman* feels like reading Chinua Achebe.
New Angles	• New Angles analysis brings a new perspective to something people assume is already understood. It asks the reader to look at a text in a new way. *Example claim: House of Cards* isn't about politics. It's about marriage.

Figure 1.2: Types of Analysis

"... That Explores ..."

Traditional, academic literary analysis students are taught in school does not explore; it is the artifact of prepared and hardened thinking. A student begins with a hard-and-fast take on the text and walks through the way the text demonstrates that idea. By contrast, Abby Rabinowitz (2016), a professor of writing at Columbia University, characterizes the job of a writer of analysis this way: "Being a writer has little to do with arguing a claim to the bitter end and everything to do with acknowledging that an argument worth making is full of complications and contradictions—that there are no simple truths" (np).

True analysis, the kind written by professionals and that people *choose* to read, looks closely at a topic as a way of exploring its nuances, its tiny details, its contradictions. When a writer does this—grabs a text and holds it up to the light to see all of its sides—she ends up probing the meaning instead of proclaiming it. By the end, both the writer and the reader have arrived at a new, deeper understanding of the text.

"... A Text."

Teachers are often encouraged to get the right book in the hand of the right student at the right time. This is when reading magic happens. The same is true for writing; in authentic analysis, those "right texts" are the texts students will choose to analyze for themselves.

As you can see from the examples in the chart earlier, we use the term *text* broadly. While the word historically connotes something written, we've loosed the ship from its moorings and consider a *text* to be *anything that has a beginning, middle, and end that can be broken down into smaller pieces and studied.* This broadening of the definition of "text" is what allows students to write about dance, sports, art, video games, television, music, fashion, sports cars, and, yes, books.

As you move through this book and encounter the many examples of exciting, authentic analysis, consider what might be possible if we broaden our definition so that students' analysis becomes more about "loosing" a text, "releasing" its nuances and meaning, and setting ideas free.

CHAPTER TWO

toward a new understanding of analysis

I n Chapter 1, we presented a new, broader definition of analysis. In order to understand how we arrived at this new definition, we need to think about how analysis has traditionally been taught. Our seniors have had a lot of experience writing analysis in school, so we asked them to sketch an image that displays what they think about when they hear the word "analysis." Here's what we saw when we studied their images:

- Analysis has been a series of idea assembly lines, formulas, seek-and-finds, and clinical strategies to uncover the one, objective "deeper meaning" of a written text.

- Many drawings revealed the influence of an authority—a teacher—determining if their analysis is "right" or "wrong."

- Many depicted the work of analysis as scientific—finding data, looking for patterns. James Moffett (1994) calls this an attempt to "scientize literature" (22). Coincidentally, almost half of the students' images included a magnifying glass.

- All the drawings focused on analysis of *literary* texts.

What do these sketches reveal about the experience of analysis in the high school classroom? For the most part, the humanity has been squeezed out of it, joy is absent, and objective rights and wrongs prevail.

This is a far cry from an explorer setting out to make discoveries and share them with others.

But this is the way it has always been. Our students' experience of English class is similar to generations of English students before us. The close study and interpretation of texts has been the central work of literature courses since Plato and Socrates. Until the late 1960s, high school and college English courses were strictly focused on literature, and analytical writing in the English classroom was "usurped as an instrument for evaluating reading" (Moffett 1994, 23). The critical literary analysis essay has been the dominant mode of writing in high school English classrooms since the mid-twentieth century when New Criticism took hold of the academic literary world.

New Criticism, a rejection of "old criticism," which largely focused on reading texts in relation to their historical and biographical context, attempted to make literary study more like science as readers explicated a text through close reading. The goal: to identify the parts and pieces of a text and then figure out how they work (Delahoyde 2011). In mechanically examining the text-and-nothing-but-the-text, students are instructed to ignore their own human experience and response to their reading. (*Never* use the first person, for goodness sake!) A detached, clinical touch in writing has not only been valued but encouraged.

Things haven't changed much: Enter many high school English classrooms today, and, for the most part, you will still see a "writing program that services the reading program," focused on churning out essays of literary analysis to prove that texts have been read and understood (Moffett 1994, 23). We ask students to develop a thesis statement about a text. (Sometimes we give them the thesis statement.) We ask them to compare and contrast or to unravel the theme. Analysis in the secondary English class means *literary* analysis.

The Problem with *Just* Literary Analysis

Imagine being an explorer pitching this expedition to a potential patron:

> *We want to take a very expensive boat filled with a large crew and lots of supplies. We will risk lives and a lot of your money. And, if we arrive at our intended destination, we will be exploring a land we discovered sixty years*

ago. A land we've explored time and again for the last handful of decades. A land we already know like the backs of our hands.

It's doubtful that many investors would jump at this opportunity. After all, what would be the point? Where's the adventure? Where's the discovery? What's to be gained?

For English teachers, literary analysis is the exploration of this well-known land. It's what we love. It's where we feel comfortable. Through our own academic experiences, "we understand the value of writing as a way of learning literature because we have had the experience . . . of coming to know the texts we have written about differently" (Blau 2003, 152). And it might seem like the way English class is *supposed* to be—our territory is the Land of Literary Analysis. Why would we go anywhere else?

Certainly, we believe there is a place for authentic, meaningful analysis of literature in our classrooms, the kind of literary analysis you just encountered in Chapter 1. Not only has literary analysis been at the heart of our academic tradition, but closely reading and deeply unpacking literature is a cognitively complex and extremely rewarding endeavor. And we want our students to experience this—to come to know a text differently through writing about it.

That said, we think there is *more*. Our classroom analytical writing also needs to make new discoveries.

Literary-analysis-only is far too limiting. But there is another problem. More often than not, students' literary analysis is lackluster. Let's be honest—we have struggled in the past to pull strong literary analysis out of our students. We bet you have, too. (In fact, it might just be why you picked up this book.) At best, students write perfunctory essays that regurgitate the ideas discussed in class. These essays have all the right parts and pieces in the right order, but they lack voice, spirit, insight, revelation, heart. They lack a person on the other side of the page. Like students who dutifully follow a formula, teachers feel frustrated, bored, and uninspired. This isn't what any of us envisioned when we imagined our students digging into literature and crafting pieces of writing. Where did we go wrong? Let's explore why this literary-analysis-only approach falls short.

Students Don't Have the Authority to Write Literary Analysis Well

College English majors are (small-time) literary experts. We get the tropes and know the lingo. After years of study, we have read what has been said before, and we intuitively know what makes our own arguments float. We bring a lot of content knowledge to the table before we ever begin the writing process. We don't have to learn how to read and interpret literature as we write. We just write.

Moreover, when we were students, we had a stake in the analysis we were writing—not just because we wanted to make the grade but because we loved the texts themselves. This passion coupled with our knowledge gave us authority to commit our claims about literature to paper.

Most of our students don't come with this authority, though. Many are not passionate about the literature they are assigned in school, and none of them have studied long enough or read widely enough to effectively enter the bigger conversation about literature. We ask our students "to be an authority on something they know little about. The writer is pinned to the ground by a topic and a voice wrestled out, which of course leads to stilted, awkward writing" (Kittle 2008, 31). They are not collegiate academics; it shouldn't surprise us that they can't write like them.

Imagine being asked to write an analysis of the stock market. If you are like us, this would take an incredible amount of detailed research—first, to understand the basics of the stock market. Then, to consider the current trends. And then to develop theories about what might be leading those trends. We would need to read a lot of stock market analysis to learn the lingo and conventions of economic analysis. And this is all before we could ever dream of sitting down to draft something. How would we feel? Overwhelmed? Unqualified? Completely adrift?

Many students have this relationship with literature. They don't know the basics, so they have to play catch up. They spend most of their mental energy attempting to parse out patterns and make theories about content they do not fully grasp. Because our students don't have the content knowledge they need to successfully analyze literature, teachers play catch up, trying to teach content and writing skills simultaneously. Neither the literature nor the writing wins.

Writing Instruction Is Sacrificed on the Altar of Literature Instruction

How do you teach a student everything she needs to know to think critically and creatively about *The Sun Also Rises* and also teach her everything she needs to know to write a meaningful, nuanced, and fresh analysis of the book? Perhaps if we had all year to study this one text, we could do it. But the realities of our classrooms make this impossible. And while we might revel in Hemingway immersion, many of our students would surely suffer.

Facing the need to teach a text and to have students write about it and to move swiftly through a packed curriculum, one of two things tends to happen. Either the teacher focuses on the literature at the expense of the writing (which is assigned as an afterthought rather than taught), or the teacher waters down the writing requirements so that students can be moderately successful.

We haven't just seen this—we have done this! In her third year of teaching, Rebekah found herself at the helm of a tenth-grade inclusion class in which students struggled with the very basics of reading and writing. Her task was to teach *Of Mice and Men* and have students compose a literary essay. After slogging through weeks of comprehension activities, she decided to give students a template for a three-page essay. She created lines where students could fill in their synopsis of the text, a one-sentence thesis statement (certainly the last sentence of the first paragraph!), topic sentences for each body paragraph, a quote from the text, an explanation of the quote, and a conclusion. This helpful document turned out to be five pages of outline for a three-page paper.

This is what we do when we give our students a task on which they cannot succeed—we water down. We control, control, control. In the absence of critical thinking and true analysis, we give fill-in-the-blank outlines, hand students thesis statements, offer up formulas until we think they can be successful. Ultimately, none of our objectives for either the literature or the writing are met. When we ask students with little literary knowledge to write analysis of that text, we are asking them to learn two challenging things at once. And that just won't lead to success. We might win in one court but only when we forgo the other.

Traditional Literary Analysis Has Limited Relevance to Students' Present—and Future—Lives

At NCTE 2015 in Minneapolis, we met teacher Jennifer Brinkmeyer (@jjbrinkmeyer). As we chatted about writing workshops and mentor texts, she expressed a frustration with literary analysis writing that we think is nearly universal. She had been studying *Romeo and Juliet* with her students, and after weeks of reading and discussing the text, priming them with engagement activities, and making connections to their own lives, students needed (according to her curriculum guide) to write about . . . motifs in the play. The frustration was visible as Jennifer exclaimed, "Is this really why we spent six weeks studying this?"

We have felt that frustration, too. We work hard to get our students to engage with literature—especially classic literature. We tell students that we study literature as a way of understanding the world, our history, our culture, others' experiences, ourselves, but then the writing products we assign don't reflect those new understandings. The writing starts—and stops—at the text itself.

Few educators have advocated for students to be able to write about the passions of their own hearts like Donald Murray. He reminds us that:

> *Our students want to write of death and love and hate and fear and loyalty and disloyalty; they want to write the themes of literature in those forms— poetry, narrative, drama—which have survived the centuries. They want to write literature, and we assign them papers of literary analysis, comparison and contrast, argumentation based on subjects on which they are not informed and for which they have no concern. (Murray 1977, 146)*

Here's the thing: traditional, academic analysis is only published in university literary journals, written and read by professional academics. Outside of academia, this kind of writing does not exist. So, when we focus solely on this mode of analytical writing, what are we preparing students for? Life as an English professor, a small percentage of the 3.7% of professional academics in the United States (Bureau of Labor and Statistics)?

When we invite students to write analytically about a text, they engage in critical thinking and stretch their analytical muscles—a worthy exercise in and of itself. But if students' written analysis never extends outside of the realm of literature, we fail to help them see the relevance of English class in their lives, and as a result, we fail to develop versatile writers who can write for multiple occasions and purposes.

Students need practice making claims about a wide variety of "texts," finding evidence that isn't solely quotes from a book, and discovering structures that make analysis crystalize in many different disciplines. They will not be in English class forever (the English major itself is on a rapid decline); students must practice analytical writing about more than just literature (Flaherty 2015). If a writing curriculum centered purely on literary analysis lacks relevance to the students' experience of a text, it also lacks relevance to the other kinds of analytical writing they will need to do in their education and in their career.

The point is this: there is more to analytical writing than *just* literary analysis. We need a bigger vision for what analytical writing can look like in our classrooms—one that encourages writers to explore new places, plays on students' passions, prepares them for future writing, engages their minds, and truly reveals deeper understanding of the text at hand.

But Isn't Literary Analysis Our Job?

Research, literary analysis papers our students have written over the years, and our guts all tell us that we need to find a balance between teaching literary analysis and analysis of nonliterary texts. The standards are singing the same tune. From the Common Core to individual state standards, analytical writing objectives are centered around skills, not literature.

Figure 2.1 synthesizes the writing skills detailed in the Common Core Standards (CCSS). Two of these standards (9–10.9.A–B and 11–12.9.A–B) link reading instruction to students' writing tasks, but the others do not specify what students should write claims about. What the standards *do* detail are the main skills of analytical writing: making claims, supporting claims with evidence, logically organizing ideas through a unifying structure, considering one's audience. And the standards specify that students should use a meaningful process for writing.

What follows are our takeaways from studying these standards.

Content

- Make claims.
- Distinguish claims from counterclaims.
- Support claims with evidence.
- Write with a sense of organization and style that is appropriate to and aware of the task, purpose, and audience.
- Write analysis of literary fiction and nonfiction texts studied as a class.

Writing Process

- Use elements of the writing process (planning, drafting, revision).
- Conduct research to solve problems and answer questions.
- Gather information from relevant sources.

Figure 2.1: Writing Skills of the Common Core Standards (9–12)

Students Need Not **Only** *Analyze Literature*

As long as students are receiving ample practice in writing claims, supporting those claims with evidence, and organizing their ideas, they will be meeting the standards. Nowhere do the standards—Common Core or state—indicate that students should be writing solely about literature in English class.

Since two standards do ask that students incorporate their reading into their writing, we are not advocating that teachers erase all literary analysis from the plan book. Analyzing literature in writing is a skill that should and must be practiced in English class. But it isn't the only one.

We need to strike a balance between asking students to make claims about literary texts and other texts—sports, movies, art exhibits, sports games, music. Even when teaching literary analysis, we need to make that writing authentic and true to what real writers do.

The Process Teaches the Product

The standards include using elements of the writing process—choosing a topic, planning, drafting, revising, publishing. When we assign students to write about a text we've chosen and ideas we have preselected and in a structure we have determined for them, we are essentially giving students a Get Out of Planning Free card. Perhaps this is why many students wait until the night before to draft their papers. When your teacher hands you the topic or the text, she has done what many writers would say is the hardest part of writing—honing in on an idea and planning its development. How is a writer supposed to discover his process when his writing assignments preclude some of the most crucial steps in that process?

Furthermore, giving students texts and topics doesn't match what professional writers do. While it's true that many writers (of newspapers and magazines especially) are assigned topics by their editors, these writers have chosen to work for these specific publications and have chosen to write within a certain content area. Professional writers are also given free range to explore and develop the topic in whatever direction their research leads and in the structure that works best. Most of our students have not signed up to write about literature. But when it's required, shouldn't they choose which aspect of a text to explore—especially if we want them to engage in the assignment in a meaningful way?

Finally, the process objectives ask that we invite students to conduct research to solve problems and answer questions, which causes us to ask: Whose problems? Whose questions? Ideally, the students'. If we want students to write authentically about literature, we must lead them in choosing their own texts—literary or otherwise—and in pursuing research that will help them answer their own questions and solve their own writing problems. Writer and college composition professor John Warner writes, "If we want students to truly write well . . . we must require students to engage in a much more rigorous curriculum centered on the most important skill all writers must practice: making choices. Writers choose what they want to write about (subject), who they want to write to (audience), and why they're writing (purpose). . . . Instruction that ignores these dimensions will prevent students from developing meaningful writing practices" (Strauss 2017).

Authentic Analysis: Exploring a Bigger World Through Passion

If a writing curriculum focused on literary analysis, with chosen texts and topics and thesis statements, sorely limits our writers, what else can we do? How do we teach the skills of analytical writing that students will need to read and write for the rest of their lives?

Remembering that literature is "only one way of viewing the world" (Murray 1968, 117), we add more territory to our expedition. We keep some literary analysis. But, rather than being formulaic and devoid of voice, we find examples of literary analysis in the wild—the kind that demands the writer bring his experience to bear on the text and build connections about how the text impacts people, communities, our world. Thinking and writing that demands investment (the kind of writing you saw in Chapter 1 in the "By Heart" piece) is far more difficult and cognitively rigorous than the analysis students are used to writing.

And then we do more. We tap into our students' myriad passions and start adding sports analysis, film analysis, television analysis, political analysis, and music analysis. We broaden our students' view of analytical writing so they can be more successful. To understand the role passion plays in effective analysis, consider Bryson, a student in Rebekah's ninth-grade class.

English was Bryson's least favorite class. By far. A pencil never felt comfortable resting between his fingers. The blank page, the blank screen—both made his heart beat faster, the walls edge in a bit closer. So, with sweat beading on his brow, he would ask to get some water, to leave the room, to get away. This was his pattern for years: Do whatever is necessary to hide, avoid the writing, even if it meant taking a zero on the assignment.

Rebekah struggled for months to connect Bryson with writing, but she listened as he debated stats from last night's games with his friends, and she peeked at his blog reader full of sports writing. Bryson's passion was college basketball. In his free time he watched games, scoured stats, read articles, rehashed with friends.

"What could you write about college basketball?" she asked him one day. "Is there something you feel strongly about? Something you'd like to think about more closely? Something you wish your friends would understand?"

He mulled this over for a bit. After class, he lagged behind, inched over to her desk, and said, "I could write about Ben Simmons. I think he's actually really good even though he didn't make it to the tournament."

"OK! Try that," Rebekah replied.

He did. And Bryson, who wouldn't string together a sentence all year, started his sports analysis with this:

Ben Simmons is the best freshman in college basketball history that didn't make it to the NCAA Tournament. I believe that Ben Simmons is not to blame for coming short of the tournament. Although the Tigers didn't have an outstanding record as they did in years past, only going 19-10 this season, this is the first time since the 2012-2013 LSU Tiger season that they haven't had a 20+ win season.

Besides having the potential number 1 draft pick in the 2016-2017 NBA draft, it was a really tough start for the Tigers this year. With a weak non-conference schedule in the beginning of the season, these losses to three non-Tournament teams immediately set LSU back. Once Victor became eligible in December, LSU showed some life, opening in the SEC with a 2-0 record by beating

continues

> Kentucky and Vanderbilt. In spite of their struggles as a team in the beginning, Simmons' averaged 13 points per game, 17 rebounds per game, 7 assists per game, and was shooting 28% from the field and 60% from the free throw line.
>
> Ben Simmons wasn't to blame this season because Simmons could be the first All-American to miss the NCAA Tournament since Davidson's Stephen Curry in 2009, although Curry played in a traditional one-bid league and lost his final conference tournament. Simmons also could be the first No. 1 overall draft pick to miss the Tourney since Pacific's Michael Olowokandi in 1998. The difference is that Curry and Olowokandi played in the NCAA Tournament in prior years.

What transformed Bryson from writing-dodger to sports analyst? Allowing him to write from his own expertise and analyze one of his passions.

No matter where your students begin as writers—full of confidence or full of avoidance—unleashing them to explore the topics and texts they are passionate about can transform your classroom and transform their writing.

Writing Instruction That Transfers to Any Content

Something wonderful happens when we stop putting all our energy into teaching the symbolism in *Heart of Darkness* just so students can write about the theme of the novel. Instead, when we invite students to bring their individual expertise to English class, we all get to fully focus on one thing—writing instruction.

When we used to teach only formulaic literary analysis in our English classes, our students went to history class or to their next English course and that "learning" was lost. Students viewed the steps of analytical writing as "the steps of writing in Ms. Marchetti's class" or "how we write about *Of Mice and Men* in Mrs. O'Dell's class." The rules didn't transfer—or at least, students couldn't see the application of the skills in their other classes.

When we shift from teaching formulas to teaching the tools of analytical writing—passion, ideas, structure, authority—the skills are isolated, highlighted, practiced, repeated, revised, and mastered over time. And when students write from their passions and expertise, they can focus on mastering those tools instead of trying to simultaneously learn and master content. These are the same tools students will need when writing analytically in any content area and about any topic. When they write a piece analyzing the causes of World War II, they will access these skills. When they analyze the findings of their science experiment, they will access these skills. And if they someday need to analyze Hamlet's soliloquy, they will be able to do that, too.

We trade one-size-fits-all literary analysis for more instructional time, sharper focus in our lessons, and buy-in from our students. Oh, and better writing.

Writing with Authority, Life, and Relevance

Donald Murray wrote that "students will write well only when they speak in their own voice, and that voice can only be authoritative and honest when the student speaks of his own concerns in his own way" (Murray 1974, 129). When students choose their topics for analytical writing, we give them the opportunity to speak of their own concerns in their own voice.

In the past, when we asked all students to write literary analysis of a given text, what we received wasn't even academic writing in the true sense. We read an approximation, a "parody of genuine literary discourse" (Blau 2003, 4–5). It just isn't a language that students own yet.

But students do own the language of video games. And basketball. And music. And dance. Students are already fluent in the language of their passions. When we give them permission to use that language in their writing, we allow them to pursue topics "which satisf[y] the reader's curiosity with authoritative knowledge. The student is an authority on many subjects . . . and the teacher should make no judgment of which subject is worthy of the writer's attention. All subjects are, for the student must write from his own knowing and his own caring" (Murray 1973, 153). Caring matters because even when students lack expertise, if they care about a topic and are curious, they can research to acquire the knowledge needed to write about it authentically and meaningfully. In Chapters 4 and 7, we will share ideas for helping students who have curiosity but not expertise write about their topics.

The Power of Passion: A Student Example

Henry, a senior, lives at the opposite end of the writing spectrum from Bryson; he loves to write, and he always has. He spent most of his high school career learning writing formulas, though. And while his ideas have always been nuanced and brilliant, the writing experience itself was devoid of the creative problem-solving that motivates him. In his senior year, Henry was given the chance to write analysis of anything—anything!—that he loved and knew well.

Henry chose to write about a text he knows inside and out, the video game *INSIDE*. We're sharing his piece in its entirety and uninterrupted to give you a sense of what passion can do for student analysis. Sit back for a minute, and watch Henry explore *INSIDE*.

INSIDE's Superior Storytelling Skills

In 2010, an independent videogame development studio called Playdead released *LIMBO*, an atmospheric, 2D puzzle-platformer. In the game, you play as a young boy, who must traverse an eerie, monochromatic landscape in search of his lost sister. After its release, *LIMBO* quickly gained critical acclaim, and won several awards, including the VGX Award for Best Independent Game. Now, years later, Playdead has finally released *LIMBO*'s spiritual successor: *INSIDE*.

The similarities between *LIMBO* and *INSIDE* aren't hard to spot. Both star a silent, prepubescent antagonist, who must traverse a bleak, nightmarish landscape while solving physics-based puzzles. But how are the games different? How has Playdead evolved since 2010?

In my opinion, the biggest and most important difference between the two games is that *INSIDE* has a far more driving and immersive story than *LIMBO* did.

This isn't saying much, of course, since *LIMBO* didn't really have any story at all. In *LIMBO*, the game opens with your character waking up in the middle of a dark forest. Then, you start walking right, until you come across a puzzle you need to solve. You solve the puzzle, and then you start walking right again. Rinse and repeat. And then occasionally something spooky happens.

That summary might seem a little unfair, but the point I'm trying to make is that *LIMBO* wasn't exactly brimming with plot.

Of course, some would argue that having any more of a story would ruin *LIMBO*'s eerie, mysterious tone. After all, nothing in the game is really supposed to make sense. The whole game takes place in a bizarre, ethereal plane of existence, completely unlike our own, populated by giant spiders, mind-controlling worms, and homicidal, Lord-of-the-Flies-esque preteens. There's no rhyme or reason as to why the world is like this, it just is. That's what makes it so disturbing. The fact that the game is so unpredictable adds to the general feeling of unease.

However, there's never any payoff. The game just keeps throwing new stuff at you until it suddenly ends, and you're left feeling sort of underwhelmed. I admire that *LIMBO* wanted to make the player feel as helpless and underprepared as possible, but towards the end of the game, it felt as though they were just putting in more weird stuff for the sake of being weird. Although I had started the game fully invested and eager to solve the mysteries of this strange new world, as the game went on I found myself slowly becoming less interested in the story, as I began to realize that I wasn't going to get any answers. *INSIDE* does a good job retaining the same mysterious element, while also making sure the player has a reason to stay interested.

continues

In *INSIDE,* the story is still left mostly up to interpretation, but it's definitely more clear than in *LIMBO.* You are a child infiltrating some sort of evil government facility, which is run by a nondescript shadowy organization. This organization conducts numerous inhumane experiments, including the apparent zombification and enslavement of massive amounts of people. You must escape the facility while avoiding capture. What your character is doing there in the first place is not explained, but already this is far more context than *LIMBO* ever provides. Additionally, all this exposition is gathered visually, through observation and inference on the part of the player, instead of by some expository text panel or dialogue. I appreciate this, because it harkens back to the way *LIMBO* threw the player into the game completely unprepared and left them to figure things out by themselves. This organic means of delivering exposition also means that different players may interpret the game's story differently, which I also like because it means that no two players will have the exact same playing experience.

Thanks to this small amount of information, I immediately became far more invested in the story. Now, when the game threw something strange and surreal at me I thought, "Ooh, I wonder how that ties into the story," instead of just thinking, "Oh, hey, another spooky thing. Great." By providing me with even the slightest hint of a storyline, *INSIDE* had my mind racing, trying to fill in the plot holes based on all the strange things I encountered inside the facility. Every new discovery held much more weight, because I was able to contextualize it. The

BEYOND LITERARY ANALYSIS

mysterious tone of LIMBO was still there, except now I felt as though I was actually solving the mystery as I played.

Something else that managed to get me fully invested in the story of INSIDE was the unnamed main character, who I consider to be a far more relatable protagonist than the original Limbo kid. In LIMBO, your character was a total blank slate; a mute character with all the charm and personality of a cardboard cut out. The idea, I assume, was to make the character easier to project upon, as is the case with most silent video game protagonists. However, I found it pretty difficult to connect with the character when he was so completely unfazed.

In LIMBO, the main character sees some pretty messed up stuff: giant flies feasting upon the corpses of those who were there before him, children's bodies dangling from trees, a giant spider impaling fleeing children with its sharpened, chitinous appendages. But no matter what, he always faces the oncoming threat with the same lifeless, bored eyes. Of course, it's a little difficult to emote when your face is completely cloaked in shadow, but even his body language remained neutral at all times. The most he would do was glance briefly in the direction of whatever horrible thing was bearing down on him, before losing interest and staring straight ahead again. When I first started playing, his complete apathy towards everything around him wasn't all that noticeable. However, by the time he was hopping across a makeshift bridge of water-bloated corpses with the same vacant expression one has when thinking about what they should have for dinner that night, I was beginning to wonder if I was playing as some sort of sociopath. This

continues

general apathy took away from the death scenes as well. Although they were very gruesome, they lacked any kind of emotional impact, because the character looked just as disinterested getting impaled on a spike as he did doing anything else.

I found it basically impossible to become that invested in the story when the main character himself acted as though he couldn't care less, and would rather be at home watching TV. *INSIDE* rectifies this, thankfully, as its protagonist is far more expressive.

In *INSIDE*, the protagonist is characterized through a variety of character animations. When you notice something worrying coming up ahead, or just to the side of you, then he will oftentimes turn his head towards it in a concerned fashion. If you're about to make a particularly difficult jump, he might peer over the ledge you're about to hurl yourself off of, his stance uneasy, but his fists balled in determination. There's even some minimal voice acting. For example, if your character is particularly distressed, his breathing might get heavier. If he takes a bad fall, he'll cry out in pain. If he sees something particularly unsettling, he might let out a small whimper.

All of these subtle noises and animations do an excellent job of turning the game's faceless protagonist into a genuinely relatable character. As I was playing, I found myself actually feeling bad for the little guy, and I realized that I really wanted to see him succeed. The more attached I grew to the silent main character, the more immersed in the story I became. I never really felt that kind of connection with the kid from *LIMBO*. In *LIMBO*, I basically just saw him as a tool to solve puzzles, and if he died I just thought "oh well, let's try that again," and restarted. But when the kid from *INSIDE* died, I felt genuinely bad, as though I had failed the character in some way. Then, once I restarted, I did my best to keep him from dying again.

INSIDE manages to tell an immersive, well-crafted story while still retaining the air of mystery that *LIMBO* had. Its plot is more cohesive, and its main character is far more relatable. I highly recommend both games, but I can say without a shadow of a doubt that *INSIDE* is by far my favorite. I look forward to seeing what else Playdead has in store in the future.

Take off your teacher hat for a minute. How did that feel to you as a *reader*? Did you enjoy Henry's voice? Were you interested in his exploration? Did you want to keep reading? Were you convinced by his claim? Did you walk away with a new discovery?

This is authentic analysis. Henry's passion and knowledge about video games enabled him to write analysis he truly enjoyed, enabled him to share something he felt *needed* to be shared. It enabled him to use his expertise to craft writing that is undeniably smart, detailed, compelling, and packed full of voice.

This is what we want for all of our students. And for yours.

CHAPTER THREE

the essential tools of analysis

O K, by now you have a million thoughts running through your head. Maybe you like this idea of expanding your analytical writing world, raising the level of student writing by connecting to their passions, and elevating their writing to the level of professional analysis. Or maybe this scares you. No matter where you stand, we're sure you're wondering this: If you are no longer teaching students to write eerily similar pieces of analysis on the same piece of literature, what *are* you teaching? You will shift your focus from teaching content to teaching the tools that will enable writers to explore any text.

Sharpen the Focus of Teaching

Whether a close reading of how the music in a video game impacts the player experience, a character analysis of Holden Caulfield, or a commentary about how Lady Gaga has revolutionized the pop music world, all analytical writing has a few essential elements in common.

Naming the essential tools of analysis sharpens the focus of our teaching and brings clarity to our curriculum. Students need consistent practice using these tools so they can explore texts in any content area:

- *Passion.* The writer's compass. Passion is the writer's wholehearted investment in the text she is exploring. Deeper than just admiration, the writer takes her subject seriously, full of conviction that it matters.

- *Ideas.* The places the writer explores. Ideas encompass everything the writer considers and discusses—claims, reasons, evidence.

- *Structure.* The maps a writer uses to chart her course. Structure includes the writer's focus, paragraphing, how she leads and concludes, and visual structure tools.

- *Authority.* The writer's know-how that enables her to explore a text. Authority speaks to a writer's content knowledge, tone, word choice, and use of grammar and conventions.

We've shown you literary analysis in the wild with Anna North, and we've shown you what student analysis can look like when a student gets to explore his passion. Now let's focus on the four essential tools of analysis and see what they look like in another piece of professional writing.

What follows is an analysis (originally for air on NPR's *Fresh Air*) about the way music functions in the Netflix series *The Get Down*. The music embedded in the piece transforms it, of course, so you'll want to listen to it on your computer or your phone as you follow along with the text. A simple Google search for "Hip-Hop Meets Disco on the Electrifying Soundtrack to *The Get Down*" will get you there.

This example of authentic analysis is a great one for us to dive into together. It analyzes the kinds of texts that students love (television, music). It's relatively short, especially compared to a lot of analysis, so it's great for younger students or students with short attention spans. It includes an audio component to support struggling readers. And we just love Ken Tucker. He's one of our all-time favorite mentor writers because his writing is clear and concise but also beautifully crafted.

This is a good time to point out to you that this article (and all of the articles we share throughout the book) will no longer be hot-off-the-presses by the time you read this, so you may decide not to use it as a mentor text. Still, even if you decide the texts are not relevant enough to hand to your current students, they will help you frame your understanding of what different kinds of authentic analysis look like. Part 3 of this book is chock-full of examples of real-world analysis just like this on the topics student writers frequent most!

Hip-Hop Meets Disco on the Electrifying Soundtrack to *The Get Down*

By Ken Tucker, *Fresh Air*, NPR

[Sound bite of song "Hum Along and Dance" as performed by Janelle Monae]

It would've been easy to slap together a soundtrack album for *The Get Down*. Just take some of the period hits that punctuate many scenes from the Netflix series such as The Trammps' "Disco Inferno" and Garland Jeffreys' "Wild in the Streets" and shove it out there for nostalgists and newbies alike.

But like the TV show itself, there are multiple layers to this *Get Down* soundtrack, intentionally disorienting fusions of past and present and a dreamlike mood that hovers over the music like a fog . . .

[Sound bite of song "You Can't Hide" as performed by Zayn Malik]

One of the things I like about *The Get Down* TV show set in the late 1970s is that it doesn't sneer at disco in favor of what would become hip-hop, unlike much of the rock music establishment of this era, which despised dance music. Rap music pioneers recognized that these pulsating rhythms could be thrilling.

The Get Down understands just how glorious the greatest disco was to the point of creating a credible would-be hit of the era. Herizen Guardiola plays the romantic lead, Mylene, who wants nothing more than to be a disco queen on the order of Donna Summer or Gloria Gaynor. To do it, she records "Set Me Free," which sounds like a lost classic, but it's actually a new song composed for *The Get Down* . . .

[Sound bite of song "Set Me Free" as performed by Herizen Guardiola]

The Get Down's most prominent producer-director is Baz Luhrmann who specializes in going over the top in movies such as

Moulin Rouge and his adaptation of *Romeo and Juliet*. He's working with technical advisers such as the music scholar Nelson George and the pioneering hip-hop DJ Grandmaster Flash—so important, he's portrayed by an actor as a key character. Luhrmann mixes true facts with heightened invention.

When *The Get Down* needs an example of inspirational rapping, the production comes up with nothing less than something called "Black Man in a White World (Ghetto Gettysburg Address)," an invented manifesto that's a collaboration between Michael Kiwanuka and the rapper Nas . . .

[Sound bite of the song "Black Man in a White World" as performed by Nas and Michael Kiwanuka]

A prime example of the way *The Get Down* plucks older music for its new purposes and thus operates precisely the way original rap music did. Appropriating beats from earlier R&B is the song "Cadillac." It takes the 1976 track "Love Is in the Backseat of My Cadillac" by the great British group Hot Chocolate and turns it into a different sort of hip-hop via the contemporary singer Miguel. Oh, and Cadillac is also the name of one of *The Get Down*'s characters, so it all becomes doubly witty . . .

[Sound bite of song "Cadillac" as performed by Miguel]

The Get Down as a TV series is uneven, often electrifying and moving, sometimes florid and corny. The soundtrack to *The Get Down*, however, is an almost pure delight, a rapper's delight as the title of a Sugarhill Gang song once termed it. It captures moments from forty years ago and brings them decisively into the present.

You might have read Tucker's piece and wondered if it is analysis. Remember that we defined analysis as a piece of writing that explores a text. Does he do this? Tucker explores music as it is used throughout a television series in his review. The series has a finite number of episodes and musical numbers (a beginning, middle, and end), and it can be broken down into smaller pieces for closer study—the music that populates the background of the action, originals created specifically for the show, and "older music used for new purposes." Tucker further explores the impact of the music as it elevates the overall quality of the television show, making it more "delightful" than "florid and corny."

This is a piece of writing that explores a text—it's analysis! In it, Tucker uses all the essential tools of analysis.

Understand the Tools of Analysis

PASSION

Ken Tucker is a professional (and very well-regarded) film and music critic. His passion is written all over his business card. But with this particular topic, Tucker is thoroughly and dynamically engaged throughout the review.

Even when he's writing about the soundtrack of a Netflix series, Tucker takes his subject seriously. He demonstrates his passion for smart music-and-television mashups as he acknowledges the "multiple layers" of the soundtrack. Rather than writing like a soulless analysis robot, Tucker acknowledges his experience and bias by directly telling his reader "things I like" about the soundtrack and that it leaves him with "almost pure delight." His emphatic language throughout the review—"pulsating rhythms could be thrilling," "just how glorious the greatest disco was," "often electrifying and moving, sometimes florid and corny"—communicates his excitement for the subject at hand.

IDEAS

This piece of analysis is replete with textual evidence—song lyrics. But this isn't the only kind of evidence Tucker employs. He also uses comparisons and allusions to flesh out what this album is and isn't.

Tucker has a strong claim, but it doesn't appear until the end of his review—he writes his way into it. Setting us up early on for the soundtrack's depth (". . . There are multiple layers . . . disorienting fusions of past and present . . ."), Tucker actually presents his reasons for liking the soundtrack and evidence of the soundtrack's credibility before presenting his ultimate conclusion on the album:

> The Get Down as a TV series is uneven, often electrifying and moving, sometimes florid and corny. The soundtrack to The Get Down, however, is an almost pure delight, a rapper's delight as the title of a Sugarhill Gang song once termed it. It captures moments from forty years ago and brings them decisively into the present.

Notice that it takes Tucker three sentences—an entire paragraph of his review—to fully express his perspective on how the soundtrack informs the television show. This is another vast departure from the one-sentence, three-part thesis statement so many students are taught to write.

STRUCTURE

In his lead, Tucker engages the audience's expectations by saying that while it would have been easy to slap together a clichéd disco soundtrack, the producers of *The Get Down* do more.

Tucker spends multiple (short) paragraphs unpacking and deepening ideas throughout his piece. Take the introduction, for example, broken into two short paragraphs. The first sets up the expectations for the soundtrack (a simple re-counting of iconic disco tunes). The second paragraph contradicts that, ex-plaining what the listener gets instead (a soundtrack of "multiple layers" and "disorienting fusions").

Tucker delights in *The Get Down* soundtrack for two main reasons: It values both disco and rap as genres, and it uses older music for new, innovative pur-poses. These reasons are not neatly contained in two, equally long body para-graphs, though. Rather, Tucker's focus is on the way the show values the musical styles it represents. It takes him nearly four paragraphs to move through this idea. He begins by showing the representation of disco in the show, then dis-cusses the pedigree of the music production, and follows with a discussion of the original rap music. His discussion of the show's sampling of older music is shorter—one paragraph.

Tucker also uses multiple paragraphs to explore every angle of his first rea-son—that both disco and rap are given equal respect and credibility on this soundtrack. Each paragraph deepens that reason, giving a sense of "Not only this, but also . . . !" that propels the reader through the review. That it can take multiple paragraphs to develop an idea may come as a surprise to students in whom the "one idea per paragraph" mantra has been ingrained. While Tucker's piece is logical and organized, it is far from formulaic. He spends as long as he needs to spend on each idea until it is completely realized.

AUTHORITY

A lot of writing with authority comes down to knowledge—how thoroughly you know your subject and how you share that knowledge with the reader. Tucker shows his vast musical knowledge by connecting *The Get Down* soundtrack with music history. He mentions that the show takes disco seriously "unlike much of the rock music establishment of this era, which despised dance music," and he acknowledges that rap pioneers of the day also saw the value of disco's rhythms as they crafted their own genre. He again nods to the show's historical accuracy when he writes that the way the show appropriates older music for new purposes "operates precisely the way original rap music did." Tucker further connects the fiction of the show to the fact of history as he alludes to Donna Summer and Gloria Gaynor as real-life mirrors for the show's lead, Mylene. He clearly knows the big hits of the disco era as he mentions "Disco Inferno" and "Wild in the Streets" in his first paragraph.

As a music expert, Tucker speaks to the integrity of the original songs on the soundtrack, calling "Set Me Free" an original disco tune, "credible," and sounding "like a lost classic." He describes an original rap number, "Black Man in a White World (Ghetto Gettysburg Address)," as "inspiring."

Tucker's understanding of the modern film and music scene is displayed in his explanation of the producers' impact on the music—a combination of Baz Luhrmann's over-the-top direction, Nelson George's technical help, and DJ Grandmaster Flash's hip-hop credentials.

We get the sense that Tucker knows his time is brief in a radio review, so he wades into this topic without diving too deep; while he gives examples from the soundtrack and insights into its significance, he moves quickly between ideas.

He also shows an obvious awareness of the audience of his forum for publication—*Fresh Air*. Tucker seems to understand that *The Get Down* might not be an obvious choice for his audience. Knowing that NPR listeners tend to be older, he focuses on the heavy significance given to disco music on the soundtrack and the influence of disco on the hip-hop featured on the album. For this same predominantly well-educated and culturally engaged audience, Tucker elevates his subject to make it worthy of their time. Connections to musical history and insight into the show's "multiple layers" appeal to this audience. At the end of his review, he does nod to the crowd who might discount this show by acknowledging that it is occasionally "florid and corny," but he validates the soundtrack as "almost pure delight."

Jargon throughout like "track" and "beats" subtly shows that Tucker speaks the language of music, and, thus, the reader knows his opinion can be trusted.

Analysis Is Everywhere, and Your Students Can Write It

Broadening the definition of analysis gives students opportunities to write about the topics on which they are experts, topics that interest them, topics on which they have something to say. When we engage them with multiple opportunities to share what they know and allow them to explore a wide range of texts, they can learn and eventually master the essential tools of analysis. These skills will serve them whether they are writing about literature or history or video games or the NBA finals.

And this is key. Because when we look at the world of writing, the writing that pours through our Twitter feeds, the articles we dog-ear in *The New Yorker*, most of it is analysis. Writers closely read literature and films and music and dance and politics and video games and current events and sports. Writers analyze everything. When we teach our students these skills in contexts that allow them to be successful, we give our students access to the wide world of analysis and prepare them to engage in those conversations as writers for the rest of their lives.

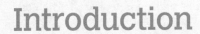

Introduction

ALTHOUGH THEY AIMED TO DARINGLY SAIL INTO THE
UNKNOWN, EXPLORERS NEVER SET OFF ON A WHIM.

Months and sometimes years of preparation ensured that they would have what they needed to give them the best chance of successfully traversing the world both discovered and undiscovered: a seaworthy ship that could cross oceans, the knowledge of experienced pilots and cosmologists, partial maps drawn by those who had explored before them, and navigational instruments like compasses, astrolabes, cross-staffs, and quadrants. They didn't know exactly what they would find or how they would get there, but explorers' ships were stocked with tools that would make discovery possible.

Section 2 of this book provides tools that will make your students' exploration possible.

In these chapters, you will find four essential tools every student explorer needs for successful analytical writing: passion, ideas, structure, and authority. We share some problems student writers often face as well as solutions—ways teachers can support writers' growth.

Explorers' discoveries challenged the accepted knowledge of the known world—they broke perceived boundaries of the physical world and the boundaries of understanding that separated the ancient world from the modern one. Analysis born out of our students' passions breaks boundaries, too; and so, in each chapter, we offer some boundary-breaking activities and techniques intended to help your students explore their topics and write the kind of analysis the world wants to read. The kind that changes our understanding.

Each chapter is divided into two parts: Activities for Exploration and Discovery and Crafting Techniques. In the first part, we share activities that will help your students explore the particular tool we are highlighting; these activities can work as minilessons for the whole class, in small-group work, or in individual writing conferences. In the second half of the chapter, we share crafting techniques that will help you name (and give you eyes to see more and more on your own!) the techniques professional writers use to hone this tool and show your students how to use them in their writing.

You are the master pilot; you have sailed these seas (or seas like them) many times before. So, you won't find a formula for instruction here. Use one strategy per writing study, or use all of them; read this section from cover to cover, or dip in and out as students' needs arise. You know your students better than anyone, and you will know what support they need.

CHAPTER FOUR

exploring passion

P assion is the writer's compass. Through our passions, we discover new writing territories to explore and find ways to express the ideas and thoughts and questions in our hearts.

Throughout this chapter we will use the word *passion* to mean the pastimes, experiences, and people our students hold dear. Even the most disengaged student is passionate about something, and we can leverage that passion to help nurture her writing life.

The Problem and the Solution

In Chapter 2, we detailed how students' writing lacks meaningful knowledge, purpose, and heart when their passions aren't at the forefront of their writing—especially their analytical writing. And in Chapter 3, we cast a vision for what's possible if we bring passion and analytical writing together.

But even once we all agree that passion belongs in analysis, other problems can crop up.

- Students don't know *what* they are passionate about.

- Students have too many passions and struggle to narrow them down.

- Students have passions but don't know enough about them to write authoritatively.

- Students don't know what they want to analyze within their bigger passion.

The solution to helping our students pinpoint passions that matter is to give them some experiences and classroom routines that encourage them to dig around in their hearts and minds to see what they care about, what they know about, what they have to share with others (see Figure 4.1).

If You See That Students . . .	Try This
Aren't sure what they are passionate about	• Zoom in on a Heart Map (p. 47) • Scavenger Hunt for Passions (p. 49) • Mine Childhood Passions (p. 50).
Have passions that are too big for one piece of writing	• Zoom in on a Heart Map (p. 47) • Passion Blogging (p. 56).
Need to explore different sides of their passion to find a topic	• Zoom in on a Heart Map (p. 47) • Digital Reading (p. 53) • Passion Blogging (p. 56).
Have passion but need deeper knowledge	• Digital Reading (p. 53).

Figure 4.1: Strategies for Exploring Passion

Activities for Exploration and Discovery

Adolescents can give the impression that nothing interests them—everything is boring; everything is beneath them. But we know that underneath that hard facade lurk unique hobbies and deep curiosities. Our job is to work as an archeologist, uncovering the passions that sit just below the surface.

Students have been systematically taught to remove themselves from analytical writing entirely. Sadly, they probably haven't brought their passions to class in years. And so, they will need time, space, and a few strategies to help them explore the things that make them tick, to narrow them down, and to look at them more closely.

Zoom in on a Heart Map

Georgia Heard (2016) writes that "when we zoom in on our heart maps, the details of our stories come into focus" (109). We think those "stories" should include analysis, too. Many students have used heart maps in the past as a way to explore possible writing topics. So these same heart maps can help students take the passions of the heart and find topics for analytical writing.

STEPS

1. Students examine their heart maps and choose one area of deep passion or interest.

2. Students create a second zoomed-in heart map that focuses solely on that passion and then makes it more specific.

3. Students use different areas of the zoomed-in heart map to brainstorm analytical writing topics.

EXAMPLE

Dylan, a ninth grader, created a heart map at the beginning of the year (Figure 4.2), which demonstrated a wide array of interests: family, writing, theater, his faith, music, pets, school. He pulled "theater" out as a topic of particularly deep passion and created a second, zoomed-in heart map exploring his interests just within theater (Figure 4. 3).

Based on his new, specialized heart map, Dylan brainstormed some possible topics for analytical writing.

- How *Wicked* changed the face of Broadway theater

- The effectiveness of *Hairspray*, Live! versus stage productions of *Hairspray*

Figure 4.2: Dylan's Original Heart Map

Figure 4.3: Dylan's Zoomed-In Heart Map

- Why the Altria Theater is the perfect venue for a musical
- A review of *Matilda*.

THINGS TO CONSIDER

No heart map? No problem! If your students don't already have heart maps, don't worry! You can spread this activity out over two warm-ups: day 1, create a broad heart map; day 2, create a zoomed-in heart map.

Time for a conference? Not every student will be able to move as quickly from the zoomed-in heart map to topics for analysis as Dylan did. But don't worry! Writing conferences can help steer a student's heart toward a specific writing topic, and Chapter 6 will provide even more support for moving from ideas to analytical writing topics.

Scavenger Hunt for Passions

In *Falling in Love with Close Reading* (2014), Chris Lehman and Kate Roberts remind us of this universal truth: We closely read the things and people we love. So, spending just a few minutes closely examining the stuff of our lives can reveal our passions. This scavenger hunt takes students through their belongings as way to uncover where their hearts are.

STEPS

1. Have students grab their notebooks and choose a few of the following locations: backpack, locker, car, phone camera roll, calendar/planner.

2. In their notebooks, students should log every single item they find in each location.

3. After they have completed the log, students should look for and highlight any patterns they notice.

4. The highlighted items represent areas of passion that can be developed into topics for analysis.

EXAMPLE

In about ten minutes, Grace searched her backpack and iPhone camera roll on her scavenger hunt. Here's what she found:

- A novel
- History textbook
- Folder with papers
- Two Spanish workbooks
- Planner
- Pencils
- Calculator
- Phone
- Headphones

- Glasses

- Screenshots of quiz answers from Buzzfeed quiz

- Book covers

- Pictures of my brother

- Pokemon pictures

- Food

- Flowers

- Friends

- Anime characters

- Rain drops

- Lego creations.

From this master list, Grace noticed that she returned time and again to cartoon/anime characters, books, and school. Inspired to write a piece of personal connection analysis, Grace considered the ways a beloved anime show helped her cope during a difficult time.

> *Fairy Tail completely changed my life for the better. I began watching it when I needed it the most. It altered my black-and-white thinking to a more open and understanding way of life. It gave me unique friendships that I wouldn't be able to find in everyday life and opened my mind to a whole new culture. Fairy Tail gave me hope when I thought there was none, and it gave me light every time I was in the dark.*

The pictures on her phone helped Grace zoom in on something she loves so that she could analyze a text she was passionate about.

THINGS TO CONSIDER

Get a buddy. Some students have trouble seeing the patterns emerge from their own lists, so they benefit from having a peer or a teacher look at the items they have found and extrapolate big ideas from it.

Mine Childhood Passions

The things we love when we are little have a way of sticking with us when we're grown—even when we haven't consciously thought about them in a long time.

Asking our teenage writers to take a trip back to childhood can yield a bounty of passions they might be eager to dig into once again.

1. Ask students to recall their childhood passions by using the questions below as notebook prompts or as a questionnaire.

   When you were younger . . .

   - What did you want to be when you grew up? (At three or four? At nine or ten?)
   - What were your favorite toys, games, or activities?
   - What did you watch over and over and over again?
   - What did you enjoy pretending?
   - What did you know everything about?
   - What were your favorite childhood books?
   - What were your favorite sections in the library?
   - What did you like learning about from an older sibling or friend?

2. From this list of possibilities, students should highlight or circle ideas that still feel exciting to them years later as potential topics for analysis.

EXAMPLE

Here's a glimpse at Andrew's notebook as he worked through these questions. When he was younger, Andrew . . .

- Loved watching baseball
- Wanted to be an architect in preschool
- Showed an interest in history (since middle school)
- Remembers good times playing baseball at the little league.

Because baseball appeared twice in this list, he honed in on baseball as a possible topic for analysis. From there he was a bit stuck, though, so he asked for a conference. Rebekah probed into Andrew's relationship with baseball: What position did he play? What's the best game he has ever played in? What's his favorite thing about baseball? Who is his favorite player right now? Who is his favorite player of all time? What team did he love watching as a child?

Andrew became more animated as he talked about his beloved St. Louis Cardinals and his favorite player, Chris Carpenter. It was clear—Chris Carpenter was his text! Here's the first paragraph of his piece.

> *Chris Carpenter is one of the greatest pitchers in recent MLB history. If a freakish injury hadn't put such a sudden end to his career, in my mind there is a chance, even though it is a small chance, that he would be in the hall of fame. While he wasn't like Cy Young or Nolan Ryan, he was still an extraordinary pitcher. During his ten years of pitching for the St. Louis Cardinals, he played in three All-Star games and helped the Cardinals to win two World Series championships, and he also helped the Toronto Blue Jays to win one World Series during his time in Toronto.*

THINGS TO CONSIDER

Phone a friend. Chatting with siblings, parents, or grandparents can be helpful here, so students should feel free to take these questions home and get input from those who have known them the longest and the best.

Classroom Routines to Deepen Passion

We live our passions.

One of our deepest passions is teaching. It's what we live and breathe at work and at home. And, so, when we're not standing in front of a classroom of students, we continue to nurture that passion: by discussing it, tweeting about it, reading articles on education news, devouring professional books on instructional design, and highlighting psychological books about the way children learn.

Because we have a passion, we want to learn more and know more. And by continually nurturing it, the flame is fanned.

If our students have a true passion, they are probably already nurturing it in a variety of ways. That video game they love steals their after-school and weekend hours. They travel around the state to play that sport. They spend their lunch period debating the ending of that movie they love.

We can teach students to take the passions they are already nurturing and explore them in ways that will make them better writers of analysis. Deepening passions takes time, so we rely on two classroom routines—digital reading and passion blogging. You can implement these routines for a single unit, but they can also become a fixture of your classroom all year long, constantly feeding and fueling students' interests so that they are always ready to analyze their passions.

Digital Reading

Every English teacher knows that the best way to learn more about something is to read about it. Students do lots of reading in English class, as a large group, in literature circles, and in independent reading, but the living, breathing, ever-changing world lives online these days. Inviting students to read digitally about their passions connects them with the up-to-the-minute conversation on the topics they love most.

The writing we find online is also the kind of writing students will be doing themselves. Digital reading has the added benefit of doing some of the modeling and structural priming that will help student readers transition to the role of student writers as they analyze their passions.

THE ROUTINE

Next you will see the instructions we give students for digital reading. The process begins as students use blog search engines, recommendations from friends, and their Twitter feed to curate an RSS reader (we love Feedly!) full of promising sites. These reading lists will grow and grow as students find new sites that inspire them.

INSTRUCTIONS FOR STUDENTS

Independent Digital Reading

Why Digital Reading?

- Most of the reading we do these days (both students and adults!) happens online: articles, tweets, blogs. We need to get acquainted with this world of writing.

- Professional writers share their work online—the same kind of writing you will be doing.

- Digital reading can help us learn about the topics we are interested in.

continues

The Assignment

- Read digitally for at least two hours per week.

- Every two weeks, you will create a story on Storify to share your most interesting reading and your thoughts about it.

- You can follow your classmates on Storify and read their stories as well to get ideas for further reading!

- You will link to at least five of your favorite articles and add a brief commentary that should consider:

  - Questions the article raises

  - Pieces of writing that you might develop based on that article

  - Ideas or topics you want to explore in future reading

  - What drew you into this piece of writing

  - A mentor sentence from the article

  - Ideas for how you might use this article as a mentor text.

You might use these sentence starters to help you get started:

- This article makes me wonder . . .

- I'm curious about . . .

- Based on this article, I might write . . .

- I was instantly hooked by this piece of writing because . . .

- The most interesting elements of this writing are . . .

- A sentence I might like to mimic is . . .

- I might use this piece as a mentor text for . . .

- Because of this article, I would like to continue to read about. . . .

We don't police the two-hour rule for reading or insist that students look at a certain number of sites; our goal is simply to engage them in the world of digital writing. We find that students consistently read much, much more than this. Like us, they get sucked in.

There are so many benefits to digital reading: Students are constantly learning about their passions, they are reading tons and tons of great writing (most of it nonfiction), they are absorbing language and techniques to use in their future writing, they are identifying potential mentor texts along the way, and students love it (it is consistently the class routine they report liking most in our classes).

But digital reading can also be a great litmus test—proving whether or not the writer is truly passionate about the topic as he thinks he is. Henry thought he wanted to write a piece of sports analysis about his favorite basketball team, the Washington Wizards. But his digital reading told a different story. As he read pieces of basketball analysis, Henry realized that while he does love his team, it wasn't a passion he wanted to write about. Instead, he found himself engrossed by product reviews of expensive basketball shoes. Doing more reading to deepen his passion for basketball revealed that his heart wasn't in it as a writer; his reading directed his writer's heart elsewhere. We point out an escape hatch to our students and remind them that they can always revise their ideas in favor of something they are more passionate about.

EXAMPLE

Zach and Mary Kate both used digital reading to learn more about their topics of interest. Zach loved Drake, but wanted to learn more about the critical reception of his latest album and also needed to learn a few more techniques for describing music. Mary Kate is a tech nerd (in the best possible sense), so she constantly reads about the latest gadget releases.

Here are excerpts from one of their digital reading syntheses from Storify. Notice how both students learn more about their interests while getting ideas for future reading and writing.

An Entry from Zach's Digital Reading Story:

Article: "*Views* Is the Sound of Drake at His Best, Worst, and Drakiest," *The Verge*

I chose to read this article because Drake's new album has been blasting through my earbuds for the last five days, and I wanted to know what the critics had to say. The article made me curious if Drake's style change was something that made his lyrics deeper and more relatable, but added unnecessary parts to the music. I also wonder if Views will sell as well as his last albums even though it isn't as aggressive or emotional. The most interesting thing about this article is that the author tries to make it seem as if Drake has no real style in the album, but I thought it was a really good mix of aggression and emotion. Because of this article, I want to continue to read about new music.

An Entry from Mary Kate's Digital Reading Story:

Article: iPhone 7 Release Date, News, and Rumors, *TechRadar*

I would have been excited for the iPhone 7 to come out, but now that I've seen what it looks like I don't think I am anymore. The headphone jack is going to be replaced by a Bluetooth or a lightning port, which I personally don't like that much. I'm excited for the dual cameras; I think they will improve the quality of taking pictures so much. People take photos for everything on their phone, so it's good that they're making improvements to the quality. I like how this article organized the sections with separate headers; it made the article easier to navigate. If I ever get an iPhone 7 myself, I want to write a review on what I like and dislike about the new phone, along with some new features I would want to see in a future iPhone.

Passion Blogging

It seems almost every day someone we know is launching a blog. Blogs are born out of passion. People begin blogs because they want to explore something they love and share this love with readers who care. It's likely that some of your students and colleagues are already blogging and that you will have blogging experts to help support you if blogging is new to you.

A passion blog serves all the students in your room—those who already have identified passions and those who are sitting there waiting for passions to find them. In *A Writer Teaches Writing*, Donald Murray (1985) asserts that "behind each writing purpose is the secret excitement of discovery: the word, the line, the sentence, the page that achieves its own life and its own meaning. The first responsibility of the writing teacher is to [help students] experience this essential surprise" (8). A blog is a low-risk place to explore thinking where students can write their way into discovery and try on different styles and texts before they commit to a more formal piece of writing.

You can use this as a standalone writing study (four weeks of passion blogging with a new post due every few days) or as a regular classroom routine that follows students throughout the school year.

THE ROUTINE

Next you will see the instructions we give students for passion blogging. We should note that at times, a Discovery Blog transforms into a Heart Blog when a student finds a topic she wants to return to again and again. Both blog forms, though, help students see their interests in many lights, which helps them explore what they already know and what they want to know more (and write more!) about.

INSTRUCTIONS FOR STUDENTS

Passion Blogging

Many people take up blogging to explore a passion and share it with others who have the same passion. This semester, you will have an opportunity to launch a passion blog!

Your passion blog can take one of two forms:

- *Heart Blog:* This is a fixed blog format where you choose one specific topic (video games or skiing or reading) you are passionate about.

- *Discovery Blog:* This blog format is open in the sense that you can explore multiple topics, using writing to discover your true passions. (You can write about video games AND skiing AND reading).

The heart blog will allow you to really deepen your knowledge about something you love, while the discovery blog invites you to explore many different topics. Either way, you will be writing about topics that excite and inspire you!

continues

The Details

You will:

- Do some thinking and writing to decide what topic(s) you want to blog about.

- Create a blog in Weebly.

- Write one post every two weeks. Posts will be due in your Google turn-in folder. At that point:

  - I will provide feedback.

  - You will revise your post to incorporate feedback.

  - You will post your writing to your Weebly blog by the next class period.

- Each time, there will be a new writing focus—a new genre to try, a style to mimic, a feature to include. As you explore your passion through blogging, you will also be building your writing repertoire.

Because we want our students to explore lots of different approaches to writing about their passions, at times we give them different ways to focus their writing energies. Here are some of the writing focuses we used for passion blogs this year:

- Curate a list (top 10s, best ofs, reading/viewing lists)

- Write a how-to

- Give a review

- Explore a controversy/debate

- Present the take-aways of an experience

- Share memories and personal connections

- Interview someone

- Tell "everything you need to know about...."

The fact that blogs live in the real world of the Internet is part of the appeal and a big reason why students are energized by this routine. Students share their writing with a real audience of classmates and others to get feedback: What do readers really like? What posts are they most interested in? What do they seem to want to know more about? Within the classroom, reading a classmate's blog also generates new writing ideas!

Once a few posts are under their belts, writers can reflect on what they have enjoyed and what they might want to expand into a longer piece of analytical writing about a chosen topic. This usually happens naturally, but it can also be a great conversation to have in a writing conference.

EXAMPLE

Evan is an aficionado of all things "nerd culture"—superheros, comic books, video games. For him, a big part of the joy is developing theories about their deeper meaning and the ways these texts connect. Unsure about a topic for a bigger piece of analysis, he tried a lot of different ideas on for size in his blog *Geekdub Theories*. Here are a few of his posts:

- Review of *Star Wars: Aftermath*
- *Halo 6* Predictions
- How to Create a Movie or Video Game Theory
- Best Theories about *Star Wars*, Video Games, and Marvel.

Looking back at his blog, Evan noticed that his "*Halo 6* Predictions" post was much longer than any of his others—he'd said a lot, and he hadn't even written everything that was in his head! This seemed like it could have great potential as a text for a piece of analysis. Here's an excerpt:

My theory includes characters from the newest Halo game that came out last month, Halo Wars 2, which is a standalone game from the main story but is said to tie in and have a large impact on Halo 6. At the end of this game, a character named professor Ellen Anders gets trapped on one of two remaining Halo Rings. The ring teleports to a mysterious planet and a Guardian suddenly appears overhead. At the end of Halo 5, it is revealed that Cortana has found a Halo Ring and taken control of it. I think that the main characters in this game and their ship, the UNSC Spirit of Fire, will meet up with the crew of the Infinity and the Arbiter's army to take back Earth from Cortana. The reason that I think this is because the story of Halo Wars 2 seemed to tie in so much with Halo 5, I don't see how these characters can still stay in their own isolated story for Halo 6.

Evan planned to use this informal blog post as a foundation for a more formal piece of analytical writing, "What *Halo Wars* 2 and the Ending of *Halo 5* means for *Halo 6*."

From Passion to Powerful Writing

Today, we take the difference-between-life-and-death necessity of the compass for granted. Most of us don't even use maps anymore and rely on our phones to give us turn-by-turn navigation. But remember how essential the compass was to the explorers aboard a ship: to know where they were headed, to keep their purpose at the forefront, to keep the ship upright, to achieve their goals, the compass was everything.

Passion is everything to a writer—the most indispensable tool of exploration. Student writers still need opportunities to learn how to use that tool, particularly within the classroom. But after we give students a few strategies and routines to help them identify and articulate their passions in powerful writing, the transition from heartfelt interest to writing becomes second nature. Now, when they feel strongly about a product, a performance, a game, they think, "Hey! I could write something about that."

CHAPTER FIVE

exploring ideas

F or writers of analysis, ideas are the new territories where exploration happens, where thoughts are loosed and set free. Like an explorer sets out to discover new places, writers of analysis set out to discover and discuss new ideas about a text.

We are using the term "ideas" to mean the original thoughts a student has about a text he is analyzing. Throughout the chapter, we will use several other terms that fall under the umbrella of ideas. For clarity, we have defined them in Figure 5.1.

	Definition	Student Example
Topic	The generalizable category under which the student's ideas fall (i.e., sports, music)	Basketball
Text	Anything that has a beginning, middle, and an end and can be broken down into smaller pieces	Kevin Durant's trade
Idea	The original thoughts a student has about a text he is analyzing	How fans feel about Kevin Durant's trade

continues

Figure 5.1: Helpful Terms for Exploring Ideas

	Definition	Student Example
Claim	A specific, contestable statement a student makes about a text	Fans are demoralized by Kevin Durant's trade
Evidence	The facts, anecdotes, and quotations a student uses to support her claim	Durant's statistics, quotes from commentators, comments from fans (message boards)

Figure 5.1: Continued

In this chapter, we will provide strategies that help students develop ideas about the texts they are analyzing, hone them into claims, and support them with evidence.

The Problem and the Solution

For explorers, the stakes are high. There is a lot to be gained, but there is also a lot to be lost. Exploration is not for the faint of heart.

And so, when we get discouraged by what we see in student analysis, it's often due to a shortcoming in the exploration of ideas, a failure to fully engage in the daring adventure that is analysis. When students' writing is tired and stale and incomplete and anemic, it's usually because they aren't exploring anything at all.

As we discussed in Section 1, too often students write about topics on which they don't have sufficient content knowledge or expertise to write about well. But, beyond a simple lack of passion and deep knowledge of the text, student writers also tend to play it safe in their analysis—wading into the shallows instead of taking the risk of a deep dive. They write what they believe they can write successfully, but more often than not, this leads to formulaic regurgitations of ideas they have heard before. In *The School Essay Manifesto* (2005), Tom Newkirk argues that the certainty students (and teachers) strive for in analytical writing is gained at a cost: "The writer can achieve certainty—but only by stressing the obvious" (39).

In part, our students live in fear of grades and so they avoid risk-taking. But many also live in fear of the very hard work of writing analysis. As a result, we get 150 nearly identical papers on our desk. Sure, this makes for tedious assessment, but, worse yet, it shows that our students haven't been doing the heavy cognitive lifting of analysis. They are exploring lands that have already been discovered.

This isn't the only problem in the realm of idea exploration, though. Our student explorers also have a tendency to arrive in a new land, hop off the ship, take a five-minute tour of the immediate shoreline, and declare the territory thoroughly scouted. They want to claim the conquest, but they aren't *actually* looking to map out the terrain.

We fight against "the obvious" by pushing our students to find fresh claims. But we give our students' analysis short shrift when we stop there. Recently, we asked teachers on Twitter to share the biggest hurdle they face in students' discussion of ideas. Resoundingly, teachers responded: Even if students have interesting ideas, they don't know what to do with them. They restate. They paraphrase. They dance around their ideas. But they don't really dig in, open them up, and analyze them.

To move well beyond the obvious into the fresh and the nuanced, our students must be "looking at ideas from different directions, shaking them, pushing them until they fall over, pulling on them to look at their roots" (Newkirk 2005, 28).

Let's find some ways to help students do just that! (See Figure 5.2.)

If You See This in Students' Writing . . .	Try This
Ideas that are stale regurgitations of class discussion	• Choose a Text to Analyze (p. 64) • Question-Flooding Your Topic (p. 66) • Find an Angle (p. 67) • Fire the First Three (p. 69) • Survival of the Freshest (p. 70) • Challenge the Status Quo (p. 72) • Evidence Inquiry (p. 74).
Lack of focus	• Choose a Text to Analyze (p. 64) • Question-Flooding Your Topic (p. 66) • Find an Angle (p. 67) • Survival of the Freshest (p. 70).

Figure 5.2: Strategies for Exploring Ideas

continues

If You See This in Students' Writing . . .	Try This
Ideas that aren't fully fleshed out	• Justify Your Evidence (p. 77) • This and That (p. 79) • They Say, I Say (p. 80) • Shifts and Changes (p. 81) • Talk Back to Evidence (p. 83) • Introduce Evidence with Discussion (p. 84) • Combine Evidence and Discussion (p. 86).
The same old research	• Survival of the Freshest (p. 70) • Evidence Inquiry (p. 74) • Justify Your Evidence (p. 77).

Figure 5.2: Continued

Activities for Exploration and Discovery

To support students in discovering new ideas, we offer strategies that push them to think beyond what comes easily to mind and expand the kinds of ideas writers of analysis are "allowed" to explore in their writing.

Choose a Text to Analyze

In Chapter 1, we defined a text as anything that has a beginning, middle, and end that can be broken down into smaller pieces and studied. While this definition truly expands students' writing territories, they still have to find texts that are manageable and can in fact be broken down into smaller parts and analyzed.

STEPS

1. Show students the chart below (Figure 5.3).

2. Explain why the items on the left are not texts.

3. Point out that the items on the right are texts because they have time boundaries (a beginning, a middle, and an end) and can be broken down into smaller pieces.

4. As a whole class, or in writing groups or with partners, have students evaluate their chosen texts against the definition of a text.

5. Through conferences, help students narrow too-big texts or find new texts that better fit the definition.

Not a Text	Text
Movies	• *Hidden Figures* (one specific movie) • Movies by Quentin Tarantino (a director's oeuvre) • This summer's new releases.
TV shows on Netflix	• One episode of *House of Cards* • Season 4 of *House of Cards* • Netflix's new original programs released this month.
Rap music	• Kendrick Lamar's new album • Kendrick Lamar's "sound" • Trends in rap music in 2017.
Steph Curry	• Steph Curry's performance during the NBA finals • Golden State's season • Steph Curry's basketball career.
Video games	• *Halo 5: The Guardian* (one video game) • The *Halo* series • The mechanics of *Halo 5: The Guardian*.
Books	• *Between the World and Me* (one book) • Elena Ferrante's Neapolitan novels • Dystopian young adult fiction released this year.

Figure 5.3: Text or Not a Text?

While a student could certainly craft an *argument* about movies or rap music or a particular athlete, strong analysis depends on the writer's ability to closely examine the smaller parts that make up a text; the nonexamples on the left of the chart simply are too broad.

EXAMPLE

Lauren's Original Text		Lauren's Final Text
The history of women's soccer	After using the chart and conferring →	The breakout performances of five young players on the US Women's soccer team

Figure 5.4: Lauren's Original and Final Texts to Be Analyzed

Question-Flooding Your Topic

Inviting students to bring their passions to the writing table opens up topics that have never before been explored in the English classroom. But this can also be like opening a big can of worms as students bring many big and broad topics to the table. A question flood helps move students from broad topics (baseball, reading, video games) to specific texts that can be analyzed and ideas about those texts.

STEPS

1. Present students with the following question stems:

    How has _____ impacted _____?

    How does _____ affect me?

    What is the meaning behind _____?

    How has _____ changed over time?

    How is _____ related to _____?

    How else might we look at _____?

    How does _____ do _____?

    Why does _____ work this way?

    Why does _____ have this effect?

2. In their notebooks, invite students to use the question stems to flood their topic with as many questions as possible.

3. When students have exhausted all possible questions, they should go back and circle the most interesting questions.

EXAMPLE

In Figure 5.5, we show an example of one question flood about the pop singer Adele. We used this as an example for students before we set them free to go on their own.

THINGS TO CONSIDER

Scope, a conferring point. Once students have developed a set of questions that spark their interest, you may need to confer with them to discuss what writing is possible given the length of the study and the scope of the assignment. For example, to explore the question, "Why is Adele popular?" would require extensive knowledge about music—not just Adele's but her contemporaries'. A typical

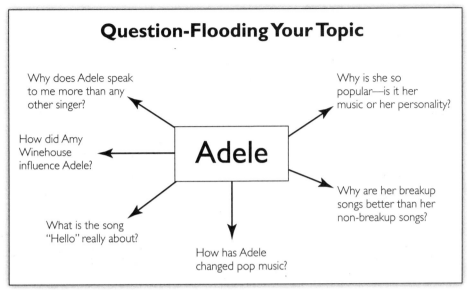

Figure 5.5: Model of Question-Flooding

three-week study of analytical writing would not allow enough research time. A smaller, more manageable topic, such as "What is the song 'Hello' really about?" would be better suited to the scope of the study. However, if you have planned a larger research-based analytical writing project, students might consider questions of bigger scope.

Find an Angle

Students can stare endlessly at a blank screen waiting for a title to reveal itself. We often encourage students to write the title last, letting the writing itself reveal possibilities. But in analytical writing, the title is often the giveaway: It reveals the writer's attitude toward the text and the angle she'll take to explore it. Asking our students (particularly our most reluctant writers) to try on titles for size at the get-go helps them focus their idea and find a way into writing with confidence.

STEPS

1. Send students to a site known for a variety of awesome analytical writing. (We're partial to *The Ringer* as our one-stop shop.)

2. Ask students to identify and jot down five titles into which they could fit the text they are analyzing.

3. Students use the five mentor titles to craft titles about the text they are analyzing.

4. Looking at the titles they have developed, students should choose one and try drafting around it.

EXAMPLE

A student identified the final game of his 2016 JV football season as the text he wanted to analyze, but then he was stuck. The text was narrow enough for him to tackle successfully . . . but how? In a writing conference, Rebekah recommended this strategy, and within five minutes, the student had identified three titles from *The Ringer* that could serve as mentor titles (Figure 5.6).

Title from *The Ringer*	The Student's Title
The (Continuing) Evolution of Steph Curry	The (Continuing) Evolution of the Titans JV Football Team
The 10 Most Important Takeaways from Day 2 of the NCAA Tournament	10 Takeaways from the 2016 Titans JV Football Season
The Secret Lessons of the NBA Playoffs	The Secret Lessons of the Final Game of Our 2016 Season

Figure 5.6: Mentor Titles and Student Titles

Newly focused and confident about what to write, the student chose his favorite—The (Continuing) Evolution of the Titans JV Football Team—and started drafting!

THINGS TO CONSIDER

Pick a title, any title. For this strategy, encourage students to ignore the content of the mentor texts. If they are writing about movies, encourage them to consider titles from sports analysis and literary analysis and video game analysis. In fact, students shouldn't even need to read the writing—just study the title. The purpose here is simply to use titles as a way to identify an angle for analysis.

Be a model. We find it particularly helpful to quickly model this strategy for students so they can see what it sounds like to substitute a different text into a few existing titles. We show them how any title—related to their topic or not—can help them clarify their angle. We worked with our same Adele example and specifically chose articles from *The Ringer*'s Major League Baseball page to model our thinking (Figure 5.7).

Title from *The Ringer*	Our Title
How *Everything, Everything* Is Changing Young Adult Fiction	How Adele's "Hello" Is Changing Pop Ballads
Lowriders Is More Than a Car Movie	"Hello" Is More Than a Pop Ballad
The Transfiguration Is a Coming-of-Age Vampire Movie That Doesn't Suck	"Hello" Is a Break-Up Song That Doesn't Suck

Figure 5.7: Possible Angles for a Piece Analyzing Adele's Song "Hello"

Fire the First Three

In Fire the First Three, students bring their initial claims about their texts to the table and then ruthlessly cut them, drilling down to ideas that are original.

STEPS

1. Set a timer for five minutes.

2. Students quickly jot down all the possible claims that come to mind about their text.

3. When time is up, tell students to cross out the first three claims on their list.

4. Students choose a claim from the remaining claims on their list.

We want to acknowledge students' first line of thinking (usually found in the first two or three claims), but chances are good that these are the claims we have all read over and over again. So, we tell students to eliminate the first three. You could ratchet this up or down by having students eliminate the first five claims or just the first claim, depending on what your students are ready for.

EXAMPLE

A student chose to write about the Star Wars franchise. Here are the claims that came to mind:

- Star Wars is a classic film franchise.
- Star Wars plays out the battle of good versus evil.

- Star Wars is better than Star Trek.

- *Return of the Jedi* is the best Star Wars movie.

- Darth Vader is the worst character in *any Star Wars* movie.

- The original Star Wars movies focus on characterization while the new Star Wars movies focus on action and plot.

- Star Wars paved the way for *Guardians of the Galaxy*'s popularity.

His first three claims are pretty trite and have probably already been written. Claims five through seven, on the other hand, say something fresher—something more worth pursuing.

THINGS TO CONSIDER

Speed is key. Speed is key here because we want to access students' surface-level thinking.

Sound impossible? Does this sound intimidating? Impossible for your students? Don't worry! If students have chosen topics based on their passions and interests, these most-obvious claims will come quickly. When students can't think of more than one claim, it's often a good indication that they should try a different topic or need to spend more time investigating the topic outside of class.

Use it again and again. This same strategy can also help students later as they mull over their evidence. Have them list all the pieces of evidence that come to mind, or that they have researched, and cross out anything that is trite. We want a writer's big ideas to be unique, but we also want them to use interesting, compelling evidence!

Survival of the Freshest

In Survival of the Freshest, students brainstorm as many possible claims as they can think of about a common text they are analyzing. This activity ensures that your students explore different ideas even if they are analyzing the same text (for example, at the end of your *Catcher in the Rye* study, you have asked all of your students to analyze Holden; or several of the students in your class have chosen to analyze Steph Curry's performance in the NBA finals). The nature of the game ups the ante and pushes students toward increasingly out-of-the-box ideas.

1. Have students list three possible claims about the text they are analyzing.

2. Then, have students list three more.

3. If you really want to bump up the challenge, ask students to add three more. (Students are easily overwhelmed if you ask them to come up with six to nine claims out of the gate, but chunking them in threes can yield deeper thinking.)

4. Have students switch lists with a partner.

5. Call on a student to share one claim from her partner's paper.

6. The teacher should say, "Raise your hand if your partner has that same claim or something similar to it."

7. Instruct the students who have raised their hands to strike through that idea.

8. Depending on the number of students and the number of claims they have listed, play three to six rounds, eliminating duplicate claims in each round.

9. The student with the most remaining claims "wins"!

EXAMPLE

Figure 5.8 shows an example of a survival of the freshest board from a senior in a class studying the poem "1914" by Wilfred Owen.

THINGS TO CONSIDER

Play mode. This game could be played with a small group of students writing on similar topics or with a whole class engaged in a similar kind of analytical writing.

Make a game board. While this could easily take the form of a list in students' notebooks, the game feel is heightened when you create a simple 3 × 3 "game board" like

Figure 5.8: Example of Survival of the Freshest

the one in the example. The boxes also provide a helpful visual goal for writers as they push themselves to think of original ideas.

Play more! Survival of the freshest becomes more effective the more you play as students become increasingly competitive and increasingly creative in their thinking.

Use and use again. Just like Fire the First Three, students can use this activity to help them develop claims about a text and again later to help them identify fresh pieces of evidence that will persuade their audience.

Challenge the Status Quo

Knowing those tried-and-true ideas about a text can be helpful when we use them to push the boundaries of students' thinking. When we invite students to challenge the status quo (the generally accepted interpretation of a text), we acknowledge the easy analysis that students tend to reach for first and then intentionally seek to disrupt it.

STEPS

1. Present the student with a "status quo" idea about the chosen text.

2. Ask the student to identify all the possible evidence (from notes, primary text, reading, personal experience, etc.) that supports this idea.

3. Next, have the student look for any information that might deepen the status quo claim, adding a new layer or dimension.

4. Then, look at any "leftover" evidence—anything that doesn't immediately support the status quo idea.

5. List the "leftover" evidence on a clean page in the notebook.

6. Look for a pattern in the new list of evidence to devise a fresh claim about the text, a claim that doesn't rely on the status quo.

EXAMPLE

"My professor assigned a paper analyzing a William Carlos Williams poem. But we can't use a 'status quo' claim. Our claim has to do something more. What do I do?!"

We received this plea from Katie, a former student, in her first semester of college. And, remembering our own travails as English majors constantly in search of an idea no one had ever had before, we chuckled. Of course a "status quo" claim wouldn't suffice; of course her professor wanted more. But Katie wanted what all of our students want; she wanted a sure thing. A tried-and-true claim that would absolutely work.

Using the challenging the status quo strategy above, Katie rose to the challenge with Williams' "Landscape with the Fall of Icarus," coming up with a claim that pushes beyond the very common (and clichéd) reading that Williams' poem points out Icarus' relative insignificance. Here is Katie's claim:

> *Rather than simply detailing Icarus' dilemma, Williams focalizes the surrounding scene, concentrating on the activities of a nearby farmer and the sea. By accentuating Icarus' environment, Williams offers an alternative to the status quo: that the irrelevance of Icarus' death does not stem from individuals' deliberate choices to disregard him, but from the preoccupation of society as a whole with more urgent interests. Williams then deepens this premise even further by challenging Icarus' apparent isolation from civilization, proposing the idea that he identifies more with the surrounding society than the status quo thesis contends.*

Katie's resulting idea begins with the status quo as a foundation, but then she twists it and deepens it. She weighs multiple perspectives, holds conflicting ideas together, and embraces complications and contradictions.

In short, she avoids the obvious and, instead, embraces ambiguity.

THINGS TO CONSIDER

Sharing the status quo. Sometimes, you will find yourself telling a student, "You know, most people think that _____" about their chosen text. But this can also work peer-to-peer or in small groups. Once students have practice with this kind of thinking, they can present one another with common, status quo takes on most topics.

How will you know all the status quo claims in the world? You won't! When you find yourself outside your comfort zone, be honest and say, "You know, I'm not sure what other people say about that text. Let's do some research." Alternatively, you can ask a student to hunt for that information on his own and share it with you in your next writing conference. As we discussed above, other students in the classroom might also be able to weigh in, especially when it comes to sports texts!

Contradicting the status quo, another option. Contradicting the status quo isn't the only goal of this activity. If a student can find evidence that makes us see an old idea in a new way, then that is equally interesting and compelling. For example, Joe, a ninth grader in Allison's class, was analyzing the text *NBA 2K*, a video game. Most players note the game's lag (the noticeable delay between the player's action and the reaction of the server) but agree that it doesn't have a tremendously negative impact on gameplay; in fact, it's so negligible the player "gets used to it." Joe, however, painted this piece of evidence in a different light: "Some people will get used to it, but when you're up by one point and your man has the ball and the game lags and you lose, I guarantee you will not get used to it."

Evidence Inquiry

In English class, evidence almost always means "quotes from the text," but real writers of analysis do so much more. Donald Murray (1985) knew this, of course.

> *The writer needs an inventory of facts, observations, details, images, quotations, statistics—all sorts of forms of information—from which to choose when building an effective piece of writing (10).*

Evidence inquiry is a hands-on approach to help students see that writers of analysis don't use just the same old types of evidence; they support their ideas in varied and unique ways.

STEPS

1. Split students into small groups, and give them some scissors and three to five mentor texts analyzing similar topics.

2. Present this guiding question: What kinds of evidence do writers of analysis use?

3. Ask students to cut the mentor texts apart looking specifically for evidence.

4. When all the evidence has been found, groups work together to sort the evidence into categories.

5. Students should then use the categories to evaluate their existent drafts and note where they might need to add more evidence, or evidence of different types, to flesh out their ideas.

EXAMPLE

Mariel, Maya, and Julia all wanted to write fashion analysis, so we put them in a group together and gave them a few mentor texts.

- "The Cult of Selena and the Fiesta de la Flor Festival" from *Racked*
- "Why Edward Enninful Will Be Good for British Vogue" from *Business of Fashion*
- "Carhartt is the Uniform of Both the Right and the Left" from *Racked*.

Figure 5.9 lists the categories of evidence the girls identified from these three mentor texts.

The students also noted that the writers of fashion analysis used images extensively to support their claims and hyperlinks to connect readers to additional evidence in writing by others.

THINGS TO CONSIDER

How should students record their categories? Depending on your time constraints and your students' needs, students can record their categories and evidence in different ways. They might write their categories in their notebooks and glue the examples underneath. They might put their categories on display in a poster to share on the classroom wall. Or, if your students are very tactile learners, they might sort evidence into different jars, each representing a different category of evidence. Finally, students can write evidence on sticky notes and sort them into groups this way.

Group students according to topic. To show how writers use varied evidence to explore similar ideas, it might be helpful to group students according to the topics they are writing about. Put your sports analysts, your music analysts, your literary analysts together and give them a set of mentor texts (or have them bring their own!) that matches their topics.

But, do I have to find mentor texts for every different topic on which my students are writing? No, not necessarily! While this can be a useful (and specific) way to help students understand the breadth of evidence possibilities, your students can also see that writers use a variety of kinds of evidence with a more general inquiry using different types of analytical writing.

Textual Evidence	Example
Personal anecdote or experience	• "The first time I strolled past the store, in 2013, during my inaugural summer in New York, I had to laugh . . .'Who would buy into this?' I remember thinking. 'Carhartt isn't a fashion brand." ("Carhartt . . .") • "Though it's 2017, I feel like I am back in the '90s as I'm surrounded by Selena superfans. . . . At the Selena tribute show, I feel like I am home." ("Selena . . .")
Expert quotes	• "'There are bedrock American ideologies, and one of those is that hard work is a moral good,' Nathan Palmer, a professor of sociology at the University of Nebraska, tells me." ("Carhartt . . .") • "'I think that perhaps part of the reason that Selena's story continues to resonate is that—even though she grew up in the United States and her family had been here for many generations—it embodied the ways that Latinos don't find an easy home either in the United States or in other countries of origin where they might find themselves." ("Selena . . .")
Person-on-the-street quotes	• "Now she's a singer, and said, 'When I sing Selena songs, I feel like I'm bringing back my parents.'" ("Selena . . .")
Specific examples	• "Even Mickey, the effortlessly cool LA twentysomething female lead in Judd Apatow's show *Love*, wore Carhartt overalls in an episode." ("Carhartt . . .") • "There's also the fact that Enninful's aesthetic is, by and large, glossy and provocative. Think: Linda Evangelista on the surgeon's table . . ." ("Edward Enninful . . .")
Comparisons and connections	• "It's what my uncles up in Maine wear when going out hunting or hauling cords of wood down to the cellar." ("Carhartt . . .") • "Enninful and Shulman couldn't be more different, not least because he is an image-maker and she is a features writer and novelist." ("Edward Enninful . . .")

Figure 5.9: Different Types of Evidence in Fashion Analysis

BEYOND LITERARY ANALYSIS

Conferring points. The categories and examples identified through this inquiry can serve as a mental checklist students use to help them choose their support widely. In a writing conference, you might ask, "What categories of evidence are you pulling from in your draft?" Then have students show you where they are engaging a range of evidence.

Justify Your Evidence

Before students can artfully discuss their evidence, they need to understand its significance, but alas, you cannot be at every desk every time a writer needs to talk through how she will discuss a piece of evidence. In your absence, students are prone to one-two-skip-a-few thinking—*they* see what the evidence reveals and how the pieces fit together, and, assuming everyone else does too, they forego explanation altogether. So, in lieu of thirty you-clones running around the room, may we offer some questions that will do some of your conferring work for you?

When presenting a piece of evidence, the writer asks herself questions to help spark a deeper exploration and discussion of the evidence.

- Why does this piece of evidence matter?

- How does this piece of evidence support or demonstrate my idea?

- What do I see in this evidence that I want my reader to see, too?

- What is the effect of this evidence?

- How does this evidence confirm our expectations?

- How does this evidence challenge our expectations?

Students in our ninth-grade classes highlighted evidence in their drafts in Google Docs and then answered one or more of these questions in a comment on the side. This important first step prepared writers to craft their discussion of evidence into the body of their paper using the techniques we offered. Figures 5.10 and 5.11 are two examples.

Students can copy these questions into their writer's notebooks and refer to them there, but since they will be using them often you might consider making these questions more permanently visible. Print the questions on sticky notes that students can tack onto their computer screens. (You can quickly search

> This evidence matters and demonstrates my claim because it comes directly from the new president of the company and shows her plans for the company in the future and how the company is changing from previous ways

With the tragic death of Lilly Pulitzer in April of 2013 and with new management in control of the multimillion dollar company, Lilly Pulitzer is evolving and breaking its old ways. Over the past few years Lilly has opened multiple new stores around the U.S., allowing for the already well known, name brand to become even more popular and wanted by consumers. President of the Lilly Pulitzer Company, Michelle Kelly said, "We see unlimited opportunities in terms of where we could grow."

I think this spike in popularity was mainly due to the one time deal with Target. When news reached the public that Lilly merchandise would be partnering up with Target many people became eager, including myself. Many excited shoppers showed up hours before Target opened, creating large lines hopping for a chance to get Lilly products. On the day of the sale the merchandise was gone within only a few short number of hours. Also Target's website crashed.

Figure 5.10: Caroline's Evidence Exploration

> What I see in this evidence that I want my reader to see in it too: that the fans were not happy and they did unecessary actions

"Russell, what's you're thoughts on the Kevin Durant trade" Russell responds to this by saying "no matter what decision he makes we will remain friends, and everything is gonna work out." Russell handled this like an adult should while some fans responded very immaturely with Durant's decision by burning his jersey, and even his shoes:

https://www.youtube.com/watch?v=p2cUeyYlze8&scrlybrkr=f2ffd206

Figure 5.11: Mario's Evidence Exploration

online for a template for this!) Or, create a digital version that students can copy and paste at the top of their document or into a Google Docs comment.

You can also switch it up by having students use these questions to interview one another as a kind of focused peer revision.

Once students understand the evidence they have available, it's time to start thinking about how they will discuss it.

Crafting Techniques for Articulating Claims

"I know what I think, but I don't know how to write it!"

We hear this constantly from writers at all levels. Students who are new to analytical writing often exist in a tangled mental forest of ideas. They have things to say (lots of them!) but which things? And in what order? And how do they find words for all of those messy ideas inside their heads? Students trapped in the forest—writers who can't yet see the trees—shy away from untangling their thoughts. It's much easier to default to the easy claim. But because we don't want a failure in articulation to scare students away from deep analysis, we offer them some guides from professional writers who have successfully explored them before.

There are many ways to use these techniques: Share one with a student during a writing conference ("It sounds like you're trying to use the 'this and that' technique. Here's what it looks like . . ."), in small groups, or as a menu of options in a whole-class writing lesson on discussing your evidence.

We offer students options, not mandates or one-size-fits-all formulas. Showing students techniques helps them explore ways of expressing complicated ideas about a text. We also encourage students to use these techniques as a launching pad for writing rather than a finish line—transforming them as their own ideas deepen and expand.

This and That

With "This *and* That," writers show the multidimensionality of a text: It is not just one thing. Using this technique, writers generally assert one level of meaning about the text and then go deeper by making that claim even more specific.

This technique is the equivalent of the "Say more about that . . ." writing conference strategy we so often use with students: It takes a valid and workable idea and then makes it more sophisticated by addition. These three sentence frames each get to the same contrast; students may "try on" all three and choose the sentence that best captures their idea.

_____ *is* _____, *but also* _____.

Sometimes _____, *but also* _____.

Even though _____, *occasionally* _____.

One of the great themes that threads its way through Toni Morrison's work like a haunting melody is the hold that time past exerts over time present. In larger historical terms, it is the horror of slavery and its echoing legacy that her characters struggle with. In personal terms, it is an emotional wound or loss—and the fear of suffering such pain again—that inhibits her women and men, making them wary of the very sort of love and intimacy that might heal and complete them.

—*Kara Walker*, review of Toni Morrison's *God Help the Child*, *The New York Times*

Art—its creation, its importance, its impact on identity and freedom—is perhaps the central theme of *I'll Give You the Sun*. The book celebrates art's capacity to heal, but it also shows us how we excavate meaning from the art we cherish, and how we find reflections of ourselves within it.

—*Lauren Oliver*, review of Jandy Nelson's *I'll Give you the Sun*, *The New York Times*

The biggest focus is her vocals—they blossoms in the song, showing the soulful, soothing side of her voice as well as the powerful, vibrant side.

—*Jeanie*, grade 9

They Say, I Say

The "They Say, I Say" technique for stating claims has been popularized by Graff and Birkenstein (2014) in their writing textbook of the same name. The versatile technique acknowledges the status quo claims of others and then adds to them, spins them, complicates them, or completely dismisses them. "They say, I say" gives writers the latitude to explore commonly addressed ideas about a text and then add their own voice to the conversation. Here are some sentence frames for this technique.

While many people think _____, I think _____.

It is often said that _____, but actually _____.

It may seem that _____; however, _____.

EXAMPLES

In *The Scarlet Letter*, Hester Prynne may seem a victim and an object, but she also shows great personal strength. She survives.

—Andrea Seabrook, "Hester Prynne: Sinner, Victim, Object, Winner," NPR

Loss doesn't make people stronger. The way we cope with loss, that's where we see true character growth. The loss of a loved one, of a relationship, of a job, of trust, of sanity—these are challenges that reveal what type of person we truly are, what we'd like to be, and how hard we're willing to work to get there. Everybody in *Firewatch* is coping with loss in one manner or another.

—Derrick Sanskrit, "*Firewatch* Sees Relationships Rise from the Ashes of Loss," A.V. Club

You could argue that The Weeknd is one of those one and done pop artists, the artists who get a glimpse of fame for one hit song, but aren't talented enough for the long haul, but I strongly disagree. . . . His most recent album *Starboy* was a success and is a turning point in his career that says he is here to stay.

—Luke, grade 9

Shifts and Changes

The "Shifts and Changes" technique reveals a text's evolution as meaning is made, transformed, and revealed to the audience. In this kind of claim, the text begins one way but then changes into something else—something surprising, stronger, more specific. Ideas expressed in this way have a movement that is the opposite of "this *and* that" claims. Rather than becoming more specific and pinpointed in its claim, these claims tend to widen and become more universal.

The more you consider _____, the more _____.

At first _____, but over time _____.

Over the course of _____, _____ became _____.

EXAMPLES

The more you consider this strange little masterpiece, the more suggestive it becomes, shifting from a single incident at a beach to a tiny allegory of loneliness and the desire for human connection.

—*Michael Dirda, "Michael Dirda on the Misunderstood Poet Stevie Smith,"*
The Washington Post

No Man's Sky (released in its original form in August of 2016 by indie studio Hello Games, and updated just a couple weeks ago) is a bauble, an amazement that borders on magical in its opening hours, becomes almost hypnotically comfortable at a certain point, then simply majestic in its scope and incomprehensible size.

—*Jason Sheehan, "Reading the Game: No Man's Sky," NPR*

At first this similarity could seem like an accidental lack of variation between characters, but Day even says late in the book: "It's strange being here with you. I hardly know you. But . . . sometimes it feels like we're the same person born in two different worlds."

—*Jay, grade 9*

Crafting Techniques for Discussing Evidence

When we study the analytical writing of professionals, we see that a great writer never leaves the reader in doubt about what she should be seeing or understanding in a piece of evidence. Rather, the writer acts as an engaging tour guide, pointing out elements of interest, showing what's important, exploring what it all means. Often, this is where the deepest analysis actually happens. What do writers talk about when discussing a piece of evidence? They consider:

- What the evidence means
- How the evidence affects the idea being presented
- How the evidence affects the text itself.

However (and probably not surprisingly at this point) this discussion doesn't follow any rigid format: It's not necessarily one to three sentences, and it doesn't always immediately follow the evidence. So, in the absence of absolutes, here are some options—techniques we have gleaned from the pros to help students add meaningful insight to the evidence they present in their analysis.

Talk Back to Evidence

One way writers move from evidence to a discussion of that evidence is to use "this" or "that" plus a power verb (Figure 5.12) to begin exploring the effect of the evidence in the text. Using this technique, writers will place the discussion in its traditional spot—immediately following each piece of evidence. This technique helps students move away from restating what a piece of evidence *says* to focusing on what a piece of evidence *does*.

	Power Verb Possibilities from Mentor Texts	
This	Amplify	Issue
	Become	Launch
	Build	Look
	Change	Make
	Contain	Render
That	Convey	Represent
	Emphasize	Seems
	Evoke	Shape
	Is crucial to	Speak
	Is necessary for	Suggest

Figure 5.12: Power Verb Possibilities

That option changed the rules of combat so that I had to narrowly dodge incoming projectiles . . . until the monster blushed so much that it stopped fighting.

—*Kallie Plagge,* "Undertale Review," *IGN*

This "spokes on the wheel" doctrine, while admirable in its ambition, may alienate pockets of the population who still pledge fealty to their old lords.

—*Carolyne Larrington,* "How to Win the Game of Thrones," *1843*

This speaks to why the novel has stuck around for so long. It's not about particular scientific accomplishments but the vagaries of scientific progress in general.

—*Jacob Brogan,* "Why *Frankenstein* Is Still Relevant, Almost 200 Years After It Was Published," *Slate*

In Korea, [Thames] would be found before games sitting quietly by himself with his baseball bat, mentally trying to visualize what he is about to do in this game. This would heavily contribute to his success due to him believing in himself, knowing that he will do well no matter what happens.

—*James, grade 9*

Introduce Evidence with Discussion

The discussion and explanation of evidence sometimes occurs *before* the evidence itself is even presented. What is the advantage of this? It shifts the focus away from the evidence itself and onto the writer's own thoughts, causing them to stand out more powerfully. The writer first explores what the piece of evidence might mean, how it affects the ideas being presented, or how the evidence impacts the text itself. This discussion is then immediately followed by the piece of evidence: a specific example, a fact or statistic, or a direct quote.

EXAMPLES

As they age, those players reach a level of play where they can't hack it up the middle, or they grow into bodies that are too big for up-the-middle positions, or they get old and slow and move to a corner. Donaldson and Bryce Harper are former amateur catchers, Alex Rodriguez moved from shortstop to third base in his late 20s, and first base and outfield corners are full of guys who once played up the middle but don't have the legs anymore, from Andrew McCutchen to Mike Napoli.

—*Michael Baumann,* "A Good Man Behind the Plate Is Hard to Find," *The Ringer*

In this case, the tactic didn't pan out; *When We Rise*'s finale was watched by just two million people.

—*Alison Herman,* "ABC Experiments with the MiniSeries," *The Ringer*

Whedon wanted to focus not on the pain and catharsis of grief but on how surreal and physically strange it can be. "What I really wanted to capture," he later explained in the DVD commentary, "was the extreme physicality, the extreme—the almost boredom of the very first few hours."

—*Sophie Gilbert,* "'The Body' and the Radical Empathy of *Buffy*'s Best Episode," *The Atlantic*

McCarthy's nonfiction, to judge from our only example, is recognizably his, with folksy locutions and no-nonsense sentence fragments and even, at points, the vaguely biblical grandiloquence of his earlier novels: "The simple understanding that one thing can be another is at the root of all things of our doing," he writes.

—*Nick Romeo,* "Cormac McCarthy Explains the Unconscious," *The New Yorker*

Sometimes, it seemed like Tartt would get distracted by some thought that flitted by and end up writing a whole paragraph about it before returning to the original idea. In a conversation between Richard, Francis, and their teacher, Julian, about a letter that had been left to him, Tartt goes on a tangent about typewriters that was entirely unnecessary and didn't add anything to the plot other than one more run-on sentence:

> It was impossible to write in Greek alphabet on an English typewriter; and though Henry actually has somewhere a little Greek-alphabet portable, which he had purchased on holiday in Mykonos, he never used it because, as he explained to me, the keyboard was different from the English and it took him five minutes to type his own name.

—*Brooke*, grade 9

Combine Evidence and Discussion

We've seen how writers talk back to evidence after presenting it, and we've seen how they sometimes discuss the evidence before they present it as a way of high-lighting their ideas. But, quite often, writers don't make these hard and fast distinctions; they combine discussion and evidence so seamlessly we can hardly tell the difference. Writers craft tight sentences that include both the piece of evidence and its effect, stepping up the pace of the writing and making it feel more sophisticated. Phrases such as *all of which* and *might well be understood as* help the writer combine the evidence and its discussion.

EXAMPLES

> Season 3's themes include undocumented immigration, opioid addiction in the white working class, and abortion, all of which make the story sound more didactic and responsive than it is or is meant to be.

—*Alison Herman, "ABC Experiments with the MiniSeries," The Ringer*

When they fall off the position, they often go all the way down to first base, like Napoli and Joe Mauer did, because years of erosion made them unable to run fast enough to play shortstop or centerfield, if they ever could in the first place.

—Michael Bausmann, "A Good Man Behind the Plate Is Hard to Find," *The Ringer*

Mark Zuckerberg, who's sometimes been known to disavow the power of his own platform, might well be understood as a Frankensteinian figure, amplifying his creation's monstrosity by neglecting its practical needs.

—Jacob Brogan, "Why *Frankenstein* Is Still Relevant, Almost 200 Years After It Was Published," *Slate*

All of these elements together describe Frida's depression and claustrophobia around her many miscarriages. We have the red ribbons strangling her. We have the monkey symbolism for her miscarriages and lost sadness. We have her monochrome expression and color scheme, drawing attention to only her.

—Marina, grade 9

Wicked has received three Tony awards, seven Drama Desk awards, and a Grammy, all of which show how impressive the cast and the directors are.

—Dylan, grade 9

Oscar Robertson, who averaged 31 points, 10 rebounds, and 9.7 assists while playing 43 minutes a game, might well be understood as a rookie who was given the ball almost every possession of the game in an NBA era ('60s) but is regarded as one of the weakest players ever in terms of aggression and competition.

—Jack, grade 9

When the evidence requires nothing more than a brief mention, writers sometimes use em dashes to combine evidence with discussion. It's a slick two-in-one trick that highlights the writer's critical thinking while quickly presenting evidence, too. This technique works well with short lists of evidence and very brief specific examples.

EXAMPLES

By making Selina frustrated and small and unappreciated in a different way with a different set of scenarios that could play out—lobbying, campaigning, writing her memoir, speaking, or getting another job entirely— *Veep* has played to its strengths without repeating itself.

—Linda Holmes, "'Veep' Reinvents Itself in the Shape of a New Humiliation," NPR

But all this beauty—the sensuality of the camera movements, the slowness of many of the scenes, the lovely hush that descends over the final act—is more than just a matter of style or virtuosity.

—A.O. Scott, "*Moonlight*: Is This the Year's Best Movie?" *The New York Times*

Plenty of these speeches—Ray's, in particular—have been memorable and hilarious.

—Emily Nussbaum, "Goodbye *Girls*: A Fittingly Imperfect Finale," *The New Yorker*

The spirits that coexist with humans are just one magical element of the book that the book has—others being fish falling from the sky and talking cats. These are completely mythical, but Murakami has weaved them seamlessly into the storyline that it hardly seems unreal—they're reality.

—Jeanie, grade 9

CHAPTER SIX

exploring structure

L
ike explorers, writers don't always know where they're going. They don't know where to start the writing or where it will end. They don't know how many paragraphs their final piece will have, or if it will have sections with subheadings. In other words, writers don't always have a structure when they start. Structure, like a partially drawn map, is something they make and remake as they go along.

The Problem and the Solution

Think about the last set of analysis essays you read. Did some or all of the essays

- Have five paragraphs?
- Begin with a question or expert quote?
- Have a three-part thesis?
- Present the thesis statement at the end of the last paragraph?
- Regurgitate the main points of the essay in the conclusion?

And did you want to pull your hair out? Did you say a prayer to the god of student writing and ask for mercy? Did you nearly die of boredom?

Now imagine a different scenario. Imagine a new stack of analytical writing in which no two essays look the same. Essays with

- Varied numbers of paragraphs
- One-sentence paragraphs that "pop"
- Narrative writing peppered in between the claims and evidence
- Evocative titles and subheadings
- Conclusions that truly leave you with something to ponder
- Paragraphs that build and take you on a journey.

This second stack of essays is not unachievable: Students will make interesting structural choices if we let them. We have to start by throwing away easy formulas and showing students the structures that real writers use.

Those of us who assign the five-paragraph essay and other formulas have our writers' best interests at heart. Formulas can help solve writing problems quickly. "How long does this paper have to be?" Five paragraphs. "How many examples do I have to have?" At least three.

Five-paragraph and other formulaic writing tasks also make grading easy. Is the claim at the end of paragraph one? Check. Does the student have at least three quotes? Check. Does the conclusion reiterate the claim? Check. Formulas are easy to spot in writing; assessment is straightforward.

But while formulas may make our students' and our jobs easier, they are inauthentic (and boring!). They don't really engage our students in the kind of problem-solving writers must do. In *Dynamic Teaching for Deeper Reading* (2017), Vicki Vinton explores the dangers of giving students formulas: "We offer students scaffolds that act as shortcuts for more complex work . . . but, I have to wonder if, by focusing on what's easy and expedient rather than on what's complex, we don't shortchange them in the long run" (5).

The structure of a piece of writing should develop organically during the writing process, but when we assign specific structures, we prescribe a way of thinking and rob students of an essential experience. Instead, we must expose them to copious mentor texts so they can see how real writers structure their writing. We need to give them tools for trying on different structures and knowing whether a structure works. In short, we need to equip students with strategies to solve their structure problems. Figure 6.1 details a few ways to tackle the diverse issues related to structure that we might see in a piece of student writing.

If You See This in Students' Writing...	Try This
Lackluster leads and conclusions	• Sticky Note Choices (p. 103) • Drop the Reader Into a Scene (p. 109) • Make a Personal Connection (p. 110) • Immerse the Reader in Media (p. 112) • Soft Echo (p. 124) • End with an Image (p. 125) • Zoom Out (p. 126).
Connections between ideas are confusing or not present	• Structure Cut-Up (p. 99) • Use a Conjunction (p. 114) • Make a Smooth Segue (p. 115) • Question and Answer (p. 116).
The writer's claim is hard to find	• Visualize It (p. 92) • Create (and Follow!) a Roadmap (p. 96) • Structure Cut-Up (p. 99) • Claim Up Front (p. 105) • The Single Paragraph Claim (p. 106) • Theme and Variations (p. 106) • The Ta-Da! Claim (p. 107) • Sections with Subheadings (p. 122) • Sections without Subheadings (p. 123) • Zoom Out (p. 126).
Poor pacing	• The Single Paragraph Claim (p. 106) • One Idea: Multiple Paragraphs (p. 117) • Mini Paragraphs (p. 119) • List-a-Graphs (p. 120) • Sections with Subheadings (p. 122) • Sections without Subheadings (p. 123).
Formulaic structure	• Create (and Follow!) a Roadmap (p. 96) • Structure Cut-Up (p. 99) • The Single Paragraph Claim (p. 106) • Theme and Variations (p. 106) • The Ta-Da! Claim (p. 107) • Make a Personal Connection (p. 110) • List-a-Graphs (p. 120) • Sections with Subheadings (p. 122) • Sections without Subheadings (p. 123) • End with an Image (p. 125) • Zoom Out (p. 126).

Figure 6.1: Strategies for Exploring Structure

Activities for Exploration and Discovery

To us, structure is the very hardest part of writing. It requires a bird's-eye view of the writing and a comprehensive understanding of what is happening and how it is happening in order to figure out where it should go in the piece. Furthermore, finding the right structure also requires us to do something that doesn't always come naturally—see our ideas from someone else's perspective. After all, while idea development is all about the writer, structure is all about the reader and making ideas easily understandable.

Students need to literally see what it means to explore different structures: to "try on" different formats and see how they affect a piece of writing. The activities below encourage playful, experimental structure work that will help students make intentional decisions about structure in their analytical writing.

Visualize It

Many of our students' notebook pages are filled with doodles and storyboards and cartoons that illustrate ideas and possibilities for writing—they just might not know it yet. Although sketching is more commonly used to plan for narrative writing, it can be a transformative tool for exploring structure possibilities for analytical writing. The magical book *Infographic Guide to Literature* (2014) by Joanna Eliot inspired us to *use* infographics as a prewriting tool to help students think about structuring their writing.

Infographic Guide to Literature is a collection of infographics that explore literature from many angles. Our favorites are the ones that analyze a theme, symbol, or pattern in a single work. In "What's the Weather Like," Eliot explores the role of weather as mood in forty classic texts. *Wuthering Heights*, *The Seagull*, and *Lord of the Flies* are among some of the novels printed atop a dark storm cloud, symbolizing the "madness" and "emotional turmoil" of these works; *The Strange Case of Dr. Jekyll and Mr. Hyde*, *Hamlet*, and *The Fall of the House of Usher* are titles sketched across a gauzy patch of fog, symbolizing the "confusion" and "stasis" of these works.

This book provides examples of visual analytical mentor texts that can help our students think about possible structures for their writing.

STEPS

Students should have already developed an idea or working claim for their analysis and gathered information; instead of planning for an essay, they will plan an infographic first.

1. Present individuals or small groups with a set of infographics.

2. Ask students to study the infographics, paying special attention to how information is organized.

3. Once students have a sense of what infographics are and how they function, they can experiment with different formats for organizing their information visually. Some may have success mirroring the structure of an infographic they studied; others may invent new structures.

4. Remind students that the focus is on exploring different ways to organize their information, not on creating the perfect infographic.

EXAMPLES

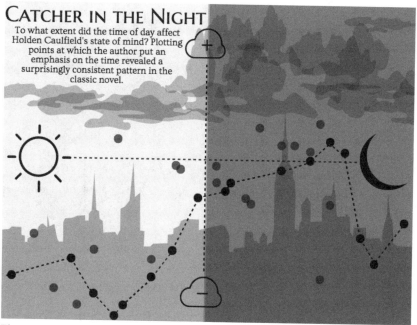

Figure 6.2: *The Catcher in the Rye*–Inspired Infographic

My claim is that Holden's sanity follows a certain pattern throughout the day, improving during the evening, but then dropping before the sun rises again. My infographic supports my claim because you can see a clear rise and fall in the plotted points, shown by the darker spots and dotted line. The infographic shows data for all the times in the book that could be clearly marked—meaning when the time of day could be easily determined. I noticed this curve in mindset while reading the book, and I wanted to illustrate it using real data.

—Lindsay, grade 9

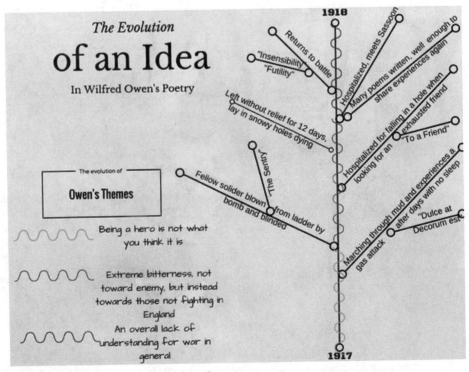

Figure 6.3: Wilfred Owen–Inspired Infographic

The purpose of my infograph is to show how Wilfred Owen's themes throughout his poems evolved over time due to certain events. Basically, I am claiming that as Owen experiences more and more throughout the war, it greatly influences his poetry. I personally despise looking at a list of dates in history class and then analyzing the outcome, but I really feel like the events that Owen experienced are important and deserve to be remembered. I tried to make these events interesting and easy to comprehend when showing their influence on the theme so that it isn't a list of dates to analyze.

—*Emma, grade 12*

THINGS TO CONSIDER

Make your own graphic organizer. In a way, asking students to organize their gathered information into some kind of infographic is akin to asking them to create their own graphic organizer. The thinking we are after is to identify and try multiple ways of grouping and presenting information, not graphic design.

Building a knowledge base. Easel.ly, a web-based infographic creator, has a primer on the seven common types of infographics. This list may provide a helpful framework for students.

Rough versus polished. While our students spend a lot of time polishing their infographics, a simple sketch of an infographic is sufficient for helping them plan possible structures for their writing. Before Lindsay created her infographic in Piktochart, she made a basic sketch of it in Google Draw (Figure 6.4). She could have easily drawn it in her notebook with a pen or pencil, too.

Can this *be it?* Yes, it can. The book *Infographic Guide to Literature* is proof that real writers create infographics to analyze a text. Last year, Rebekah's students created infographics, instead of writing essays, as a summative assessment. After looking at mentor texts, students developed an infographic around Wilfred Owen's poetry (a single poem or multiple poems) and then worked in pairs to

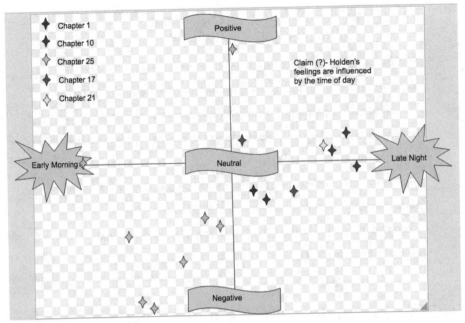

Figure 6.4: Lindsay's Infographic Planning

make their thinking visible. Students loved a visual approach to literary analysis and reported that they had to think in new ways in order to move away from words and into images. Their brains were stretched.

Next steps. Once students have designed an infographic, they need to think about how their visual plan might translate into an essay. For instance, Lindsay's infographic might inspire one of two structures: She could organize her analysis around a few key moments of depression in *Catcher*, or she could organize the essay around the two themes of light and dark.

Create (and Follow!) a Roadmap

In this activity, students study and map out the structures of various mentor texts. Then they choose one structure to emulate.

Thinking about mentor texts as literal maps concretizes structure while reminding students that there isn't just one way to get from Point A to Point B. Maps contain many routes for the driver to explore.

STEPS

Here are the instructions we provide students.

Mapping a Mentor Text's Structure

Think about the road trips you take—on vacation or to "away" games. What do you routinely do along the way? When you stop, what do you do? If you were to make a "map" of one of your road trips, what activities would be on it?

Maps can reflect where we've been and also guide us where to go. Mentor texts are a "map" of how to write—where to go first, second, and what to include on your "trip."

Today, you will study and create a map for a few different mentor texts and then experiment using the structures you uncover in your own writing.

1. First, study your mentor text through the lens of structure. Use this question to guide your discussion: How do writers of analysis structure their writing?

2. Write your answers in the margin of a mentor text.

3. After you are finished discussing the structure, grab a piece of poster paper. At the top, write your mentor text title. Then, draw a large road.

4. To plot the "stops" of your trip, consider what is happening in each paragraph and how you might represent it visually. For example, you might illustrate the claim with a giant exclamation point (because claims are bold and contestable and exciting).

5. When you are done, you will present your map to the class.

EXAMPLES

A group of ninth graders mapped out the structure of the NPR article, "Henry Fleming, Reluctantly Wearing the Red Badge," a character analysis of Henry Fleming from the *Red Badge of Courage* (Figure 6.5). Based on Allison's suggestions,

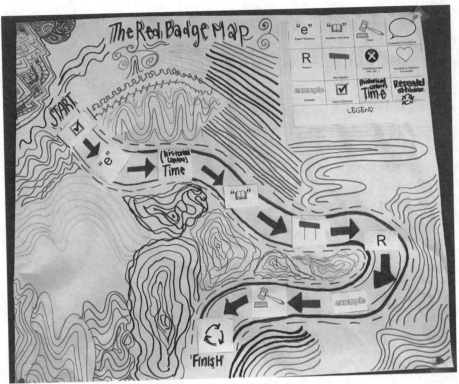

Figure 6.5: Structural Map of Mentor Text

the students added two of their own icons to the legend: an icon that indicates a repeating structure, and another to show the author's use of historical context.

THINGS TO CONSIDER

Structurally diverse mentor texts. Give students a set of essays from the same column or magazine with vastly different structures. The first time we tried this exercise, we were in the middle of a literary analysis unit of study. Students were using essays from NPR's "In Character" series as mentor texts. We selected three texts for this exercise; two have clearly defined subsections, and the third is a multiparagraph essay without larger sections:

"Troy Maxson: Heart, Heartbreak as Big as the World" by Allison Keyes

"Jo March: Everyone's Favorite Little Woman" by Lynn Neary

"Henry Fleming: Reluctantly Wearing 'The Red Badge'" by Elizabeth Blair.

Scaffolding for younger or less experienced students. When using this activity with our ninth graders, we provide a scaffold that our upperclassmen don't need. Instead of inviting students to create their own symbols, we provide a legend for them, complete with icons for claim, reasons, ideas, transitions, and so on (Figure 6.6). We then give students a packet with one or two rows of each icon. Students cut and paste icons onto their hand-drawn maps. Notice the blank boxes on the legend inviting students to draw in their own icons as needed.

Structure Cut-Up

If essays are "word houses" (Heard 2014, 38), then re-structuring an essay is like remodeling a house. If you've lived through a remodeling, then you know how messy things get as walls come down, entryways seal shut, and dust coats everything. But the magic lies in the mess. One day, light streams in through new windows, and the dust begins to lift. As you settle into your new space, the wait feels worth it.

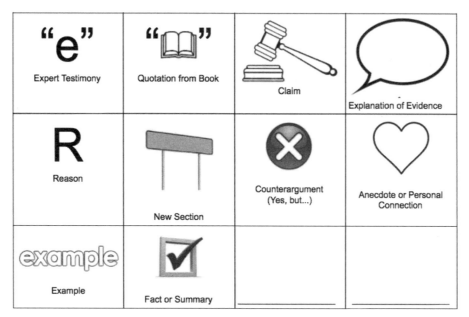

Figure 6.6: Legend for Scaffolded Structure Map

In this activity, students physically cut up the pieces of their essays and shuffle them around to explore other possible structures. Expect your floors to be covered in scraps of paper and sticky notes as students break down the walls of their writing and reenvision its design.

STEPS

Here's the how-to we give our students.

INSTRUCTIONS TO STUDENTS

Steps for Restructuring Your Essay—Remodeling Your "Word House"

If essays are "word houses," then restructuring our essays is a little bit like remodeling a house.

Remodeling a House	Restructuring an Essay
Blowing out the back of the house	Expanding the heart of your piece
Knocking down walls	Removing paragraphs and sections that don't fit
Adding a room	Adding paragraphs and sections to develop your idea
Reconfiguring the flow of the house	Changing the order of ideas
Adding columns or walls	Adding subheadings or section dividers

Today you are going to explore other possible structures for arranging your ideas. Here's how:

1. Print out your draft.

2. Cut up your draft into smaller pieces. A smaller piece might be:

   a. Paragraphs

   b. Small sections

3. Move the pieces around on your desk (or floor!) to explore various arrangements. Consider the chart above as well as some of the following suggestions:

   a. Move your claim to a different position.

   b. Find a way to make your best paragraph your lead.

   c. Split large paragraphs into smaller ones.

   d. Leave a space where you think you might need to add more discussion or evidence.

   e. Move a piece to the side if you realize it doesn't fit anymore.

   f. Write subheadings on sentence strips or sticky notes, and add them to your piece.

4. While you play with different structures, think about:

   a. What doesn't belong?

   b. What do I need more of?

   c. Which transitions need to be reworked as a consequence of this shifting?

5. Create at least two different possible structures.

EXAMPLE

Figure 6.7: Students Restructuring Their Essays

THINGS TO CONSIDER

Transitioning. One consequence of moving the pieces of writing around is that you disrupt the transitions that united paragraphs. The section in this chapter called "Artful Transitions" will help your students with the work of crafting new transitions that support the revision work they've done.

Paper versus computer? Obviously, pieces of a draft can be moved around by cutting and pasting them within a Word document. However, remodeling an essay on the computer doesn't have the same impact as moving the pieces around on a desk. The physical computer screen is limiting—you can't use the space that lies beyond it—and students who limit their reshuffling to the computer screen won't see all the possibilities.

Talk it out. Once students have imagined different structures, they can talk with writing partners or groups about their options, weighing the strengths and weaknesses of each one:

- How are the two structures different?

- Which structure showcases your idea most effectively?

- Are there elements of each one you could combine into a third variation?

- What parts of your writing would you need to combine, delete, or add to if you chose one structure over the other?

- What did you learn about your piece through this activity?

For homework or in class the next day, students begin revising their drafts with their new structure in mind.

Sticky Note Choices: Leads and Conclusions

Angela Stockman, executive director of the WNY Young Writer's Studio and author of *Make Writing* (2015), taught us the possibilities for bringing a makerspace philosophy into the writer's workshop. One place that a maker mentality is particularly helpful is when thinking about the way different leads or conclusions can work in a piece of analysis. Rather than just thinking about options, we need to help writers try different leads and conclusions on for size. Sticky notes are the perfect tool for helping students get physically engaged with trying different leads and conclusions in a piece of analysis.

STEPS

1. Students choose a few lead or conclusion strategies to try in their piece of analysis. These strategies could come from the mentor texts you are studying as a class or from the techniques for leads and conclusions we share later in this chapter.

2. Students write the name of each technique on a separate sticky note and create a column on the desk.

3. Students write their own version of each kind of lead on separate sticky notes and place them beside the strategy sticky note.

4. Students can pick up each sticky—now with a lead or conclusion written on it—and "try it on" in their writing, whether it's on paper or on the screen. They can read their piece with each kind of lead or conclusion attached and see which work well, which don't, and what they like best.

Henry tried three different leads for his *Catcher in the Rye* character analysis (Figure 6.8).

Holden is a teenager that fears the road ahead.	Fearful, friendless, and young, Holden is fearing what happens next in his life.	Holden is like me how I dread the day. My family and I grow up and the friends around me, but unlike Holden I have a little bit of excitement.

Figure 6.8: Henry Tries Lead Options

THINGS TO CONSIDER

Color, color everywhere. Colored sticky notes can enhance this activity by providing students with a way to code the different parts of their essays: Lead strategies might be written on blue sticky notes, and conclusions on green sticky notes. Colored sticky notes really make an impact when students play with the position of each one, trying it at the beginning, testing its impact toward the end of the piece, and so on.

Keep those stickies. We always encourage students to keep leftover sticky notes in their notebooks, in case they change their minds later or to serve as models for leads and conclusions in future writing.

Crafting Techniques for Structure

Structure can mean a lot of different things. We would like to invoke the definition of structure that Georgia Heard provides in *The Revision Toolbox* (2014). Structure is:

> those tools that have to do with planning, rearranging, and organizing a text. The structure of a piece of writing includes a plan for the organization; a focus; the arrangement of text; the introduction or lead and the conclusion; and even organizational units such as paragraphs and chapters. (39)

Most young writers associate structure with paragraphing—and it does include paragraphing—but it also encompasses so much more. Students need to first learn all that structure can mean and do before considering the structure of their own writing.

Focus

All analytical writing has a focus, a specific idea the writer wants to communicate to the reader. Traditionally, we have taught students that the focus should be communicated to the reader early on in a thesis statement or claim—a single sentence that communicates their overarching idea. We've told them to put this main idea in the first paragraph, preferably at the end.

But a close study of real-world analytical writing shows us that writers don't always follow these rules: Some use their claim as their title; some put their claim in a bold, single-sentence paragraph; some play with variations on a claim throughout the piece of writing; some work their way up to a claim at the end of the piece. The techniques below present different possibilities for communicating the focus of a piece of analytical writing.

CLAIM UP FRONT

You need not look far to identify the focus of many analytical essays: Writers often make their title their claim. Sometimes an intentional fragment and sometimes a complete sentence, titles-as-claims leave no room for misunderstanding the focal point of the piece. This structure is particularly advantageous for digital readers who won't have to bother with clicking on a link to see what a piece is about: They can simply read the title. This technique is also a go-to for inexperienced writers struggling to find the right place to state their focus; you can hardly go wrong with right up front and center.

Examples

- "Steph Curry, the Prophet of Basketball" (*The New York Times*)

- "*Guardians of the Galaxy, Volume 2*: A Good But Lesser Sequel" (*Variety*)

- "Why *Little Women* Is Still the Best Christmas Movie" (*Vogue*)

- "How Streaming Changed the Gaming Ecosystem" (NPR).

THE SINGLE PARAGRAPH CLAIM

Another way to bring attention to your claim is by putting it in a single-sentence paragraph of its own. Similar to the claim-up-front move, the single-paragraph claim emphasizes the main idea by putting it on its own line. Writers who give us their claim in the title or in its own paragraph make it easy for digital readers to scan and decide if they want to devote time to reading the whole article. Following the claim is, of course, a thorough discussion of evidence.

Students love this technique because it's simple to use, and it feels like it's breaking a long-held writing "rule" that a paragraph needs five to eight sentences.

Example

Although the storyline might span the universe, it's the internal dysfunction of generations of Skywalkers that is the root of the problem—and which pushes the plot forward.

In short, Star Wars is an open-ended cycle of science fiction films about bad parenting.

—*Jeet Herr*, "Star Wars Films Are Not About Good vs. Evil.
They're About Bad Parenting," *New Republic*

THEME AND VARIATIONS

Sometimes writers hide the claim. It's not the title, it's not in its own paragraph, and it's not the last sentence of the first paragraph. It's everywhere and nowhere.

Like the classical music form that consists of a melody, or theme, followed by variations of that melody, the "theme and variations" writing technique allows a writer to introduce her topic at the beginning of the piece and explore it from a few different angles, ultimately inviting the reader to infer the claim or big idea of the text.

To try this, ask students to begin with a big question about their text. Then, they should develop a few different answers to that question using different angles or lenses (perhaps first a historical lens, then a feminist lens, then a personal lens). Each of these answers will eventually become a subheading to be explored in the body of the essay.

Example

In a character analysis of Henry Fleming, the protagonist in *The Red Badge of Courage*, writer Elizabeth Blair uses discrete sections to explore Henry's state of mind during war ("Henry Fleming Reluctantly Wearing 'The Red Badge,'" NPR). While Blair doesn't explicitly state a guiding question in her character analysis, we can use her section subheadings and focal points to infer that she might have been exploring a question like "What does Henry Fleming reveal about courage?"

Figure 6.9 shows the structure of her essay.

Section Subheading	Section Focus
(Introduction)	Gives background information about the book and Henry Fleming, a young man looking to make his mark in the war
Battle of Chancellorsville	Depicts the Battle of Chancellorsville—the battle that *Badge* is likely based on—as a bloody, chaotic battle in which many soldiers ran for their lives
Cowardice Is Complicated	Presents cowardice as a complicated emotion
From "Youth" to "Man"	Discusses Henry's transformation throughout the book

Figure 6.9: Subheadings and Section Focus

THE TA-DA! CLAIM

Some writers build up to their claim over the course of a piece, presenting it as the final "ta-da!" Sometimes it's literally the last line. When writers put their claims at the end, they force the reader to stick with them as they build to a final conclusion.

Examples

Both examples presented here are the final paragraphs of much longer pieces of analysis. We recommend you find them on the internet and take a peek at how the writers build to these claims.

The Expanse isn't going to come home with a sack of Emmys, and it's not going to redefine the genre the way *Star Trek* did, but it's an incredibly well-shot, well-acted drama that, while based in familiar ideas and sci-fi tropes, still manages to take us to places we've never been before. It's not *Firefly*, and it's not *Battlestar Galactica*. But it makes me feel the way I did watching those shows for the first time, and that's even better.

—Michael Baumann, "*The Expanse* Steals Gracefully from
All of Your Favorite Shows," *The Ringer*

Like *Hide and Seek*, *Little Nightmares* confidently captures the exhilarating fear of waiting to be found by something that's hunting you. But it also replicates the alien horror of being a child that doesn't understand what's happening to and around them, and of a seemingly familiar environment turned into a series of opportunities for safety and danger. Smart, grotesque and never-endingly weird, this is a very different, extremely welcome kind of horror game that left me wanting more than its brief five hours provides.

—Joe Skrebels, "*Little Nightmares* Review," *IGN*

Engaging Leads

Most teachers teach students the power of a good lead to hook a reader, some-times giving them ideas like "start with a quote" or "begin with a rhetorical ques-tion." Many times when students write analysis, though, they seem to drop this strategy, instead settling for a boring and generic opener usually full of facts and needless background.

What follows is a collection of strategies for writing a compelling lead, one that entices the reader to keep reading. At first glance, these strategies may not seem so boundary-breaking. The dropping-a-reader-into-a-scene move is reminiscent of Nancie Atwell's "begin inside" poetry lesson. Sharing your personal experience is a suggestion we often share with our seniors who are drafting college essays. But when it comes to instructing students in the art of analytical writing, these strategies *are* a bit unusual. When was the last time you instructed your students to begin their *Of Mice and Men* essays with a personal anecdote or YouTube video?

DROP THE READER INTO A SCENE

In this strategy, writers take a page from the narrative playbook and drop their reader into a scene as if they were writing fiction or memoir.

Examples

> On a crag of volcanic rock, overlooking the wastes of Udun, I crouch silently in the rain, watching the orc hordes of Mordor milling around below me.
>
> They march and they argue. They taunt their human slaves and, when they pass close enough, I can hear them talking about me—Talion, called Gravewalker, murdered Captain of Gondor brought back to life by magic and the influence of my mostly invisible elf/wraith buddy, Celebrimbor, who is a ghost that lives in my head.
>
> —Jason Sheehan, "Reading the Game: *Shadow of Mordor*," NPR

> "Cow!" says Jo Thornton Harding, as a black-and-white bovine, caught on the edge of a tornado, sweeps, legs flailing, in front of the truck she's sharing with her soon-to-be ex-husband, Bill "The Extreme" Harding.
>
> The creature is swept out of view. And then: "Another cow!" Jo says.
>
> "Actually," Bill replies, "I think it was the same cow."

It's an exchange that, apologies to *Casablanca* and *Gone with the Wind*, may well be the best bit of dialogue in American cinematic history: elegant, sparse, ironic.

—Megan Garber, "The Spin Zone," *The Atlantic*

MAKE A PERSONAL CONNECTION

Personal pronouns everywhere will celebrate the day we invite our students to open a piece of analysis with a personal experience or connection. Analysis and personal writing aren't mutually exclusive. The claims we make about texts are rooted in our own personal responses to the text. Telling writers to excise all personal pronouns—and ultimately their personal connections—from their analysis writing is the equivalent of telling them their response to the text doesn't matter.

When writers lead with a personal connection, they often share the context that prompted the writing—a political event, the release of a new movie or video game, or a disturbing news story. Historically, students have written in response to a class assignment—the occasion for the writing has been school. But if we want our students to write authentic analysis we have to invite them to respond to real events that move them, and then we have to show them how to leverage this personal connection for their leads.

Ask students to think about what brought them to this text: Did the latest video game just arrive at your door via Amazon Prime? Were you watching *Seinfeld* reruns instead of doing chores? Did your best friend hand you a book she had just finished and say, "You have to read this"? Did your parents drag you to the movies? Have students write a little about what prompted the writing and see if it might work as a possible introduction.

Alternatively, students might explore the memories that surround the text they're analyzing or how it connects to parts of their past and present. Jotting down some memories might also point the writer toward a lead.

Examples

And so . . . . I scrutinized Manning's every muscle twitch after the Denver Broncos' first drive stalled at the New England Patriots' forty-eight-yard line. As he did his typical stiff-legged trot to the sideline, I saw no trace of the

trademark Manning pout but rather the confident posture
of a quarterback who knew that he was fortune's favorite.

—Brendan I. Coerner, "Reading Peyton Manning," *The New Yorker*

I met Anne Shirley first, though whether it was on the
page or through the interpretation of Megan Follows, I
can't recall. Either way, I quickly acknowledged our kinship:
garrulous and gawky, passionately devoted to our dearest
girlfriends, and eager to love those who loved us—not to
mention some that didn't. Her delicate nose was the focal
point of her wobbling vanity; mine, contrastingly, seemed
a curse designed to condemn me to torment. But we both
plotted out our lives according to storybook conventions, and
our first attempts at authorship were similarly bathetic.

—Rachel Vorona Cote, "Are You an Anne Shirley or an Emily Starr?
In Praise of L. M. Montgomery's Lesser-Loved Heroine," *LitHub*

A learner's permit is not far into my future, and I am
terrified. It also doesn't help that whether it be my parents
discussing how much they look forward to not having to
drive me around anymore, or my friends expressing their
excitement about getting their own permits, I hear about it
at least once a day. I still have two months to go before that
trip to the DMV comes, but with these constant reminders,
my anxiety continues to build and build and build.

It's not that I'm particularly scared about the responsibilities
that come with being on the road—I consider myself able to
handle such things. Rather, it's clear to me that I am more
afraid about what a permit entails. With a learner's permit
comes a driver's license, and with a driver's license comes

junior year of high school. Before I know it, I'm middle-aged, with a full-time job and a family. This isn't really a bad thing—I know that. Yet I am still *so scared* of not being a kid anymore—and thanks to *The Catcher in the Rye*, I know that I'm not alone."

—*Sydney, grade 9*

IMMERSE THE READER IN MEDIA

Most writers who analyze a text have been moved, changed, or provoked by that text. We're thinking of Joe who spent thirty hours this weekend playing the newest video game. Or JaNiece who is spellbound by the cover of Kendrick Lamar's album *To Pimp a Butterfly*.

Writers who lead with media are looking for their readers to react—to be moved, changed, or provoked by the text they are about to explore. With the start-with-media technique, writers lead with that video, clip, photo, song, or other visual or audio medium as a way to let readers experience what they experienced—and then read all about it.

Examples

"Yeah, that was pretty cool," Andrelton Simmons said. "I liked that one."

I'd just asked him about a play from April 8, when he'd leaped to corral a wayward throw from first-baseman Jefry Marté, then twisted down to lay a last-second tag on a diving Jean Segura.

[Video showing Segura out at third on an overturned call]

In addition to the incredible coordination and presence of mind it takes to make a play like that, this tag stands out for two reasons: First, nobody watching the play live thought Segura was out, except Simmons.

—*Michael Baumann, "Andrelton Simmons Is Peerless," The Ringer*

Here, have a clip of Neymar being awesome. Sorry, Nacho.

[video clip]

Here, have another one.

[video clip]

One more? Okay, fine. One more.

[video clip]

Honestly, I wouldn't blame you if you went down the Neymar highlight rabbit hole and never came back. Of course, soccer matches aren't highlight reels, and if there's been one criticism of Neymar, it's that you wouldn't be missing much just by watching his YouTube clips.

—Mike L. Goodman, "No Messi, No Problem: Neymar Becomes a Superstar," *Grantland*

Wednesday morning, March 15, 2016, hip-hop rapper Kendrick Lamar released the cover of his new album, *To Pimp a Butterfly*. The cover full of black males caused an uproar. People wondered what Lamar was aiming to say. His fans, specifically his white fans, were shocked and didn't understand the meaning of this cover. But what was the problem? Why was there such a big deal about the cover of this specific album. Was the cover secretly dissing the American justice system?

[photo of *To Pimp a Butterfly* album cover]

The cover features a group of shirtless black males on the front lawn of the White House. But there is so much more meaning beneath the surface of this image. If you look deeper into the image, there are three details that Lamar put into the album cover to diss the American justice system.

—JaNiece, grade 9

Artful Transitions

Accomplished writers have mastered artful transitions—transitions that truly help guide the reader from one idea to the next while maintaining the same level of craft as any other sentence in the piece. Sentences that begin with "Another reason is" are artless and boring; our students can do better. And transitions don't just occur between paragraphs; they show up between sentences and larger sections of writing, too. Figure 6.10 will help students choose the best technique for the type of transition they need.

Strategy	Works Best Between . . .		
	Sentences	Paragraphs	Sections
Use a conjunction	×	×	
Make a smooth segue		×	×
Question and answer	×	×	

Figure 6.10: When to Use Transition Techniques

USE A CONJUNCTION

For their entire English careers, most of our students have been forbidden to begin sentences with coordinating conjunctions. But real writers do it all the time, especially to indicate how ideas build upon one another.

If you think about it, conjunctions are natural transition words: The job of a coordinating conjunction is to show a relationship between ideas. "And" is used to connect two similar things, "but" is used to show a contrast between two things, and "for" is used to show the cause-and-effect relationship of two things.

This technique wins major brownie points with students because it's concrete, it breaks a common teacher rule, and the sleekness of the transition is truly audible when read out loud.

Examples

The rice grits, a lesser-known culinary cousin to corn grits, were made with Carolina Gold rice, a quality product that needs only butter and salt to shine. And the insouciant smear of black squid ink rimming the white dinner plate? Jackson Pollock would surely nod in approval.

—*Jo Lord,* "East Coast Provisions Reimagined, Rebranded, and (Mostly) Remarkable," *Richmond Times-Dispatch*

There's a case that Rodgers's 36-yard pass to Jared Cook that got the Packers to the Dallas 32 with three seconds left is the most impressive throw in playoff history. Not most dramatic, mind you — there's always the Immaculate Reception or the Helmet Catch or even Fourth-and-26. But as far as being impressive goes? Rodgers's throw is in the conversation for number one.

—*Kevin Clark,* "The NFL Game of the Year: Packers-Cowboys Finally Delivers a Payoff Classic," *The Ringer*

As he walks away from the NFL, he definitely leaves a legacy; however, he also cuts his own career short. Megatron most likely had his own personal reasons to hang up his cleats. But he should have, as the classic saying goes, left it all on the field.

—*Zach,* grade 9

MAKE A SMOOTH SEGUE

Sometimes writers use conversational elements to improve the flow of ideas. In this technique, writers use "speaking of" or a pronoun to refer to an idea mentioned in the previous sentence or paragraph. Although undoubtedly less formal than most of the transitional strategies we have taught our students in the past, a smooth segue gives the reader a feeling of sitting at a table with the writer as she talks out loud between sips of coffee.

Examples

Below, we have pointed out the smooth segues in italics. The emphasis is ours.

> The service this time? Still not what the food and decor deserve.
>
> *Speaking of the decor,* the place is all exposed ductwork, old brick . . .

> —*Jo Lord,* "East Coast Provisions Reimagined, Rebranded, and (Mostly) Remarkable," *Richmond Times-Dispatch*

> The story may be new to most viewers, but the manner in which it's told will be familiar to all but the youngest.
>
> *This* is not necessarily a bad thing.

And

> [Mr. Costner] desegregates the NASA bathrooms with a sledgehammer and stands up for Katherine in quiet but no less emphatic ways when her qualifications are challenged.
>
> *It's a bit much, maybe,* but Mr. Costner, as usual, does what he can to give the white men of America a good name.

> —*A. O. Scott,* "Review: *Hidden Figures* Honors Three Black Women Who Helped NASA Soar," *New York Times*

QUESTION AND ANSWER

Writers often pose rhetorical questions they want readers to think about, but as a transition technique, the writer poses the question and provides the answer. This is a helpful way to assert the writer's opinion as well as transition between two sentences or paragraphs.

Examples

> But as far as being impressive goes? Rodgers's throw is in the conversation for number one.

> —*Kevin Clark,* "The NFL Game of the Year: Packers-Cowboys Finally Delivers a Payoff Classic," *The Ringer*

The service this time? Still not what the food and decor deserve.

—*Jo Lord*, "East Coast Provisions Reimagined, Rebranded, and (Mostly) Remarkable," *Richmond Times-Dispatch*

Paragraphs and Sections

By the time they reach high school, most students are comfortable paragraphing their writing. They understand that paragraphs are organizational units that divide long blocks of text into shorter sections, helping readers navigate through the writing. What else have our students typically internalized about paragraphs? A few things:

- One idea per paragraph

- The main idea is the first sentence

- Paragraphs should be five to seven sentences long

- Each paragraph needs one to three pieces of evidence.

This is the knowledge our ninth graders bring with them in the fall. But when we study copious examples of real analytical writing, we see these rules don't always hold true. Sometimes a writer needs more than one paragraph to fully explain an idea. Just like the claim, the paragraph's main idea isn't always featured in the first sentence; sometimes it's not explicit at all. And the more analytical writing we pore over, the more we see today's analytical writers using short-and-sweet paragraphs rather than long, drawn-out, hard-to-swallow paragraphs that take multiple readings to understand.

Here are some ways to disrupt your students' traditional ideas about paragraphing and raise the level of their writing.

ONE IDEA: MULTIPLE PARAGRAPHS

Big, chunky paragraphs aren't fun for the reader or the writer. The brain can handle only so much information at once, especially on the web, where so much published writing lives today. But when students have been told to contain one idea per paragraph, their paragraphs snowball in size.

There is a better way. Two paragraphs. Or even three. To explain the one idea in depth. Real writers do it all the time.

Another reason writers might choose to break one idea into smaller paragraphs is because they have a surplus of evidence and they want to do each piece justice, fully explaining how it supports their claim. Paragraphs that are over-loaded with evidence and discussion are bound to lose the reader's attention.

Conveying one idea across multiple paragraphs disrupts another false understanding our students have about paragraphs: that each paragraph should contain at least one piece of evidence. Sometimes it takes a writer a whole paragraph to describe the evidence, and another just to discuss it.

Examples

What *Fuller House* is like on its own is beside the point; it matters only in reference to the original. This reboot . . . is the ultimate product of our nostalgia culture, the perpetual virtual high school reunion of Throwback Thursdays and "Things Only a '90s Kid Would Know" listicles.

So your personal experience of *Fuller House* will depend on how it interacts with your memories. If you loved *Fuller House*, I can no more review this experience for you than I could your first kiss or your grandmother's cookies.

—James Poniewozic, "*Full House* Sequel Is a Forced March Down Memory Lane," *The New York Times*

The most obvious similarity to the Bible is the character of Jon Snow. If *Game of Thrones* can be compared to the Bible, then Jon Snow is the Christ figure at the center. Jon Snow is born of humble birth. The supposed illegitimate son of Eddard Stark, he is at the bottom of feudal society. Though wealthy from his connection to nobility, he is unable to inherit any property or titles.

Jon joins the Night's Watch and assumes the role of Lord Commander. Soon afterward, he lets the wildlings, tribes of barbarians north of the Wall, into the safety of the southern lands. Just as Jesus fed five thousand, Jon Snow looks down at the mass of people gathered at the wall and negotiates their resettlement into Westeros.

However, Jon's greatest similarity to Christ is the circumstances of his death. He is brought out and stabbed by his own men for his good deeds. Just as Jesus had his charge written on a sign above his cross ("King of the Jews"), Jon Snow has his charge written on a post. He is stabbed in front of the sign.

The next couple of events are eerily similar. Jon Snow is resurrected. His wounds stay with him. Jon Snow walks around with stab wounds in his stomach similar to the holes in Jesus' hands and side. In the biblical story of Thomas the Apostle, Jesus shows him the holes in his hands and side to prove his resurrection.

—Max, grade 12

MINI PARAGRAPHS

A mini paragraph is a paragraph under five sentences (sometimes they're a single sentence). Mini paragraphs present information in quick bursts, rather than long drawn-out passages, improving the readability of a piece of writing. Today's digital readers crave this kind of visual scaffolding. Short paragraphs are easier on the eyes and the brain.

Mini paragraphs stand out because of their length, so writers often use them for conveying the claim or other important ideas. Because they're short, writers pay careful attention to word choice and punctuation in mini paragraphs. Like poetry or short fiction, every choice matters. These little gems pack a punch.

Examples
Each example is a single paragraph in a longer text.

The other Jane—Jane Austen—would not have been amused.

—Michiko Kakutani, "Curtis Sittenfeld's Eligible Updates Austen's Pride and Prejudice, The New York Times

Dear White People is full of specificities, references, and utter realness that you didn't know you needed, so much so that it can catch you off guard, like stumbling across a pitcher of water and suddenly realizing you've been thirsty for decades.

—*Pilot Viruet, "Dear White People Is Hilarious, Real, and Necessary," Vice*

The Baltimore Orioles are once again, shockingly, in contention for the World Series this year. Their starting pitching is awful and they have extremely slow players, but they keep winning and winning.

—*Will, grade 12*

LIST-A-GRAPHS (PARAGRAPHS IN LIST FORM)

Here's another thing you see in "analysis in the wild" that might seem horrifying at first: Writers bullet their evidence, inundating the reader with one piece after another, in list form. A fairly casual move, presenting evidence in a list can really help a writer drive home a point. Lists say, "There is so much evidence here in support of my point, you can't possibly refute it. So let me keep throwing it at you."

Examples

Would you like some more LaMarcus stuff? I have some more LaMarcus stuff. Here:

* LaMarcus is the worst jump shooter in the playoffs among all players who've taken at least fifty shots.

* LaMarcus made as many shots (two) as he had turnovers during Game 1 of the Rockets–Spurs series. (I'll take this moment to point out that he's making over $20 million this season.)

- LaMarcus was a minus-thirty-six in Game 1 of the Rockets–Spurs series, a remarkable stat that's even more unbelievable when you realize he played only twenty-five minutes. (I'll take this moment to point out that he still has two more years on his contract with the Spurs.)

  —*Shea Serrano,* "The Spurs Need LaMarcus Aldridge to Rejoin the Living," *The Ringer*

President Trump is in Saudi Arabia this weekend to meet with Arab leaders, visit the birthplace of Islam, and give a speech about religious tolerance with the hope of resetting his reputation with the world's 1.6 billion Muslims. But it's unclear if a two-day visit is enough to overshadow his past statements about Islam and its faithful, with his rhetoric becoming more virulent as he campaigned for president.

Here's a look back at some of the comments that he has made . . .

- September 20, 2015: On *NBC News,* Trump was asked if he would be comfortable with a Muslim as president; he responded: "I can say that, you know, it's something that at some point could happen. We will see. I mean, you know, it's something that could happen. Would I be comfortable? I don't know if we have to address it right now, but I think it is certainly something that could happen."

- September 30, 2015: At a New Hampshire rally, Trump pledged to kick all Syrian refugees—most of whom are Muslim—out of the country, as they might be a secret army. "They could be ISIS, I don't know. This could be one of the great tactical ploys of all time. A 200,000-man army, maybe," he said. In an interview that aired later, Trump said: "This could make the Trojan horse look like peanuts."

- October 21, 2015: On *Fox Business*, Trump says he would "certainly look at" the idea of closing mosques in the United States.

—*Jenna Johnson and Abigail Hauslohner, "'I Think Islam Hates Us':*
A Timeline of Trump's Comments About Islam and Muslims," The Washington Post

SECTIONS WITH SUBHEADINGS

Subheadings are to short pieces of writing what chapters are to books. Subheadings can improve the readability of a piece of writing by capturing the essence of each section. Today, subheadings are much more interesting and creative than the subheadings we wrote for our college term papers; they have as much voice and craft as everything else in the piece.

Examples

To fully grasp how sections and subheadings are working in a piece of writing, you need to view the piece of writing in full. In these examples we include the article's title/heading and subheadings to give you a sense of how the different sections are working together, but we highly recommend searching the internet for the title and author to view the full article.

Title: "Netflix's Extremely Busy April, " by Alison Herman for *The Ringer*

Claim: "This is what Netflix has shown us it takes to build an entertainment Death Star: almost infinite breadth, strategic depth, and a willingness to wait things out when they don't immediately click."

Subheadings:

- *A Show for Everyone Is a Shower for No One*
- *Spending Big—Especially on Really Big Names—Is a Sound Investment*
- *It Is Possible to Fix a Streaming Mistake?*
- *There Is No Comedian Too Big—Or Too Small*

- *Anything Can Be a Franchise—and a Good One, Too*
- *Being Relentlessly On-Trend Has Its Drawbacks*
- *Buzz Is Fleeting, but Quality Is Eternal.*

Title: "The Mixed Blessings of the NBA Playoffs," by Shea Serrano for *The Ringer*

Claim: "The whole point is that the Celtics got a thing that looked like it was good (the number-one seed), then immediately found out it was actually bad."

Subheadings:

- *BAD, but Actually GOOD: The Pacers Getting Swept by the Cavs*
- *BAD, but Actually GOOD (but Actually It's Just BAD): Blake Griffin Missing the Remainder of the Playoffs*
- *GOOD, but Actually BAD, but Actually GOOD, but Actually BAD, but Actually . . . *Forever*: Kevin Durant Winning a Championship with the Warriors*
- *BAD, but Actually GOOD: Rudy Gobert Getting Injured*
- *BAD, but Actually GOOD: The Spurs Losing Game 4 of Their Series Against the Grizzlies*
- *GOOD, but Actually BAD: The Raptors Remembered That They're Actually Better Than the Bucks.*

SECTIONS WITHOUT SUBHEADINGS

Some writers choose to divide their writing into sections without subheadings. Section breaks may consist of extra white space, asterisks, or other ornamental symbols. Section breaks with and without subheadings achieve the same effect: They break longer pieces of writing into more manageable chunks. The difference is a matter of aesthetics: How does the writer want the section break to look on the page?

In our experience, students have really enjoyed considering how sections with subheadings or other space dividers might affect their piece; the addition of asterisks or other symbols adds an instant air of sophistication to their writing. Students can use the font Wingdings to create various ornamental dividers.

Examples

The Handmaid's Tale Treats Guilt as an Epidemic," by Megan Garber, *The Atlantic*

* * *

"The Spurs Need LaMarcus Aldridge to Rejoin the Living," by Shea Serrano, *The Ringer*

Meaningful Conclusions

Traditionally, students have been taught to reiterate their claim in the conclud-
ing paragraph—summarize their main idea, touch on their reasons one last time,
and make a quiet, boring exit. But professional writers don't rehash all their
claims in the conclusion. After studying hundreds of conclusions, we've noticed
that most writers echo their overarching idea, but their last gesture is not one of
regurgitation. It is far more interesting, thought-provoking, and resonant.

SOFT ECHO

Most writers do give a nod to their overarching idea in a conclusion, but this "soft
echo" is different from restating the claim. Writers use keywords to remind readers of their argument while giving them something new to consider.

Examples

> By the end of the book, she's basically speaking to no
> one. . . . In one chapter, she writes, with a sense of courage
> that is jaw-droppingly misplaced, "If I can help celebrate
> the fact that I'm a superengaged mom and unabashedly
> ambitious entrepreneur, that yes, I'm on a construction
> site in the morning and at the dinner table with my kids
> in the evening, I'm going to do that." And why wouldn't
> she? Who wouldn't celebrate that level of ability and
> accomplishment—except, maybe, the type of man who would
> say that putting your wife to work is a dangerous thing? The
> fundamental dishonesty of Ivanka Trump's book is clearest

in the fact that she never acknowledges the difficulty of knowing, or being governed by, anyone like that.

—*Jia Tolentino*, "Ivanka Trump Wrote a Painfully Oblivious Book for Basically No One," *The New Yorker*

In the end, Malvolio's greatest treachery is being starkly at odds with the message of the play. *Twelfth Night, or What You Will* is all about accepting life with all its wind and rain and insanity—something that Malvolio is ultimately too much of a party pooper to even consider.

—*Tom*, grade 12

END WITH AN IMAGE

Poets often use this strategy—end with an image—to bring their poems to a close. Images, particularly images of night, darkness, and endings, provide a sense of closure in a sensory way. In analysis, writers may describe a scene that is relevant to the text they are analyzing, or much like a lead strategy discussed earlier in the chapter, end with a personal connection that is grounded in imagery.

Examples

And so in addition to drawing out the darkness embedded within the text, Walley-Beckett has also included lovely and entirely concocted moments that match the sweetness of the novel, like when Matthew and Marilla ask Anne to sign her name in the Cuthbert family Bible and make herself, officially, one of them. "Shouldn't we hold hands over a running stream and pledge ourselves to each other as Cuthberts forever, or prick our fingers and mingle our blood as a symbol of our lasting devotion?" Anne wonders, by way of asking for a grand ceremony to mark the occasion, before settling instead for a celebratory glass of raspberry cordial and a signature. "With this pen," Anne says, her hands shaking, "I take you, Matthew and Marilla Cuthbert, to be my family forever, to call you mine and to be yours, for always." Then she writes down her name.

—*Willa Paskin*, "The Other Side of Anne of Green Gables," *The New York Times*

From her earliest TV appearances, like "Team" at the 2014 Grammys, she has displayed the same intense stare, anchoring her loose moves with a calmly confrontational look. It gives her focus, as well as reminding the viewer that Lorde is not to be gazed at; that she is firmly in control. When she sang the stark piano ballad "Liability" at Coachella in April, her performance was almost entirely in her face. She sat on the front of the stage, using one hand to clasp at the air, and her eyes to scan the enormous crowd slowly. As they watched her, it was as though she could see every single one of them.

—*Aimee Cliff*, "Why Lorde Is a Great Dancer," *The Fader*

ZOOM OUT

Writers zoom out to give a bird's-eye view of their topic: They explore how it is important to our culture, how it is important to more than just *this* text. This is why we read analysis of texts we don't necessarily care for ourselves—because the writers connect us to something bigger than just the text they're analyzing. An album analysis, for instance, will show why the album is important—to the artist and the listener, but also to music in general, to our culture.

Examples

Dear White People the concept was always going to face tremendous resistance and attract racist vitriol. But pouring more energy into depicting the racism its characters face than writing the characters themselves makes it hard to root for *Dear White People* the show. . . . As a series that markets itself partly based on its conversation-starting qualities in the era of #BlackLivesMatter, the show falls short of creating black characters who feel like they exist today. Drake references may be eternal, but culture evolves quickly—and *Dear White People* hasn't leveled up. Sometimes #relatability alone isn't enuf.

—Hannah Giorgis, "*Dear White People* Doesn't Know How to Reckon with 2017," *The Ringer*

Today there may be more reason than ever to find solace in fantasy. With post–9/11 terrorism fears and concern about a warming planet, Griswold says American authors are turning increasingly to fantasy of a darker kind. . . . Like the collapse of the Twin Towers, these are sad and disturbing stories of postapocalyptic worlds falling apart, of brains implanted with computer chips that reflect anxiety about the intrusion of a consumer society aided by social media. This is a future where hope is qualified and whose deserted worlds are flat and impoverished. But maybe there's purpose. If children use fairy tales to process their fears, such dystopian fantasies (and their heroes and heroines) may model the hope kids need today to address the scale of the problems ahead.

—Colleen Gillard, "Why the British Tell Better Children's Stories," *The Atlantic*

Though Holden would never tell the reader, he was afraid. He was afraid of growing up. And this fear was expressed by him through his constant questioning about where the ducks go when the pond freezes over. He didn't genuinely care about migration patterns. In his mind, he was actually wondering about where he goes and what happens to him when he grows up. "They can't just ignore the ice. They can't just ignore it," he exclaimed. He couldn't ignore his impending doom—also known as adulthood.

I need to learn to deal with my *own* impending doom, and Holden Caulfield is the perfect example of how to *not* do that successfully. He let his fears make him spiral into a deep depression that eventually takes him to a mental hospital. Rather than put myself through that, as I and other readers have learned, I need not to worry about something I can't control, as Holden Caulfield did."

—*Sydney,* grade 9

CHAPTER SEVEN

exploring authority

S uccessful analytical writing brings together wholehearted passion and extensive content knowledge. But unless a writer can clearly and confidently communicate that knowledge to readers, all is lost. No one will read the ideas or understand the unique claim. Just as explorers needed sailing knowledge before they could launch their ships, student writers need authority: the writing know-how afforded to them by deep content knowledge, strategic word choice, and thoughtful use of grammar and conventions.

The Problem and the Solution

In a midprocess reflection, ninth grader Brooke describes the challenges of writing an analytical essay about her all-time favorite band, Fall Out Boy.

> [My claim is:] The best option for Fall Out Boy now is to let their legacy remain the pop-punk-emo-rock rollercoaster that it is, before they lose who they are entirely.
>
> The most difficult part of this specific analysis was writing like I knew what I was talking about. I am by no means a music expert, but I had to be able to describe various aspects of Fall Out Boy's music intelligently....

I think what scared me away from [this idea was that] I would have to give a semidetailed review of seven different albums, all in the same genre and by the same artist, and I'm not very educated on music. I understand and love it, but I don't know every genre and every part that makes up a song, and I don't think I would be able to talk about what technically makes each album good or bad.

Passion does not guarantee expertise. People don't have to be knowledgeable about the things they love; they just have to love them. Brooke could talk for days about her devotion to Fall Out Boy; she could recount every concert she'd ever been to, sing all their lyrics from memory, and explain in basic terms why she adores them. Yet in her response above, she admits that it was difficult to "talk about what technically makes each album good or bad."

But Brooke didn't give up. An experienced mentor-text studier, Brooke looked for ways to build her authority:

I used the mentor text ["Fall Out Boy: Ranking Every Album from Worst to Best"] to help guide me with vocabulary and language, I did not gather a lot of structure from it. I learned words like "discography," and how to use "sludgier" and "fluttery" to describe music accurately. Another thing I learned from my mentor text was how to use examples to back myself up. Instead of just describing the album as a whole, draw in specific songs, other albums, and even other artists to give a comparison or contrast to what I am speaking about.

Although passion does not guarantee expertise, it's a gateway to it; students who are passionate about a text want to learn more about it. Brooke's self-selected mentor text helped build music knowledge and vocabulary. Later, she infused her draft about Fall Out Boy with some of these genre-specific words to make her ideas more specific and assert authority.

In this chapter, we will offer ways to help students build a strong vocabulary and other strategies for increasing their authority about the subjects they hold dear. The chart in Figure 7.1 illustrates a few of the characteristics of passionate-but-flimsy writing and a guide for where to look in this chapter for solutions.

If You See This in Students Writing . . .	Try This
Vague word choice	• Word Clusters (p. 134) • Tone Inquiry (p. 138) • Active Research (p. 142) • Voice Inquiry (p. 146) • Specific Word Choice (p. 151) • Breaking the Dictionary (p. 151) • Tell the Truth (p. 160).
Powerless conventions	• Usage Inquiry (p. 132) • Sentence Fragments (p. 156) • Start with a Coordinating Conjunction (p. 157) • Capital Letters (p. 157) • Proper Nouning (p. 158) • Out-of-Place Punctuation (p. 159).
No awareness of audience	• Word Clusters (p. 134) • Audience Inquiry (p. 136) • Tone Switch (p. 141) • Active Research (p. 142) • Breaking the Dictionary (p. 151) • Tell the Truth (p. 160) • Show Vulnerability (p. 161) • Talk to Your Reader (p. 162).
Inappropriate tone	• Word Clusters (p. 134) • Tone Inquiry (p. 138) • Tone Switch (p. 141) • Active Research (p. 142) • Breaking the Dictionary (p. 151) • Tell the Truth (p. 160) • Show Vulnerability (p. 161) • Talk to Your Reader (p. 162).
Little voice	• Word Clusters (p. 134) • Active Research (p. 142) • Voice Inquiry (p. 146) • Listen to the Writing (p. 148) • Eliminate the Wishy-Washy (p. 149) • Breaking the Dictionary (p. 151) • Capital Letters (p. 157) • Out-of-Place Punctuation (p. 159) • Show Vulnerability (p. 161) • Talk to Your Reader (p. 162).
Weak ideas	• Active Research (p. 142) • Eliminate the Wishy-Washy (p. 149) • Tell the Truth (p. 160).

Figure 7.1: Strategies for Exploring Authority

Activities for Exploration and Discovery

The first step to building authority in your own analysis is understanding what authority looks and sounds like in powerful writing in the wild. The exercises that follow will help students grasp a clear understanding of authority and get them thinking about how to approach it in their own writing.

Usage Inquiry

On the surface, a piece of conventional writing is easy on the eye and pleasing to read. It doesn't jolt the reader or grate against his ear. And while we, as teachers, are thrilled to see competent, "correct" writing, when was the last time you congratulated a student on a properly placed comma? The simple truth is that students must learn to write conventionally if they want to be taken seriously.

But we want much more for our young writers. We want them to possess an authoritative command of conventions that enables them to make strategic choices about how they want language and punctuation to shape their meaning.

There are many ways to teach the conventions of usage. What follows is an example of an inquiry that accomplishes two of our goals: to immerse students in powerful examples of analytical writing and to build their authority by creating an understanding of how usage conventions affect writing.

STEPS

1. Study student writing, and make a list of usage problems that crop up in your students' writing.

2. Determine what convention might help them fix this problem. Pull examples from several different mentor texts.

3. Ask students to make observations about how the convention is being used. Make a list of their observations on the board.

4. Invite students to look for strategic places in their writing for the accurate use of this convention.

EXAMPLE

In our classrooms, students were having trouble adding and discussing evidence without creating long, run-on sentences. When we studied real examples of analysis, we saw that many writers were using the em dash to add examples to their writing and explain how their evidence connects to their claim. So we decided to design an inquiry around the em dash.

The mentor text, "Why Time's Trump Cover Is a Subversive Piece of Art," by Jake Romm of *Forward* offers many ways of using the em dash.

During the lesson, we gave our students the entire article and asked them to do a first-draft reading to get a sense of what the piece is about. Then we framed the inquiry: *What is an em dash? Why do writers use them? What are all the different ways we can use them?*

Small groups of students typed up all the sentences containing em dashes. Here are just a few of the sentences they captured on a Google Doc:

> *"Paintings of seated monarchs can be seen to hold two aesthetic functions—to ground the association between the sitter and the throne, thus solidifying the metonymy, and to heighten the sense of servitude in the viewer."*

> *"By placing a portrait in this tradition, the chair assumes the role of the throne, and the sitter the role of king (or queen)—the visual effect is the same."*

> *"There are two images at play here—the imagined power-image taken from the front, and the actual image, in which Trump seems to offer the viewer a conniving wink, as if to say, look at how we hoodwinked those suckers in the front (both Trump and the viewer are looking down on those in front)."*

Then we asked students to consider all the different ways in which em dashes were being used: Where do em dashes occur in a sentence? How does the em dash affect the way you read the sentence? How would the sentence be different without the em dashes?

After small-group work, students shared their findings. The em dash:

- Gives the reader a side note/extra information

- Contains examples in list form

- Makes the reader focus because it stands out and sometimes introduces a different tone

- Can serve as a "drum roll" after which something big is going to be revealed

- Interrupts the fluid thought and therefore lends a conversational tone

- Can contain a complete sentence or a fragment, but if what's inside is a fragment, the rest of the sentence has to be complete

- Works the same way that parentheses do.

Students were then given time to find a few strategic places in their drafts to use em dashes correctly and meaningfully. Here are two sentences that show students' use of em dashes to insert evidence:

The show was simple—Bear would take a celebrity such as Shaquille O'Neal, Barack Obama, or Zac Efron, and pull a *Man vs. Wild* on them—and would take them into harsh wilderness and teach them how to survive for a few days.

—*Nick, grade 9*

Of course the mirror-image that high school is to *Survivor* can be seen in the very simplistic ways—grade and teams; returning players and friends you already have on your first day; the *Survivor* reunion show and high school reunions.

—*Bryn, grade 9*

Your students might study how writers incorporate quotations, or when to use *that* and *which*, or even broader studies of how writers use punctuation and sentence structure to create voice in their writing. The act of inquiry is itself an exercise in authority: Students are invited to take learning into their own hands while they investigate a text to learn more.

Word Clusters

As we saw with Brooke in the introduction, not having genre-specific vocabulary at your fingertips makes the analysis of a text difficult. This specialized vocabulary shows off the writer's knowledge and proves that she can talk the talk.

To build stronger vocabulary, students can create word clusters by studying mentor texts in their chosen area and creating a list of the kinds of words writers use to analyze. For example, Brooke wanted to write an analysis of Fall Out Boy's devolution, so she found writers who were writing about Fall Out Boy, or writing about how a band's sound changes over time, and made note of the words these writers used to describe bands and music.

1. Show your students this list of Starbucks orders, and ask them which drinks they would be comfortable making. Then, discuss why it would be challenging to make these drinks without a command of the Starbucks lingo.

   - Tall, Nonfat Latte with Caramel Drizzle
   - Grande, Iced, Sugar-Free, Vanilla Latte with Soy Milk
   - Triple, Venti, Soy, No Foam Latte
   - Triple, Venti, Half-Sweet, Nonfat Caramel Macchiato
   - Decaf, Soy Latte with an Extra Shot and Cream.

2. Say to your students, "Today you will go in search of words used by writers who are writing about the same topics as you."

3. Put students in groups according to their topics. For example, all students who are writing about music should work together. Hand each group a cluster of mentor texts on this topic.

4. Students should first read through to get a sense of what the texts are about. Then they should highlight the lingo—the vocabulary or jargon of their subject area—and create a list of these words and phrases in their notebooks, paying special attention to words used across multiple mentor texts.

5. Finally students should be given a chance to add their own words to this list based on their personal knowledge and experiences with this subject.

EXAMPLES

Words Bailey tracked in a Packers vs. Cowboys review:	Words Bryn tracked in a review of East Coast Provisions restaurant:
• Throw • Pass • Score • Sideline • Ball • Field goal	• Appetizer • Menu • Style • Flavorful • Palette • Entree

Figure 7.2: Student Word Clusters

continues

Words Bailey tracked in a Packers vs. Cowboys review:	Words Bryn tracked in a review of East Coast Provisions restaurant:
• Play • Game • Season • Defender • Win • Playoff • Offense/defense • Strategy • Yardage	• Presentation • Ambiance • Atmosphere • Harmonious • Decor • Culinary • Cuisine • Vibe • Service • Savor • Insouciant

Figure 7.2: Continued

THINGS TO CONSIDER

Group work optional. Students can create word clusters individually or in small groups; small-group work often yields richer word clusters with students pooling their collective knowledge.

Scaffolding. Students have varying degrees of knowledge in their subject areas. Students who have a lot of passion but less expertise should approach the task a bit differently. The chart in Figure 7.3 offers guiding questions for both proficient and beginning students.

Audience Inquiry

We believe the writers who make a connection with us, who feel like our smartest friends, who give us the sense that they truly understand us. Because they know us so well, we come to depend on their perspective.

Successful writers start with an audience in mind. Sometimes this audience arises out of necessity: "I want to write to people who have never played this video game before to convince them it is worth their money." Sometimes audience is determined by the desired place of publication: "I want to write something for Heinemann, so my audience will be practicing teachers looking for sound instructional strategies." For writers of analysis, knowing their audience is paramount. After all, leading an audience to consider their original perspective is the

For Students Who Are Topic Experts:	For Students Who Have Less Expertise:
• What topic-specific words do I see the writer using that I recognize? • What jargon do I see the writer using that I don't recognize? • What words would I add to this list based on my own experiences and knowledge of this genre? • What words are other mentor writers using to describe this subject?	• What words are unfamiliar to me? • Which of these words are specific to this subject area? • What can I learn about these words? • Where can I learn about these words? • Who in the class can I talk to about these words? • What words are other mentor writers using to describe this subject?

Figure 7.3: Guiding Questions for Word Clustering

reason they write. For analytical writing to be real and meaningful, our student writers need an audience, too. Someone other than us.

Students need to have a sense of the different types of audiences that exist for writing, and how audience informs a writer's choices. Each time they consider the audience behind a piece of writing, they are better positioned to choose an audience of their own.

STEPS

1. Give students a cluster of mentor texts from a variety of publications.

2. Working in small groups, students should determine the audience of each piece by considering these questions:

   • What do you know about this publication? Who typically reads it? Does the writing contain any clues?

   • Consider the word choice. Are the words formal? Informal? Is there a lot of challenging word choice? Is there a lot of slang?

   • Are there allusions in this piece? Consider the references. Who would understand them? Who are they aimed at?

   • How much background or context is given about the text(s) discussed? How much does the audience already know about Shakespeare?

3. From this information, students can make a t-chart in their note-books: *If the Audience Is . . . Then You Might Consider . . .*

In Rebekah's senior English class, students considered their audiences for their *Twelfth Night* analysis by first studying five pieces of professional Shakespeare analysis:

- "Hamlet Was a Bro Who Didn't Even Like Sex," by Jillian Keenan, *LitHub*

- "50 Shades of Shakespeare: How the Bard Used Food as Racy Code," by Anne Bramley, NPR

- "Forget His Coinages, Shakespeare's Real Genius Lies in His Noggin-Busting Compounds," by John Kelley, *Slate*

- "Shakespeare: One of the First and Greatest Psychologists," by Steven Pinker, *The Atlantic*

- What Was Shakespeare's Central Philosophy?" by Ed Simon, *LitHub*.

Figure 7.4 shows the noticings from one of her classes.

THINGS TO CONSIDER

A very brief word on publication. Nothing makes the writing process more authentic for students than publication, and it's the natural consequence of all the class time spent thinking about audience. We also ought to encourage our students to push their writing into the world, especially analytical writing, the dominant mode that surrounds us in this increasingly digital world. While it's great for student writers to shoot for the moon and submit their work to big, adult publishers, there are also a number of avenues for student publication that consider analytical or critical essays. Check out *Teen Ink*, the Scholastic Art and Writing Contest, *Parallel Ink*, and the *Cuckoo Review*!

Tone Inquiry

When students are unaware that every piece of writing has a tone, it often results in bland, tone-deaf writing that sounds as though it was written by robots. With analysis, much of a writer's authority comes from *sounding* like an expert. Some of this comes from word choice, but a lot of the sound is in the writer's attitude toward the subject. Conventional schoolhouse wisdom says that for analytical

If the Audience Is . . .	Then You Might Consider . . .
Genuinely interested in Shakespeare	• Making your credentials clear • Making the piece about Shakespeare—not you • Using high-level vocabulary • Writing dense, text-heavy paragraphs • Frontloading the claim, and then following with evidence • Packing in as much evidence as possible (including lengthy examples/quotes from the text) • Making connections with history, philosophy, or other intellectual pursuits • Embracing the audience by using "we" • Ensuring evidence comes primarily from the text.
General audience (not especially interested in Shakespeare, but willing to listen)	• Using a list or repeated structure to make it easier for the reader to synthesize information • Incorporating pop culture references everyone would understand • Aiming for wide appeal to older and younger readers alike • Using a faster pace—sections are chunked so that you can read them all together or individually • Relating the text to something broader that everyone cares about.
Millennials OR people who aren't interested in Shakespeare but should be	• Using a catchy title to lure in wary readers • Bringing Shakespeare down to an everyman's level • Being blunt! Being shocking! Being controversial! • Using a casual, conversational tone • Using slang • Using humor (even when discussing tragedy) • Ensuring text evidence is very short and accessible • Including elements of narrative/storytelling to connect with the reader • Incorporating pop culture references • Focusing on extratextual evidence.

Figure 7.4: Student Findings About Audience

writing the tone should be serious, formal, and detached, but a quick look at some professional analysis doesn't bear this out to be true. Consider, for example, the range of tone in these two excerpts:

> A fresh reading of *Observations* suggests that, while Moore's descriptive powers are formidable, she is primarily a poet of argument, which is to say that she is most primarily a poet of syntax—the convolutions of her long, charismatic sentences seduce us into agreement long before we've had time to consider the substance of the argument at stake.
>
> —James Longenbach, "Less Is Moore," *The Nation*

> It's fun to watch all these people cook, and it's relatively rare to watch a final three without thinking, "It would be a bummer if this bonehead emerged victorious." But *Top Chef* gets there sometimes—including the Seattle season, where Kish was also easy to root for."
>
> —Linda Holmes, "*Top Chef* Is Delivering a Satisfying Season Right on Time," NPR

You can begin an exploration of tone by simply looking through a short stack of mentor texts. You will almost certainly see that with analysis in the wild, any tone is fair game—from formal to casual to colloquial to personal to straight up irreverent. Pay attention to how, regardless of the writer's specific tone, it's almost always consistent and confident across the piece.

A professional writer probably doesn't thoughtfully tap his pencil to his chin and muse, "Today, I will adopt a wry tone in my essay." Instead, the tonal choice a writer makes is mostly subconscious and influenced by a number of factors:

- *By audience.* As students discovered in Figure 7.4, different audiences often dictate different tones. If you are writing to a younger audience, the tone will probably be more casual. If the audience is older or more educated, the tone will often be more formal.

- *By publication.* Some publications have a very strong tone of their own—*The Huffington Post, Jezebel, The Ringer*, to name a few. If students aim to write a piece that would fit a very specific publication, they would be wise to consider that publication's dominant tone. They may find that all kinds of voices are represented in their dream publication, and so they have more latitude in the way they approach their topics. But, if they find that nearly every piece has a humorous tone, an aggressive tone, a clinical tone, a sardonic tone, then they will need to make their writing follow suit.

- *By stance.* A writer's tone might be quickly and easily established through the writer's own stance toward the subject. A critic panning the latest hip restaurant in town will begin the entire writing process with a critical tone. A sports writer analyzing his beloved team's recent loss will use a voice full of gentle defense and justification. A writer doesn't always have a strong emotion toward her topic, but when she does that will influence tone from the get-go.

Tone Switch

Tone can be abstract for students at first, so it's helpful to have them examine the ways in which they naturally code-switch for tone in different situations. Later, they can adapt this same skill to their writing. This storytelling game illustrates the concept of tone and helps students practice switching between tones for different writing situations.

STEPS

1. Have students choose a partner (for this activity, it's helpful for students to partner up with a friend if possible).

2. Ask students to tell their partner their craziest school story—something that happened to them or to someone else.

3. Make a big deal of leaving the classroom: "I am going to step out of the room for a few minutes so that you can tell your stories in privacy—I definitely don't want to hear these! I'll be back in about four minutes!"

4. Leave the room, wait, and enjoy listening to the giggles and gasps through the door. (Try not to imagine the stories they are telling.)

5. When you return, ask students to tell the same story . . . but to the principal.

6. Allow students to retell their stories.

7. Debrief as a class by asking, "What did you change when your audience changed?" and "How might this affect how you write for your audience?"

EXAMPLE

Our ninth graders came alive when we used this strategy to illustrate the changes writers naturally make when considering different audiences. The activity offers students a chance to be silly and tell stories that aren't usually sanctioned in class. But it does an important job, too, in allowing students to practice the postures of considering their audience and then switching their tone to match.

We don't know (and don't want to know!) the stories our students shared, but when we debriefed as a class, they noted a number of important changes. Our students commented that they changed their word choice, and they changed the amount and kind of detail they provided. Some even reported that they sat up straighter, spoke more politely, and changed their demeanor when asked to tell their story to the principal.

THINGS TO CONSIDER

Possible modifications. This strategy can be modified to help students practice sharing their ideas with specific audiences or geared toward specific publications. Or invite students to share their idea with a classmate using serious, formal language and then again in language they would use with a friend. This can be freeing and help students move away from the staid tone they believe they are *supposed* to use when writing analytically.

Active Research: Experts and Everyday People

The word "research" conjures up images of students sitting behind computers in the library stacks, index cards in hand. And while this kind of research—seeking out and evaluating various print or digital resources, taking notes in one of the many digital research platforms available today, and synthesizing information—plays a pivotal role in the information-gathering stage of analytical writing, it's not the only kind of research that students can or should be doing.

In active research, students seek out opportunities to help build their knowledge of a particular topic or text. The more knowledge they have, the more authority they will convey in their writing. Active research also often yields important moments worth writing about.

Experts can be a rich source of information for students who want to explore outside the library. Just talking to an expert for a few minutes can shift a student's understanding of her topic. Expert quotes can also be woven into a student's writing to add authority.

It's obvious how an expert can add authority to a piece of writing. What might not be so obvious is the texture and support an everyday person can add. Sometimes an average citizen can provide the just-right quote or perspective a student needs to support his claim.

STEPS

1. Students should make a list of experts or "everyday people" (nonexperts) whose knowledge might help them better understand their topics. For example, a student writing a review of an album could ask the voice or band instructor at her school to help her describe the instrumentation in the songs. Or a student writing an analysis of a football player's career could seek help from the football coach.

2. Students should determine what kind of help they need. The album reviewer might ask for help describing the instrumentation or the quality of the singer's voice. The football writer might need help interpreting a player's statistics.

3. Students can conduct formal interviews or simply spend time with the person, taking notes to capture information and insights.

4. Direct quotes can be woven into the actual piece of writing.

EXAMPLE

Look at how professional writers use both expert and nonexpert testimony to lend additional credibility to their ideas.

Expert Testimony:

If you begin to ask why Anne has remained popular for as long as she has, you will get multiple explanations and a bounty of adjectives: She's curious. She's hopeful. She's optimistic. She's timeless. She's ahead of her time. She's imperfect, but perfectly so. She is easy to love. Everything about Anne—her disposition, her gender, her age, her provenance—is a rarity for acclaimed television. Tony Soprano, Don Draper, Walter White, Hannah Horvath, and the rest of the antihero litany are infamously challenging to love, while Anne's appeal is as plain as the freckles on her face. When I mentioned to [writer and coproducer] Walley-Beckett that Anne is a straightforwardly winning character, her initial reaction was to defend her as if from an undermining charge. "Oh, she has got some antihero stuff, which is fun," Walley-Beckett said. "She's not classically beautiful, and she has a bad temper, and she can be heedless." But then she agreed that yes, "she is a highly lovable and yummy pleasure to sit down with at night."

—*Willa Paskin*, "The Other Side of Anne of Green Gables," *The New York Times*

Everyday Person Testimony:

Though the girls mostly liked Jo and appreciated her lack of vanity, some of them felt that she presented too lofty a role model:

"[Jo] spoke her mind . . . she doesn't care what other people think," says eleven-year-old Emily Martin. "I really admire her and wish I could live up to her standards."

—*Lynn Neary*, "Jo March, Everyone's Favorite Little Woman," NPR

THINGS TO CONSIDER

Timing is everything. You will need to do some advance planning if your students are going to conduct interviews; it's usually not the kind of thing they can throw together overnight. This is an excellent over-the-weekend assignment: "Over the weekend, find your expert and everyday people testimony for your piece."

It's not the mode that matters. If face-to-face interviews are not possible, encourage students to use email or Skype or FaceTime or good, old-fashioned phone calls to connect with the people they need to talk to.

Active Research: Experiences

Students who complain that research is boring need to get out more—that is, they need to seek out experiences that might offer a new perspective or help build their knowledge of a certain topic. For his article analyzing the factors leading J. Crew's declining sales ("What Happened to J. Crew?"), *New York Times* writer Jon Caramanica visited five different J. Crew stores in New York City to see what spending time in their retail spaces could tell him about the values and problems of the company. Because he was there and saw the stores with his own eyes, Caramanica writes with a special kind of authority. Experiential action research conveys the authority of an eyewitness. Figure 7.5 details a variety of experiences that match the types of analytical writing students might be doing.

Type of Analytical Writing	Authority-Building Experiences
Sports analysis	• Attend a sports game • Listen to a sports podcast (see Chapter 10 for ideas) • Gain experience as an "announcer" at a school sports game • Play on a sports team.
Music analysis	• Attend a concert • Join a band • Take music lessons • Listen to a music podcast (see Chapter 9 for ideas).
Literary analysis	• Attend a book club • Listen to a literary podcast • Watch a documentary on an author.
Video game analysis	• Play video games (!) • Watch a friend play a game.
TV and movie analysis	• Go to the movies • Host a TV viewing party • Watch television "aftershows" and behind-the-scenes DVD extras • Listen to a podcast (see Chapter 8 for ideas).

Figure 7. 5: Ideas for Experiential Action Research

The reexperience. Depending on the kind of analysis your writers are engaged in, these experiences (that game, that concert, etc.) might be well in the past already. In this case, the experience research can be reliving that experience by rewatching game tape, researching the complete set list for the concert, viewing clips from the episode, listening to the album again, and so on.

Voice Inquiry

In terms of authority, nothing separates student analysis and professional analysis more than voice—the writer's ability to sound like himself. Sometimes wisecracking and other times serious, we love it when we get a sense of the writer's personality through his words.

In the past, we have encouraged students to "Find your voice. Go ahead. Sound like yourself when you write." But students don't know how to do that without some exploration and play. Here are several activities to help students identify voice, both other writers' and their own.

STEPS

To help our students write with passion and care, we must show them writing that sings with voice. When a piece of writing sings with voice, it is almost as if the writer is reaching through the page and speaking directly to you, the reader.

1. Select a mentor text with a strong voice.

2. Read the piece *out loud* to students.

3. As you read aloud, invite your students to underline places in the text where they feel the writer is speaking directly to them.

4. Explore how the writer does this.

EXAMPLE

Students studied a review of the video game *That Dragon, Cancer* by Lucy O'Brien (*IGN*). The game is about a family whose son has been diagnosed with cancer. Figure 7.6 shows the lines students underlined and our attempts to understand the writer's craft.

Lines That Sing with Voice	What the Writer Does
"Not everything works."	Tells the truth, even if it's hard to handle
"But for every high concept, there's a truth that grounds *That Dragon, Cancer*: The battle the Greens face is not just a matter of mourning, it's how to mourn."	Shows layers of her thinking
"They clash, then come together, then clash again."	Creates a rhythm, like a person talking
". . . swoop in and out of their lives . . ."	Unique word choice ("swoop")
"As the credits played, I felt fortunate they allowed me in."	Shows vulnerability ("I felt . . .")

Figure 7.6: Lines That Sing with Voice in "*That Dragon, Cancer* Review"

THINGS TO CONSIDER

The best mentor texts. This study of voice can be done with any number of analytical mentor texts. Figure 7.7 offers a few suggestions to get you started. Once students have studied voice and are able to name the strategies writers employ to create it, they are ready to read their own writing through this lens.

Mentor Text	Subgenre of Analysis
"Why Are There So Many Shows About Time Travel Right Now?" by Gwen Ihnat, *A.V. Club*	TV analysis
"The Crucial Importance and Splendid Madness of *Friday Night Lights* Season 2," by Darren Franich, *Entertainment Weekly*	TV series analysis
"*The Lego Batman Movie* Drags the Caped Crusader," by Glen Weldon, NPR	Movie analysis
"Searching for Salvation in Charlotte Bronte's *Villette*," by Rachel Vorona Cote, *LitHub*	Literary analysis

Figure 7.7: More Analysis Mentor Texts That Sing with Voice

Listen to the Writing

Voice is often described as "the person behind the words" (Culham 2003, 109). In this exercise, students listen for places where their writing falls flat and the person behind the words has disappeared.

STEPS

1. Listen to the writing. Students working alone can record themselves reading their writing using Voice Memo on an iPad, smart phone, or any basic recording device or application; students working with partners may read their writing aloud or have their partner read the piece out loud.

2. Identify places where the writing lulls. As the piece is read aloud, slowly and attentively, the listener marks places where the writing lacks voice. In digital documents, he can use the highlighter tool in the main menu; on paper, a highlighter or pencil.

3. After the reading, the student and her partner should discuss places where the writer's voice isn't strong. The writer should talk through her thinking while her partner takes notes, jotting down words and phrases that might help the writer add voice.

4. Revise to add voice. The writer now needs time to work through some of these marked passages, replacing "lifeless or mechanical" writing (Culham 2003, 109).

5. Listen to the writing again.

There isn't a formula or even a clear-cut strategy for adding voice to writing. To help a piece of writing sing with voice, the writer must put more voice into it—it's that simple and that complicated. A simple chart, shown in Figure 7.8, in-

Lines That Sing in My Writing	What I Did	Lines That Drone in My Writing	What I *Could Do* as a Writer

Figure 7.8: Strategies for Adding Voice

corporating the lines your students marked and their reasons for marking them, can help writers think about voice and identify strategic places in their writing to revise.

Eliminate the Wishy-Washy

No matter what, a writer of analysis always conveys confidence in her perspective—that the claim is valid and important for others to read and understand. Using first person doesn't remove authority on its own. Take *New York Times* columnist David Brooks, for example. His career in the op-ed world has been made on expressing his authoritative view of our society, and yet, here is how he opens a recent column on how buying a home is like falling in love:

> I've been thinking about the big decisions in life: How do people choose careers, colleges, spouses, and towns. Of those decisions, buying a home ranks with the most difficult . . .
>
> Like a lot of the biggest decisions, it is more emotional than coldly rational. People generally don't select a house; they fall in love with it.
>
> —*David Brooks*, "The Home-Buying Decision," *The New York Times*

Brooks' tone is comfortable. He leads with a personal musing, and yet when he gets to his claim, his language is strong. Rather than speculatively guessing or tentatively conjecturing, he boldly states his claim. We can teach students to adopt this same boldness with a simple activity.

STEPS

1. Remind students that writers of analysis must be strong and fearless with their language, and then ask them to grab their drafts and a marker or different-colored pen.

2. Slowly read through a list of wishy-washy, uncertain words and phrases. Instruct students that as you read the words, they should bravely cross them out of their drafts. These words have no place in their analysis anymore!

3. By the time you are finished, students should have much more authoritative language in their writing.

WISHY-WASHY LANGUAGE

I believe

I feel

Maybe

Might

Kind of

Sort of

Sometimes

THINGS TO CONSIDER

Added bonus. This activity forces many rereadings of each student's draft (something our students avoid at all costs if possible) and usually requires some revising and smoothing out of the newly chopped-up sentences. Tone, rereading, and revision all in one!

Partner work. Sometimes student writers don't see where they are hedging their bets. Students can trade papers with a peer and read through the lens of wishy-washy diction.

It's all about the intention. One of Allison's ninth graders smartly pointed out that Bill Simmons, one of our mentor writers, *does* use a wishy-washy phrase in his piece, "The Greatest, Best, and Most Historic NBA MVP Column Ever." Simmons writes, "I believe that Russell Westbrook will win the 2017 MVP trophy. I just don't know if it's the right pick." Simmons wrote this at a time when every sports writer was predicting this year's MVP. So, after some discussion, we theorized that Simmons uses this phrase to make his take on the MVP stand apart from others' predictions: Others believe it will be one player; *Bill Simmons believes* it will be Russell Westbrook. We agreed that writers *can* use these phrases intentionally to create a certain effect.

Crafting Techniques for Asserting Authority

Once our writers know what authority is, what it looks like in professional writing, and strategies for building their own authority, they will need some crafting techniques to get newfound authority into their writing. The techniques in this section will help your students use stronger, more specific word choice, intentionally play with grammar and conventions, and pull in their own writerly voice in authoritative ways.

Specific Word Choice

An authoritative sports writer or literary critic will have an arsenal of precise language at hand—yes, to make their writing sound "smart," but also to more carefully pinpoint and define the elements of the text they are closely reading. Specific word choice makes a writer sound like a boss, but it also enables them to perform a wider range of intellectual gymnastics as they use nuanced shades of meaning to explore ideas.

Earlier in the chapter we detailed a "word cluster" activity (p 134) in which students mine mentor texts for genre-specific language. Word clusters give students a sense of the kinds of topics they should explore in their writing; for instance, the word *decor* in a restaurant review suggests a need to describe the furnishings and decoration of a restaurant.

Word clusters also help students articulate ideas about their own texts, and they can be lifted from the cluster and placed in strategic places in students' writing. On their current drafts, have students highlight words that lack punch and power, then, replace them with stronger, topic-specific language from their word cluster.

EXAMPLE

Luke was reviewing *Starboy*, a new album by The Weeknd. Look at how he used more specific language to help him articulate his thoughts on the album (Figure 7.9).

Breaking the Dictionary: Profanity, Slang, and Pop Culture

Beware: We are about to ask you to consider letting students break some of the most fundamental commandments of formal school writing by going completely informal and (occasionally) incorporating tasteful profanity, slang, and pop culture references in analytical writing.

Luke's "Before"	Luke's "After" (with topic-specific language gleaned from mentor texts underlined)
The beat is great and the piano adds so much to the song.	The beat is absolutely stunning; the <u>high-pitched drumline</u> makes for a nice <u>modest beat</u> that hits the ear just right. There is also a <u>piano key</u> that is hit every so often in the song; it is hit in the perfect spots, and it makes the song so <u>emotional</u>. The song seems sad when the piano note is hit at a <u>lower and more depressing note</u> as the song goes on, and sometimes in the song his <u>voice drops</u> a note lower <u>in sync</u> with the piano making the song even more <u>emotional</u>.
He [The Weeknd] is a great singer.	I also like it because he sings kind of spazzy and <u>unsteady</u> at parts, and I think it's because the song is about parties and substances and that <u>unsteadiness</u> really captures that aspect well. The <u>bass</u> is a very <u>dominant part</u> of the beat, and it makes the song more <u>rich</u>.

Figure 7.9: Luke's Revisions for More Specific Word Choices

Pull up just about any mentor text, even from the most formal publications like *The New York Times* and *The New Yorker*, and you will run across these three elements of voice. It's simply a part of writing today. Writers use profanity, slang, and pop culture references for lots of reasons: to sound more like themselves, to relate to the reader, to add humor, to make useful comparisons. In every case, they are trying to communicate their ideas in the clearest and truest way possible. And since this is a technique used by professional writers of authentic analysis, borrowing these moves every once in a while lends authority to student writing by making it feel more like writing from the pros.

You may have had students ask you about including these elements in the past. "What's the right answer?" you wondered. "*Can* he use a pop culture reference there? *Can* she use that *damn*?" Our answer is always: Do professional writers? If so, yes! Or at least maybe!

These elements can certainly be controversial depending on your school and community culture. Depending on your own level of comfort, you could explicitly teach these elements using the examples below or you can just allow it to come up organically with your students.

We tend to let this topic come up among our students as they are exploring mentor texts before we dive into the conversation. And we usually discuss it more openly and at more length with older students (eleventh and twelfth graders). The choice, of course, is yours.

PROFANITY

Profanity in professional analysis is wide ranging—from casual and colloquial to abrasively in-your-face. We tend to see it more in digital writing on more casual sites (*A.V. Club, Vulture, The Ringer*) that skew younger in terms of audience. Writers love profanity for its shock value and its realism. In these examples, consider the impact of the word choices.

> When the movie originally aired, I was in seventh grade, a particularly difficult year thanks to surging hormones, an increasing emphasis on status and appearance at my intermediate school, and the fact that seventh graders were total assholes to each other.
>
> —Jen Chaney, "How *13 Reasons Why* Compares to '80s Pop Culture About Suicide," *Vulture*

> But there's no impact to any of the blows struck; even when a policeman gets a sickle-blade embedded in his skull, we don't really get that "daaaaamn" moment that action movie fans live for.
>
> —Tom Breihan, "America Had Never Seen Anything Like *Crouching Tiger, Hidden Dragon*," *A.V. Club*

> Pratt has luckily been in the habit of starring in movies that make a shit ton of money—hence the difficulty in arguing that he's not a star.
>
> —K. Austin Collins, "Chris Pratt Is Not a Movie Star," *The Ringer*

On a sad note, the late Bill Paxton plays Mae's father, who has MS, and it hurts to watch him so enfeebled, even if he's only acting. We're already reeling from another premature death this week: Jonathan Demme. Welcome to What a Shitty Year: The Sequel.

—*David Edelstein, "When It Comes to Tech Thrillers, The Circle Is Pretty Square," Vulture*

SLANG

Slang is any language that matches the conventions of everyday speech rather than formal writing. This can include slang spelling or slang vocabulary. Slang is often playful and metaphorical, adding vividness to a piece of writing.

Drake references may be eternal, but culture evolves quickly—and *Dear White People* hasn't leveled up. Sometimes #relatability alone isn't enuf.

—*Hannah Giorgis, "Dear White People Doesn't Know How to Reckon with 2017," The Ringer*

I repeat: THE HATE VIBES BETWEEN THESE TEAMS ARE SO POWERFUL THAT DUDES LIKE JONAS "I'M BLEEDING" JEREBKO AND IAN "NONSTOP INJURIES" MAHINMI ARE BEEFING NOW. Jonas Jerebko made a dirty play in a crucial playoff game! I feel like I'm watching my children grow up.

—*Jason Concepcion, "No Lay-Ups '90s Basketball Is Alive in Celts–Wizards," The Ringer*

POP CULTURE REFERENCES

In *The Unstoppable Writing Teacher* (2015), Colleen Cruz argues that pop culture plays a role in students' cultures and values "as much as ethnic, religious, and racial backgrounds" (117). In professional analytical writing, pop culture references are frequently used as allusions that deftly add layers of meaning and connection to the writer's ideas.

Emma Watson plays Mae, a young, ingenuous woman who lands a low-level but much-coveted job and gazes in wonder at the sunny, invasively social employees on its rolling grounds outside San Francisco. They're like chirpy little Stepford Techies with camera phones trained on everyone else.

—*David Edelstein*, "When It Comes to Tech Thrillers, *The Circle* Is Pretty Square," *Vulture*

Even though it's the same age as Sylvester Stallone, Steven Spielberg, and Donald Trump, the National Basketball Association looks better than all of them. Did you know that Ian Mahinmi will make almost $16 million this season . . . and he's not even one of the league's 49 highest-paid players? Hold on, I'll put that in bold italics.

—*Bill Simmons*, "LeBron Is Still Painting His Masterpiece," *The Ringer*

The song itself sounds like decades past: a pastiche of '80s-into-'90s styles like New Edition pop-and-B and New Jack Swing, crossed with the skittering, thumping 808 drums of a modern trap jam. Critics have compared "Like" to vintage R. Kelly, but more than anything I hear peak Bobby Brown, particularly in Mars' straining, high-register vocal.

—*Chris Molanphy*, "Bruno Mars' New No. 1 Proves He's the Canniest Hit-Maker of the Decade," *Slate*

Breaking the "Rules"

Through usage inquiry, we want our students to learn the many important conventions that will make their writing intelligible to others. Still, writers can assert their authority—their command of conventions—by breaking those rules for effect. After all, these aren't the written-in-stone kinds of rules that make the English language work. Rather, these are conventions (usually *school* conventions) that have been accepted as truth over time.

A writer demonstrates her power when she intentionally breaks a rule. She says, for example, "I know this isn't a complete sentence. And I don't care. This is the way I want it." In general, writers break conventional usage rules for emphasis. (We cringe when our students fall back on "for emphasis," so nudge your students to define exactly what is being emphasized in each example.)

Students love learning about breaking those usage rules that have been drilled into them for years and years. They feel rebellious. They feel like real writers. Students should be cautioned, though: Writers use each of these techniques in calculated moderation—perhaps once per piece of writing. These techniques pack a punch and shouldn't be abused.

SENTENCE FRAGMENTS

Sentence fragments are incomplete sentences that lack either a subject or a verb. The subjects and verbs here are usually understood and can be found in the preceding sentences. When you are studying intentional fragments with students, you might ask students to say what *would* complete the sentence.

> And then there are sequels that are reboots. Se-boots?
> Re-quels?
>
> —*Alissa Wilkinson,* "The Summer Movie Sequels and Reboots
>   to Watch and the Ones Nobody Needed," *Vox*

> OK, so now we're gonna get spoilery. Fair warning.
>
> —*Jason Sheehan,* "Reading the Game: *The Last of Us*," NPR

> A popular criticism of today's NBA from the Joe Budden—old-
> head set is that it is soft. Too reliant on three-pointers.
>
> —*Jason Concepcion,* "No Layups '90's Basketball Is Alive in Celts—Wizards," *The Ringer*

> In a rush of events, Troy gets broken up with by Gabriella,
> runs around on a golf course singing about his frustration,

and then is reunited with Gabriella on a stage while they
sing about love. Very romantic to the untrained eye.

—*Lauren, grade 12*

START WITH A COORDINATING CONJUNCTION

Writers begin sentences with conjunctions (*for, and, nor, but, or, yet, so*) to draw a
strong, immediate connection between two ideas.

And they can do it with whatever kinds of clothes they're
already interested in.

—*Constance Grady*, "Lorde Is the Celebrity Avatar of Pop Culture's Witch Obsession," *Vox*

And yet there's a broader range of possibility in art.

—*Alissa Wilkinson*, "Why Silly Summer Movies Matter," *Vox*

But it is, without a doubt, awesome. . . . But seeing each
subplot to its resolution slows down the overall pace and dulls
Guardians 2's jaunty thrill.

—*Alex Abad-Santos*, "Review: *Guardians of the Galaxy Volume 2*
is Marvel's Funniest Film, and Much Braver Than the Original," *Vox*

CAPITAL LETTERS

Writers might use all-caps to replicate speech (shouting, ranting). It's almost always funny.

It provided an opening for the faction that wanted Brown
to hurry up and do some all-caps COACHING.

—*John Gonzalez*, "Mike Brown Has the Best Job in the World," *The Ringer*

NOT to mention, she is out here breaking all kinds of laws
by bringing her daughter to Memphis with her FOR GOOD
without the consent of her child's father who might be a

deadbeat, but they signed an agreement and she poo-poo'd all over that thang.

—Panama Jackson, "Do You Watch *Greenleaf*? You Might Should Watch *Greenleaf*," *VSB*

I think we should feel REALLY GOOD about the Yankees and their rebuilding process right now.

—Bailey, grade 9

PROPER NOUNING

When a writer wants to make something abstract more tangible, they might capitalize it, thus turning it into a proper noun. These faux proper nouns scream, "I'm important! Pay attention to me!"

Adding the fact that toy horses are generally smaller than normal horses, not to mention fantasy horses, it seems unlikely that such a creature could beat any of the others listed here in a race. At least he's wise, though. Not to mention Real. Imagine him, all Real and worn and loved, his little legs all seamy, limping across the finish line in the dimming afternoon, long after everyone else has gone home . . . no, you're crying.

—Emily Temple, "Who Will Win the Literary Kentucky Derby," *LitHub*

A player will get the ball in a certain spot and everyone watching will instantly recognize it and know exactly what's going to happen: Desolation is going to happen; wreckage is going to happen; ruination is going to happen. A Terror Move is going to happen.

—Shea Serrano, "The James Harden Pick-and-Roll Is Nightmare Fuel for Defenders," *The Ringer*

> [Book clubs] have become a staple of a certain kind of literary life, a core part of a person's identity: You Club, therefore you Are.
>
> —Judith Newman, "Dear Book Club: It's You, Not Me," *The New York Times*

OUT-OF-PLACE PUNCTUATION

To emphasize one idea within a larger sentence, a writer might include a parenthetical exclamation point in the middle of the sentence.

> "And if Katie's mom is her Tracy Jordan—the unstoppable force that suddenly upends an already delicate work environment—then her Jenna Maroney is Portia (Nicole Richie) (!), the brazenly needy and overconfident co-anchor who constantly frustrates Chuck, the puffed-up anchor (John Michael Higgins) at the center of the show.
>
> —Linda Holmes, "The Good and Goofy *Great News* Comes to NBC," NPR

> But it's time to stop calling Pond a side project, not only because this is the band's seventh (!) album, but because The Weather is the best and most accessible distillation of Pond's unhinged appeal.
>
> —Vulture Staff, "Mac DeMarco's *This Old Dog* and 8 Other Albums to Listen to Now," *Vulture*

Human Touches

Donald Murray (1974) writes, "Students will write well only when they speak in their own voice, and that voice can only be authoritative and honest when the student speaks of his own concerns *in his own way*" (129, italics our own). Voice and authority are intertwined; if our goal is for students to write with authority, we must help them write in their own voices. But what does it mean to write with voice?

Voice in analytical writing is as important, if not more so, than it is in any other kind of writing. Because analysis writing is traditionally viewed as dry and academic, we have to make extra room in our teaching curriculum to help students find their voices and let their passion dance on the page.

Here's the good news about voice: When students are invited to choose their topics and think and write something about which they are deeply passionate, their writing is more likely to be filled with voice. However, articulating a passion and feeling a passion are two different things; and there will be many more writers who require support and modeling in order to "write in their own way."

The techniques below are best taught after students have drafted a piece of writing. Because voice is more a matter of craft and less about the thinking behind the writing, students will get more out of considering these possibilities with drafts in front of them.

TELL THE TRUTH

Let's be honest: We sometimes need to say things that are hard to hear—about a text, about ourselves. Analytical writers do this, too. This hard truth-telling makes the reader trust the writer and know that, regardless of the circumstances, this writer will speak honestly.

> On Twitter, brevity is necessary. But it isn't always the best tactic for a novel.
>
> —Tasha Robinson, "*And We're Off* Proves Brevity Isn't Always the Soul of Wit," NPR

> We're a country of women encouraged by best-selling authors and tech leaders to ask for raises, possibly after power-posing in our office bathrooms while belting out "I AM MOANA" or "Let it goooo." (We're also a country of poor or underemployed women who've never read *Lean In*, watched a TED talk, or seen *Frozen*, but more on that in a moment.)
>
> —Katy Waldman, "Spectacle and Imposter," *Slate*

But Vada's idiosyncratic antics—feigning illness, reading books that most adults skip, forcing herself into an adult community workshop—was the kind of attention-seeking I didn't feel comfortable doing myself. I read a lot, was a straight-A student, and wrote kind-of shitty (okay, very shitty) poetry, all rather unobtrusively. Rewatching *My Girl* today, I now realize what grated me so much about Vada's behavior: It was what I wanted to do but couldn't, too afraid to make myself be heard among my two sisters, as well as any number of my parents' louder concerns.

—Laura Adamcyzk, "*My Girl* Delivered Death in an Unbearably Precocious Package," *A.V. Club*

SHOW VULNERABILITY

Even though the focus of a piece of analysis is the close examination of a text, the writer's encounter with that text can provide a rich layer of evidence while also showing her humanity to the reader. Writers show vulnerability by revealing their emotions and personal experiences. It seems like being vulnerable and being authoritative would be opposing goals, but they actually work together—writers gain credibility and authority as they explore their own feelings and reactions to the texts they are exploring.

In these clothes about grief and violence, the absent body is so strongly implied that I felt I was looking at the personal artifacts of one dead woman.

—Josephine Livingstone, "The Passion of Rei Kabakubo," *New Republic*

She knows secrets about Stardew Valley that I never will, because to her, it's a map to a world she is just beginning to understand, while for me, it's a spreadsheet of a system I understood all too well.

—Jason Sheehan, "Reading the Game: *Stardew Valley*," NPR

A few weeks ago, after finishing "Lady Lazarus" and shoving it into my binder, something struck me: The way people reacted to "Lady Lazarus" in class is how our society reacts to suicide. I cannot tell you how many mental health professionals and people with mental illnesses believe suicide is selfish. . . . They reinforce an already rampant stigma by delegitimizing deep pain, sometimes their own. They treat the mentally ill as if they were dead, and as the Nazis valued Jews, only valued for the power and superiority they provide.

But people with mental illnesses are not dead. They are living, breathing, speaking people. The fact that Plath even wrote "Lady Lazarus" is astonishingly brave.

—*Anna,* grade 12

TALK TO YOUR READER

Talking directly to the reader builds a sense of fun and camaraderie into the analysis. It can enliven the writing and make it feel more like a communal event than an artifact of academia.

Holy moly, people, if you never believe anything else you read on the Internet, believe that friendship isn't therapy and therapy isn't friendship.

—*Linda Holmes,* "Missing Richard Simmons and the Nature of Being Known," NPR

Do I sound like someone freshly intoxicated by plays? Guilty as charged. . . . Take a deep breath and see a play you've never heard of and know little about, full of people you don't recognize. If you can turn on HBO or Netflix and engage with something unexpected and challenging, something not for everyone, you can do it in a theater, too.

—*Linda Holmes,* "Hey You, Prestige Television Fan: Here's Why You Should See a New Play," NPR

If you get no other FCBD book, get this one. If the store runs out of copies, rip one out of some little kid's hands, if you have to. (Don't do that.) (I'm just saying though: Them little tykes got *lousy* upper body strength.)

—*Glen Weldon,* "A Guide to Free Comic Book Day 2017: The Don't-Misses and the Near-Misses," NPR

Introduction

THE CHAPTERS THAT FOLLOW PRESENT MYRIAD RESOURCES
TO HELP BOTH YOU AND YOUR STUDENTS BEGIN TO
ENGAGE IN THE WORK OF AUTHENTIC, PASSION-DRIVEN,
EXPLORATORY ANALYTICAL WRITING.

Each chapter delves into a different subcategory of analytical writing. To choose these categories, we studied all the different kinds of texts that real writers are exploring today; we then narrowed the list to reflect the topics our students are most passionate about:

- Movie and television analysis
- Music analysis
- Sports analysis
- Video game analysis
- Literary analysis.

Each chapter in Section 3 follows an identical structure that aims to give you an overview of the subgenre, as well as specific ways to coach students in this kind of analytical writing. These chapters can be read top to bottom or in bits and pieces based on your needs. Maybe you will immerse yourself in the chapter on sports analysis to learn what you need to know to help a small group of students analyzing this season's NBA draft. Or, you might open to the chapter on movies and television on the way to school so you can help just one student find the mentor she needs to write a piece on trends in fall TV.

On the next page we've summarized the purpose of each section so you can find exactly what you need.

What Writers Explore

Think of this section as a guided tour that provides an overview of the topics that writers in each subgenre explore. If you're like us, you don't have expert knowledge of video games. So, when a student proposes a piece analyzing trends in recent video games, you may not know where she should begin, what she needs to consider, or what a reader will expect to encounter in the piece. (And, after all, this is precisely the point. It is the student's point of expertise—not ours.) In each "What Writers Explore" section, you will find the building blocks of that subgenre to help you get your own footing, alongside mini mentor texts demonstrating the discussion of each topic.

This section can be used in a number of ways, from individual conferences to small-group work and whole-class lessons. Imagine you are sitting beside a student who has written a mere two paragraphs about the recent Super Bowl but claims to be done. What other things do writers of sports analysis consider? What other topics might this student explore to flesh out his draft? Look to this section for lots of possibilities. Or perhaps you are conferring with a group of writers who need some examples of how writers describe characters. The mini mentor texts in this section will provide just the models you need.

Where to Find It

In this section we share our top, go-to sites for finding passionate, authentic mentor texts to inspire and instruct your students in each subgenre of analytical writing. You'll notice that most of the resources we provide point you to written texts that can be printed or read online. However, in some cases we direct you to podcasts. Podcasts give young writers language that will help them articulate their thoughts about a text just as printed texts do. Additionally, podcasts can be particularly helpful for English language learners who might be more successful with audio-based texts.

Key Mentors

Mentors are professional writers whose work inspires and guides our students toward better writing. While the mentor texts we provide in this book will eventually become outdated and possibly irrelevant, the mentors will continue to give and give with new texts to consider.

In this section, you will find three of our favorite mentors—writers at the top of their game, who are well-known and highly regarded in their genre, and whose work we have vetted with the toughest audience of all, students. We will share what they are known for in the field, a brief description of what you need to know about each writer, and a handful of mentor texts to get you started.

Helping students identify key mentors in the genre not only puts a face behind the writing but also gives students some starting points for finding additional mentor texts. Students can look up other pieces by these writers, follow them on Twitter, pose their own questions, and read the mentor's latest work. You might share the name of one of these mentors with a particular student during a conference, or you might share a whole-class lesson about one of the featured authors and some of his or her writing. No matter how you use this section, as a writing teacher it's important to know well the writers who are doing the work we want our students to emulate.

Ideas for Student Writing

When students spend time identifying and closely reading their passions, topics for analytical writing will naturally bubble up, but forms for those ideas can be harder to find. In writing conferences, students often say things like, "Um, I'm thinking about writing something about how this album is different from his other albums." This section will show you how to help students turn their initial ideas into strong claims. A handy chart begins with the idea "seedlings" students will likely bring to you, then moves into possible forms those ideas could take and suggested mentor texts. This chart isn't exhaustive by any means, but it's a good place to start as you help students move from doodlings, jottings, flash drafts, and big ideas into concrete forms and polished pieces.

Chapter 13: The Chapter of Possibilities

If students are writing into their passions, you'll find lots of opportunities to push beyond these five popular subgenres and explore other types of analytical writing—dance analysis, food analysis, political analysis—analysis that you can't even imagine before a student brings it to play. So, for all of the analytical writing that is yet to be written and for all the analytical writing that you cannot predict, Chapter 13 is a make-your-own-analysis-resources chapter. Here we walk you through our process for gathering resources to guide and inspire students and make it possible to teach through small-group instruction and writing conferences.

movie and television analysis

M ovie and television analysis is constantly at our fingertips, and it's one of the subgenres of analytical writing our students know best. Our students read reviews as they decide which movie to see, which TV show to skip, which new release to queue up on Netflix. They scan weighty theories and interpretations of the media they love so that they have talking points about that show to bandy about the lunch table with friends.

In our media-drenched culture, many of our students are instant authorities on multiple topics in this subgenre. They come to us ready to share why *Mockingjay* is amazing. Having begged for permission to see it, they are practiced at explaining the thematic nuances of *Mad Max: Fury Road*. While analyzing Melville's style might be a stretch for many high schoolers, chatting about tone and style in *Game of Thrones* comes more naturally. Most of our students come primed and ready, armed with latent potential, on the cusp of crafting intriguing movie and television analysis if we show them how.

What Writers Explore

These days, television and movie writing is almost as much a part of the viewing experience as actually watching. For every episode of prestige television that airs, hundreds of articles are written parsing the details, pouring over the plot, predicting what's next for the characters. Writing about the television and films we consume extends the experience—when the hour or two of runtime is up, we can spend the days leading up to the next episode or the months between installments sharing our insights and reading others' theories. Writing about TV and movies is an intellectual and emotional interaction, a way to connect with others who share a similar desire to understand why characters—like people—behave the way they do.

And then there are writers who like to go even deeper. Thinking about the direction, the lighting, the sound—all the technical choices that work together to create a whole world as real as our own that the viewer can enter.

Students who choose to write about television and film will enjoy the familiar English class territory of thinking about theme, setting, and characterization, while also exploring new elements such as visuals, acting, and direction.

Story

When writers analyze the story of a movie or TV show, they do so in many different ways. They might write about the effectiveness and coherence of the plot, the richness and believability of characters, the quality and style of the actual words in the script, or the success of an adaptation. When writers explore story they might make discoveries about the following.

THE STYLE OF DIALOGUE

Yet while Boyle, like his subject, may be the visionary who understands how to present this potentially bamboozling material to the public, it is screenwriter Sorkin who provides the dramatic source code. From the trademark quickfire walk-and-talk dialogue (Boyle calls it a "standing-up movie") to the slick sociopolitical satire, this runs on Sorkin software.

—*Mark Kermode, "Steve Jobs Review—Decoding a Complex Character," The Guardian*

THE EFFECTIVENESS AND COHERENCE OF THE PLOT

> Despite giving us some great moments that highlight the strongest members of the cast, "Marooned" doesn't offer any compelling developments in the main plot, which proves to be a problem. Instead, the main plot hinges upon Rip Hunter making one bad decision after another. How have they made this character not only boring, but an outright idiot?
>
> —Angelica Jade Bastien, "*Legends of Tomorrow* Recap: Fire and Ice," *Vulture*

THE SUCCESS OF AN ADAPTATION

> Reading Barker's book, I was struck by how incisive it is. . . . It's packed with episodes that would have been startling onscreen and with crazy-scary characters who'd have burned a hole in the screen.
>
> —David Edelstein, "*Whiskey, Tango, Foxtrot* Plays It Safe and Suffers for It," *Vulture*

THE RICHNESS OF CHARACTERS

> Claire is a fascinating character, but too much of what works in her character is wrapped up in how much of a mystery she remains, even four seasons in. . . . The new season establishes some background on who Claire Underwood is, but somehow it doesn't add up to a clearer sense of her.
>
> —Lisa Weidenfeld, "*House of Cards* Is as Enjoyable and Frustrating as Ever," *A.V. Club*

Theme

Film and television critics tie their analysis of individual elements back to something bigger, something central—the theme of the show, the big idea the viewer should walk away with, the broad arc of the storyline, the lesson that this text reveals. When writers explore theme, they might make discoveries about the following.

ALLUSIONS AND PARALLELS

Instead, the series feels hot-wired with modern parallels, which extend far beyond those baby Kardashians. Without ever mentioning the links, the creators evoke the Cosby scandal and Black Lives Matter, the debate about Hillary's "likability" and Obama's legacy, the rise of reality TV and the expansion of cable news. It's a tasty Proustian cronut that makes you remember the events of not only 1995 but 2015.

— Emily Nussbaum, "Not-Guilty Pleasure," *The New Yorker*

THE MULTIPLE THEMATIC TERRITORIES

Along with the visual nods to Spielberg, it shared his deep fascination with the fragile bond between children and parents, the failed dream of suburban safety. It was a show about grief and abandonment; on those subjects, it was sincere.

— Emily Nussbaum, "Archie's and Veronica's Misconceived
Return to *Riverdale*," *The New Yorker*

BIGGER IDEAS ABOUT CULTURE

This show has uncorked in me some deeper fear and loathing about the fate of our culture, just as it did in the late '80s, when my crowd used to watch and make fun of *Full House* as stoned and drunk college students.

— Hank Stuever, "You Already Know *Fuller House* Is Bad.
But Are You Adult Enough to Resist It?" *The Washington Post*

Visuals (Special Effects, Set Design, Lighting, Staging, Animation)

The manner in which a story unfolds on the screen is largely shaped by visual effects—the set design, colors on the screen, the way lighting is used, design in animation, cinematography, and special effects. Writers of film and television analysis zoom in, closely reading these visual moves for their deeper significance. When writers explore visuals, they might make discoveries about the following.

THE VERISIMILITUDE

> The sequence is spectacular in every sense of the word. OK, the bear is a product of an expert visual-effects team. But not for a second will you doubt you're seeing the real thing. This is one for the time capsule.
>
> —Peter Travers, "The Revenant," *Rolling Stone*

> A palpably convincing digital creation, this churning gray inundation powers straight into the little people, who panic and scatter, creating a regular day-of-the-locust free-for-all that separates children from parents, the survivors from the newly dead.
>
> —Manohla Dargis, "The Wave Is a Disaster Movie Making a Big Splash," *The New York Times*

THE DEPTH OF VISUALS

> It's all visually rich, especially the downtown area, where a foot chase undergoes a rapid shift in size when Judy pursues a suspect into a smaller-scale rodent neighborhood. As Judy and Nick's investigation continues, the city's bright pastel hues shift to more noirish tones, with streaks of streetlamp light.
>
> —Jesse Hassenger, "Clever Subtext Often Trumps Jokes in Disney's *Zootopia*," *A.V. Club*

Acting and Direction

Different than examining the role of the central characters, writers also explore the artists behind those fictional lives as they consider the actor's craft. Similarly, a director's artistic choices have a tremendous impact on shaping the stories we watch. Writers pull back the curtain on the human element behind film and television as they explore the intersection of an actor's performance and a director's influence. When writers explore acting and direction, they might make discoveries about the following.

THE NUANCE OF A PERFORMANCE

Courtney B. Vance gives a layered, subtle performance as the master showman Johnnie Cochran, Clark's most powerful antagonist—a quiet take on a bold man. . . . .The show grants him more gravitas, mainly by emphasizing the complex intersection of his private and public selves.

—Emily Nussbaum, "Not-Guilty Pleasure," *The New Yorker*

A NEW ELEMENT IN AN ACTOR'S REPERTOIRE

And then there's DiCaprio. Hidden behind a grotty beard, his words mostly reduced to grunts, he nonetheless provides a portrait of a man in full. It's a virtuoso performance, thrilling in its brute force and silent eloquence. . . . . *The Revenant* shows DiCaprio stretching his acting muscles, testing himself, eager for challenge. That you do not want to miss.

—Peter Travers, "The Revenant," *Rolling Stone*

THE EVOLUTION OF AN ACTOR'S ON-SCREEN PERSONA

I liked watching Fey, who's learning to be a real actress—to stop pulling sitcom faces and just *be*. It's fun to watch her go from helpless to hard-charging, mastering the language and trying to see past the propaganda on all sides.

—David Edelstein, "Whiskey, Tango, Foxtrot Plays It Safe and Suffers for It," *Vulture*

A DIRECTOR'S INSPIRATION

From a visual and technological standpoint, one could call it post-*Gravity*: Most of the film is set within a high-tech orbiting spacecraft, and director Daniel Espinosa (*Safe House, Child 44*) takes the weightlessness of the environment as inspiration, his camera floating constantly around the characters and down long passageways, pivoting upside down, catching majestic glimpses of the cosmos in the corner of the frame.

—*A.A. Dowd*, "*Life* Comes at You Fast When You're Being Hunted by a Hostile Octopus," *A.V. Club*

A DIRECTOR'S QUIRKS

However, the Coens' fondness for intentional anticlimax—put to pointed and poignant use in films like *Inside Llewyn Davis*, *No Country for Old Men*, *Barton Fink*, and *A Serious Man*—gets the better of them.

—*Ignatiy Vishnevetsky*, "The Coens Swipe at Religion, Counterculture, and Hollywood in *Hail, Caesar!*" *A.V. Club*

Where You Find It

Figure 8.1 lists five of our favorite go-to sources for mentor texts in movie and television analysis.

Source	Medium	Go to for . . .
A.V. Club	Website	All-around go-to site for writing about movies and television—reviews as well as larger essays and commentaries
Vulture	Website/podcast	All-around go-to site for writing about movies and television—reviews as well as larger essays and commentaries
		Vulture also has a popular podcast, the *Vulture TV Podcast*, which offers in-depth discussions of significant television series, episodes, and trends.
NPR	Website/radio	Primarily reviews and shorter pieces of analysis

Figure 8.1: Where to Find Movie and Television Analysis

Source	Medium	Go to for ...
Pop Culture Happy Hour	Podcast (no transcript available)	Listeners of this weekly podcast will find casual-but-brilliant analysis of all things movie and TV (There is also occasional music and literary analysis.); like chatting with your friends over coffee, *Pop Culture Happy Hour* is extremely accessible to students in its format while exposing students to top-rate criticism.
The Atlantic	Website/ magazine	The movie and television writing in *The Atlantic* ranges from more straightforward review-based analysis to analysis that zooms out to consider the broader significance of a particular film or series.

Figure 8.1: Continued

Key Mentors

If you want to read film or television analysis that is smart and incisive every time, look no further than Emily Nussbaum, David Edelstein, and Matt Zoller Seitz. Their prolific work will have students reading and marveling for days.

Emily Nussbaum

Twitter: @emilynussbaum
Known for: Television commentary

The winner of the 2016 Pulitzer Prize for criticism, Nussbaum's television commentary in *The New Yorker* doesn't take the form of weekly must-see drama recaps. Rather, her TV criticism—longer than most pieces in this subgenre—branches into social commentary. And her "so what" can pack a wallop, zooming far out into the broader significance of television in our culture.

Some Mentor Texts to begin with:

- "Graphic, Novel: *Marvel's Jessica Jones* and the Superhero Survivor," *The New Yorker*

- "Doll Parts: *UnREAL* Deconstructs *The Bachelor*," *The New Yorker*

- "Glee Club: Fresh Starts on *Crazy Ex-Girlfriend* and *Younger*," *The New Yorker.*

David Edelstein

Twitter: @david_edelstein

Known for: Film criticism

Edelstein's film writing (*Vulture*, *New York Magazine*) makes a great mentor text—it's smart, but digestible, and often anchored in an anecdote. Edelstein is a great mentor for student writers trying on this sub-genre for the first time. As a bonus, he is a contributor to NPR's *Fresh Air*, so students can listen to many of his reviews in addition to reading them.

Some Mentor Texts to begin with:

- "Rekindling the Spirit of a Galaxy Far, Far Away in *Star Wars: The Force Awakens*," NPR

- "*Mockingjay—Part 2* Ends *The Hunger Games* Series," NPR

- "The Fog of War Collides with the Fog of Michael Bay in *13 Hours*," NPR.

Matt Zoller Seitz

Twitter: @mattzollerseitz

Known for: Television and film criticism and commentary

For a teacher helping her students learn the ropes of analytical writing about film and television, Matt Zoller Seitz's writing (*Vulture*, RogerEbert.com) is a true workhorse, giving you a huge bang for your buck. If Emily Nussbaum works best in macro, weaving bits of ideas into a big picture, Matt Zoller Seitz's work shows students the micro, making the most out of every tiny detail in a film or show. Because Zoller Seitz critiques both film and television, his work provides a great side-by-side comparison for students—how does one writer analyze a whole work (film) differently than smaller pieces of a whole work (television episodes). Also, like David Edelstein, you can find him in the world of podcasts, smartly chatting about television on the *Vulture TV Podcast*.

Some Mentor Texts to begin with:

- "The New *X-Files* Has Plenty of Mythology, Now Bring on the Creatures," *Vulture*

- "*Fargo*'s Second Season Will Be a Classic in Its Own Right," *Vulture*

- "Review: *The Martian*," *RogerEbert.com*

Ideas for Student Writing

Student have lots of opinions about the movies they see and the television shows they're addicted to watching, but they don't always know what form those opinions should take. Our job is to help guide students from vague ideas to concrete forms.

Figure 8.2 lists the most common broad ideas students will bring to the table, a form that idea might take, and a mentor text suggestion to get them started.

Student Wants to Write About . . .	Might Take the Form of . . .	Mentor Texts . . .
A character	A piece comparing a character to real-life tropes and stereotypes	"The Psychology of Voldemort" (Julie Beck, *The Atlantic*)
	A piece exploring multiple perspectives on a controversial character	"Why It's So Hard for Us to Agree About Dong from *Unbreakable Kimmy Schmidt*" (Kat Chow, NPR)
A TV show from yesteryear	A piece on the show's lasting cultural relevance	"Donald Trump Is Still Basically Hosting *The Apprentice*" (Alex McLevy, *A.V. Club*)
An actor or actress	A piece comparing an actress to a character she famously portrays	"Is Jennifer Lawrence Katniss-ing Us?" (Jordan Hoffman, *Vulture*)
Their take-aways from a movie or show	A listicle of major lessons learned	"8 Life Lessons from *The Breakfast Club*" (Erin Mulrane, *Movie Pilot*)
The theme	A piece providing an alternate theory about the movie's theme	"Star Wars Films Are Not About Good vs. Evil. They're About Bad Parenting" (Jeet Heer, *New Republic*)
Costuming	Analysis of how the characters' styles aid their characterization	"*Heathers* Style: A Fashion Analysis of the Original Mean Girls Movie" (Tom Fitzgerald and Lorenzo Marquez, *Fusion*)
Setting	A piece analyzing how setting influences characterization and theme	"Captain America on the Potomac" (Linda Holmes, NPR)
Genre	A piece debating whether a television show is a comedy or a drama	"*Horace and Pete* Is Louis C.K.'s Take on American Melodrama" (David Sims, *The Atlantic*)
Source material	A piece on the latent themes in the source material highlighted by a particular writer/director	"*Sense and Sensibility* and Jane Austen's Accidental Feminists" (Devoney Looser, *The Atlantic*)
Trends and patterns in movies/TV	A piece on why female relationships make the best love stories on TV	"The Best Love Stories on TV Are Between Two Women" (Molly Eichel, *A.V. Club*)

Figure 8.2: Ideas for Student Writing in Movies and Television

CHAPTER NINE

music analysis

T his chapter is dedicated to all the students we've caught listening to music in class. The students with one earbud in, and the other (the one facing you) out. The students with chords tangled in their hair. "Can you please take your earbuds out?" you whisper politely from the front of the room, tapping on your ear. "Oh, I'm not listening to anything," they respond, a hint of a smile on their lips.

This chapter is dedicated to those students whose entire world is music. What would happen if we invited those students to write about the sounds and rhythms and lyrics pouring into their ears on a daily basis? What would happen if we told those students they could help others understand why their music is life-altering? And what would happen if those students discovered that writing, like music, could affect change? We don't know about you, but we'd like to find out, which is why we've included this chapter on music criticism, replete with cream-of-the-crop mentor texts and incredible writers, some of whom were sitting in classrooms just like yours not too long ago, the music flowing through them.

What Writers Explore

Music criticism isn't as esoteric as you may think. Sure, critics wax poetic on the inner workings of a song, using words like *modulation* and *cadential extension* and *arpeggiation*, but like the literary critics we're familiar (and comfortable!) with, they also comment on more universal topics like theme, tone, and historical context, engaging readers with a variety of musical backgrounds.

Professional writers of music analysis explore why the music matters—yes, to the album but also to the artist's evolution and to the people who are listening to it. Music is a language in and of itself; it reaches into the deepest parts of our souls, and writers want to explore this thing that only music can do. Music writers probe the depths of a song or an album in order to articulate the inarticulable: why that song moved them to tears, why that beat makes them involuntarily bob their head, what makes people shout "Freebird" at a concert.

A Musician's Worldview

Music critics are interested in the distinctive lens through which a musician views the world and how he chooses to present that world to listeners. Writers of music analysis explore the themes and ideas that artists return to time and time again as context—a way to situate a particular work in the broader picture of the artist's primary concerns. By zooming out, the writer presents a bigger and more detailed picture of the music's impact on the artist's career and on our culture.

When writers explore a musician's worldview, they might make discoveries about the following.

THE ARTIST'S TONE

Even in the face of tragedy ("Summer Friends"), "Coloring Book" exudes an optimism so strong it's like its own religion, while "Views" brings a short-fused, operatic pessimism to matters as trivial as belatedly answered texts.

—*Lindsay Zoladz, "Drake, Chance the Rapper, and the Millennial Divide," The Ringer*

HOW AN ARTIST DISRUPTS SOCIETAL EXPECTATIONS

There's an unspoken pressure in our society for women to "act their age," whatever that means, so maybe the most inspiring thing about Gwen is that, at her best, she's disregarded that false ideal. I didn't expect her new album to clarify exactly why I worshipped her when I was younger, but it did: She's always been the world's oldest teenager.

—*Lindsay Zoladz,* "With Her New Solo Album (and New Relationship), Gwen Stefani Proves the Value of Public Insecurity," *Vulture*

As a global superstar of the 1970s, David Bowie broke the boundaries of gender roles and sexuality. And he did so with such seeming ease, such delight, that for his fans it was suddenly imaginable to be precisely who you were—not who someone else told you to be.

—*John Nichols,* "David Bowie, the 'Apolitical' Insurrectionist Who Taught Us How to Rebel," *The Nation*

Genre

Sometimes all you need to know about a person is that they like rock. Or classical. Or hip-hop. Perhaps this is why people who write about music include a discussion of genre—simply categorizing a song, artist, or album according to genre says volumes about it. Genre reveals to the listener the many layers of a song: its structure, its history, and its influences. Writers can identify the genre of a song or album and explore how it fits or defies that category. They can explore ways in which some musicians play in and around different genres, "sampling" qualities from each, or how a musician's oeuvre has transitioned among various genres over time.

When writers explore genre, they might make discoveries about the following.

AN ARTIST'S EVOLUTION

Yorke's grown increasingly more soulful as a vocalist over the course of Radiohead's career, though he still loves the flat affect that speaks for his inner android, even on "Desert Island Disk," this album's cautiously hopeful, post-breakup call for "different kinds of love." Yet it's obvious that in the five years since *King of Limbs*, the band has registered the rise of a new kind of soul music that is as sonically experimental and emotionally unpredictable as its own twisted take on realness.

—*NPR Music Staff,* "11 Very Different Opinions About the New Radiohead Album," NPR

As they've inched away from the puckish P-Funk stylings of their early years toward a new classic rock, the quality of the music has hinged on how well the band could cut to the emotional quick.

—*Craig Jenkins,* "Red Hot Chili Peppers' *The Getaway* Is Their Best in Years," *Vulture*

Theme

In the same way a student might write about what the theme of a novel suggests about our world, music critics explore the themes of songs and albums as a way to help readers understand an artist's purpose and contributions to the world of music and beyond. When a writer explores themes in a piece of music, she is staying close to the text, asking, "What is *this* song saying?" and, "What is the message of this album?"

When writers explore themes, they might make discoveries about the following.

THE CONNECTION THE SONG MAKES WITH THE LISTENER

Jay-Z's song is for someone but his "you" is a repeating body—a person and series of people known and unknown. . . . These revelations are, in fact, spiritual, touching the most defenseless parts of each of us even as we collectively grieve.

—*Shana L. Redmond,* "Faith Under Fire: Jay Z's 'Spiritual' Is a Modern Song of Sorrow," NPR

MOTIFS AND MESSAGES

The body remains front and center in Beyoncé's early solo work. In "Get Me Bodied," on her second album, *B'Day* (2006), for instance, she tells her audience what she wants. . . . On the whole, Beyoncé's lyrics operate on a kind of continuum. The underlying message: Men will try to control you by dictating the limits of your pleasure, your ambition, your success. Get yours before they rip you off, emotionally or otherwise.

—Hilton Als, "Beywatch," *The New Yorker*

THEMATIC TONE

Beyoncé is certainly not the first person to make art that comments on race and identity in a way that feels expansive and humorous.

—Erin Vanderhoof, "Beyoncé with the Good Art," *The Nation*

Cultural Commentary

A lot of music is timeless, and critics enjoy musing on the themes and images of songs that will carry us from decade to decade. But music can also be *timely*—and critics often explore how a song or album comments on or illuminates a particular aspect of our culture today. It's a critic's job to not only consider the permanence of a song but also to contextualize it in the exact moment in which it came to be. Similarly, music critics also look at trends in the music world and think about how the music of the moment reflects the state of our world. A writer's discussion of a piece of music's commentary on culture is often related to the music's theme but with a specific, social, and outward-focused lens.

When writers explore the cultural subtext, they might make discoveries about the following.

TRENDS IN MUSIC

In 2016, repurposing old tunes for new product is no longer a vital part of the industry and, with its absence, our view of the past is slowly shifting. Yes, copious repackaging could be a mercenary practice, but music fans also benefitted tremendously by record labels' need to recycle the past.

In fact, we often don't grasp how deeply the practice has
affected our collective view of music history.

—Stephen Thomas Erlewine, "Why the Death of Greatest
Hits Albums and Reissues Is Worth Mourning," Pitchfork

SOCIAL CONTEXT

Let a Jay Z protest song serve as self-care until the next
black body is inevitably laid to rest on America's streets.

—Vulture Editors, "7 Best New Songs of the Week" (July 12, 2016), Vulture

Craft

To write well about music, critics must have a deep understanding of music and
how it works. They must be able to break down a song and explore its many layers—its rhythms, chords, and structure. This doesn't mean that writers need to
use complicated technical jargon. Music critics use metaphor and description
that make sense to them and make sense to the reader, enabling the audience
to imagine a sound that they aren't presently hearing. And like all good analysis,
music criticism must also make clear the connection between the craft of a song
and its larger meaning.

When writers explore the music itself, they might make discoveries about
the following.

CONNECTING PAST AND PRESENT

"Can't Go Back" starts with a burst of whimsical,
pitter-pattering instrumentation that's not far off from
today's cheerful indie pop; plush harmonies blossom in the
background of "Book of Love"; and the soulful "Only over
You" feels like an old-fashioned torch song.

—Annie Zaleski, "Fleetwood Mac's Mirage Is a Well-Crafted
Diamond in the Rough," A.V. Club

INSTRUMENTATION AND ENERGY

The restless double-octave guitar lick that starts "American
Girl" is the beginning of *Greatest Hits*, and it gives the

album an undeniable energy that continues through the gorgeous "Here Comes My Girl," the aching "The Waiting," and even the dopey "Don't Do Me Like That." By the time the Lynne era arrives with "Free Fallin'" and "Into the Great Wide Open," the urgency has waned, but the craftsmanship hasn't.

—David Brusie, "Tom Petty's *Greatest Hits* Record Remains the Best of the Best-ofs," *A.V. Club*

There are pianos stacked everywhere, in the swelling intro to lead single "Dark Necessities," the dramatic coda to "The Longest Wave," and the lilting breakdown in the sprightly rocker "Feasting on the Flowers."

—Craig Jenkins, "Red Hot Chili Peppers' *The Getaway* Is Their Best in Years," *Vulture*

THE STRUCTURE OF THE MUSIC

Someone could get a PhD thesis out of studying the major-minor shifts in his Beatles songs: Sometimes the change is from verse to chorus, to mark a change from affirmation to melancholy, as in "The Fool on the Hill"; sometimes it's in the middle of a phrase, as in "Penny Lane," to capture a mood of mixed sun and showers.

—Adam Gopnik, "Long Play: The Charmed Lives of Paul McCartney," *The New Yorker*

Production

Most songs aren't the musical creation of a single person. From the songwriter to the singer to the producer, songs are shaped by many professionals. And often the thing that makes a song truly distinctive is the production of it—the myriad decisions about editing parts, setting levels, and adding effects. While this might be unfamiliar musical territory for some writers in your class, others will come to the table with substantial production knowledge (we've taught many budding producers, DJs, and mixmasters in the past). Students with less prior knowledge about music production will still be able to describe the effect they are hearing, whether or not they know what it's called or how it's achieved.

When writers explore production, they might make discoveries about the following.

A SONG'S SOUND

> Gaga gets understated production from Mark Ronson. . . .
> "A-Yo," a taste of Motown handclaps and dirty talk, or
> "Dancin' in Circles," a reggae ode to she-bopping co-written
> by Beck that sounds like a No Doubt cover band who'd call
> themselves Spiderwebs or Hella Good.
>
> —*Rob Sheffield,* "Lady Gaga's Soft-Rock Turn *Joanne* Is Her Best in Years," *Rolling Stone*

> The bass-heavy production is so weighted by contemporary
> circumstance that it threatens to drag.
>
> —*Shana L. Redmond,* "Faith Under Fire: Jay Z's 'Spiritual'
> Is a Modern Song of Sorrow," NPR

SAMPLING: FOOTPRINTS OF OTHER MUSIC

> Beyoncé served as the executive producer on *Lemonade,* so
> she had power over the curatorial and visionary decisions
> that make it so distinctive. As an art object, it's layered in
> a way that a stack of books is: It's a coherent whole, but it
> has seams, sites where creative decisions stand out. From
> the Isaac Hayes (performing Burt Bacharach's "Walk on
> By") sample on "6 Inch," a song about a working girl—once
> you hear it, you can't unhear it—to the clever quotations
> of songs like Animal Collective's "My Girls" and Soulja Boy's
> "Turn My Swag On," the music bears the marks of a bunch
> of talented people getting together in a room and having a
> lot of freedom to make something enjoyable.
>
> —*Erin Vanderhoof,* "Beyoncé with the Good Art," *The Nation*

Comparisons and Influences

Artists don't make music in a vacuum; rather their art is inspired and influenced by songs and artists of the past and present. Musicians borrow from other musicians' playbooks all the time, and it's a writer's job to pick up on this kind of parroting and think about how those influences shape the music.

When writers explore comparison and influences, they might make discoveries about the following.

HOW ONE ARTIST SHAPED THE CAREER OF ANOTHER

At the height of his stardom in 1970, Haggard recorded a tribute album to Wills—he picked up the fiddle just a few weeks prior to recording, playing with enthusiasm, not skill—but his entire career can be seen as an enduring salute to Wills, a musician who saw no division between country, blues, jazz, and pop.

—*Stephen Thomas Erlewine,* "Why Merle Haggard Was a Country Game Changer," *Pitchfork*

THE BLENDING OF ARTISTS, SOUNDS, AND GENRES

The first song that jumped out at me from the muddy lily pond that is *A Moon Shaped Pool* was "The Numbers." It's like an expansive blending of Neil Young's "Old Man" with Patti Smith's "People Have the Power" with some Eurodisco strings thrown in, and the most openly inspirational call to action on this album.

—*NPR Music Staff,* "11 Very Different Opinions About the New Radiohead Album," *NPR*

SOUND INFLUENCES

"Wishful Beginnings" off of *Outside* bears the stamp of Reznor's buried-secret manner of layered production, its recurring croaking noises unnerving like the last gasps from a strangulation lost somewhere in the recording of "Reptile" or "A Warm Place."

—*SPIN Staff,* "The 100 Greatest David Bowie Moments," *Spin*

Where You Find It

Figure 9.1 lists six of our favorite go-to sources for mentor texts in music criticism.

Source	Medium	Go to for ...
NPR	Website	Album reviews and song analysis (*Songs We Love*).
Classicfm.com	Website	The host of Classic FM online radio, this website offers gobs of resources for musicophiliacs; search the Music Theory tab for short, visual music analysis.
Vulture	Website	Every week, *Vulture* editors highlight the best new music in "Songs of the Week"; once or twice a month they put out an album review.
The Ringer	Website and newsletter	An all-around-awesome mentor text database—like the cool kid at school, *The Ringer* knows just what to talk about and when; your students will love reading about what they are listening to and thinking about *right now*.
Switched on Pop	Podcast	We love Nate and Charlie's wicked smart, hilarious take on the making and meaning of music; each episode is forty-five minutes of pure analytical genius.
Song Exploder	Podcast	Musicians breaking down their own songs—it doesn't get any better than this.

Figure 9.1: Where to Find Music Analysis

Key Mentors

Ken Tucker

Twitter Handle: @kentucker

Known for: Music reviews

If webpages could be physically marked, Ken Tucker's page on npr.org would be dog-earred and stained from years of use in our classrooms. Tucker is the mastermind behind one of our all-time favorite mentor texts, a review of Pharrell Williams' album $GIRL$. With an active Twitter page, Tucker serves as a dependable, prolific, inspiring mentor for our students.

Some Mentor Texts to begin with:

- "Pharrell Williams: Just Exhilaratingly Happy," NPR
- "Beyoncé Is "At the Height of Her Powers" in *Lemonade*," NPR
- "Mitski Creates a Heightened Remembrance of Adolescence on *Puberty 2*," NPR.

Lindsay Zoladz

Twitter handle: @lindsayzoladz
Known for: Pop culture criticism and reviews

Lindsay has been the pop music critic for several of our all-time favorite mentor text clearinghouses: *Vulture*, *Pitchfork*, and *The Ringer*. Presently a staff writer at *The Ringer*, Lindsay reminds us of the coolest kid in high school who was also intimidatingly smart. In a short autobiography for *Vulture*, Lindsay honors her own mentors: "People sometimes ask me when I knew I wanted to be a music critic, and the honest answer is that I never really did. I always loved listening to music and I always loved to write, but when I was younger, Music Criticism felt like a country that was walled off to me—I'd never been issued the proper passport. I had the feeling that a lot of the music writing I encountered was talking down to me.... When I was a little bit older, I found critics—Willis and Greil Marcus and Joan Morgan and Rob Sheffield among them—who came at it with a different approach." With a strong Twitter presence and hefty oeuvre, Lindsay is easily one of our favorite mentors to share with students.

Some Mentor Texts to begin with:

- "Drake, Chance the Rapper, and the Millennial Divide," *The Ringer*
- "Nick Jonas Is Quietly Woke: How a Former Boy-Band Star Is Redefining Pop Masculinity," *The Ringer*
- "Save the Term 'Surprise' for Albums That Are Actually Surprising," *The Ringer*.

Craig Jenkins

Twitter handle: @craigSJ
Known For: Music criticism and reviews

Jenkins joined the *Vulture* team in May 2016 as the pop-music critic. Lane Brown, *Vulture*'s culture editor, describes Jenkins as a writer with "wide-ranging tastes, infallible radar, and the ability to explore big ideas while clearly explaining to readers what the music actually sounds like." We couldn't agree more. Brown's eclectic tastes are a refreshing change in a sea of pop-heavy music criticism. In addition to writing about big names, he reviews lesser known, independent artists, exposing us and our students to a variety of sounds, styles, and experiences.

Some Mentor Texts to begin with:

- "Let's Hope the New Ghostbusters Movie Isn't as Terrible as Its New Theme Song," *Vulture*

- "Desiigner Is the Song of Summer Front-Runner, Just Ahead of Drake and JT," *Vulture*

- "Blood Orange's *Freetown Sound* Is the 'Passion' of Black America," *Vulture*

- "Radiohead's Dystopic Lyrics Resonated a Little More Than Usual at MSG Last Night," *Vulture*.

Ideas for Student Writing

Have you ever listened to students talk about their favorite band or musical artist? They could go on and on forever. But talking effusively and writing smartly are two different things. We have to capture that energy and passion and help them articulate their thoughts on paper. One way to do this is to help them find a focus and then direct them toward a mentor text that's doing similar work (Figure 9.2).

Student Wants to Write About . . .	Might Take the Form of . . .	Mentor Text . . .
The evolution of a band	A look at how a band's various albums stack up	"Fleetwood Mac's *Mirage* is a Well-Crafted Diamond in the Rough" (Annie Zaleski, *A.V. Club*)
Their music idol	A piece exploring the bigger ideas an artist represents	"David Bowie, the 'Apolitical' Insurrectionist Who Taught Us How to Rebel" (John Nichols, *The Nation*)
Soundtrack/score	A piece exploring how the soundtrack does or doesn't illuminate the show or film	"*The Handmaid's Tale*'s Closing Songs Are Slyly Genius" (Jen Chaney, *Vulture*)
Listening experience	A piece exploring different ways of listening to an album	"11 Very Different Opinions About the New Radiohead Album" (NPR Music Staff, NPR)

Figure 9.2: Ideas for Student Writing in Music Analysis

continues

Student Wants to Write About ...	Might Take the Form of ...	Mentor Text ...
A singer	A piece that looks at how a musician has revolutionized the music world	"Nick Jonas Is Quietly Woke" (Lindsay Zoladz, *The Ringer*)
An album	Review of a brand-new album	"Red Hot Chili Peppers' *The Getaway* Is Their Best in Years" (Craig Jenkins, *Vulture*)
A musician's career	A piece that explores why an artist is successful	"Gwen Stefani Is What the Truth Feels Like" (Lindsay Zoladz, *Vulture*)
A song	Analysis of a song	"Jay Z's 'Spiritual' Is a Modern Song of Sorrow" (Shana L. Redmond, NPR)
Music culture	A piece exploring a new trend in music	"Why the Death of Greatest Hits Albums and Reissues Is Worth Mourning" (Stephen Thomas Erlewine, *Pitchfork*)

Figure 9.2: Continued

CHAPTER TEN

sports analysis

I f you want to know your students, look no further than the locker rooms, athletic fields, and courts at 3:00 in the afternoon. The students who sat passively in your classroom an hour earlier come alive in their jerseys and sneakers. They are in their element. They are happy. You watch as the basketball players warm up, landing basket after basket. They make things look so easy. And don't you wish you could transfer that facility to the classroom and to their writing? You can—if you connect what they're doing at 3:00 to what's happening in your writing workshop right now.

Many students who are participating in sports are also reading about sports in their free time. At the very least, they're reading and sharing statistics on players. Some of them are reading lengthier pieces about these stats, as well as thoughtful analysis about a team's season, conference playoffs, and draft picks. One surefire way to ignite curiosity and passion in your student athletes is to invite their sports into your workshop and teach them how to write the kinds of things they are reading.

What Writers Explore

A sportswriter is a sometimes fortune-teller, sometimes problem-solver, frequent armchair quarterback, and occasional cheerleader. If writers of TV and film analysis are motivated by intellectual engagement and writers of music analysis are motivated by probing emotional reactions, sportswriters are motivated by competition. They break down the performances of players, teams, games, and coaches because they are driven to figure out the most fundamental question of all sports: Who is the winner and who is the loser?

Writing sports analysis provides an outlet for students to explore their firmly held opinions in more depth than they might over the lunch table—a natural extension of their constant sports discussion and banter. In the moments between classes, our students are debating stats, and fantasy draft picks, and favorite teams. So when we invite students to write about sports, we invite them to lift their banter to the next level. When a writer begins to uncover the patterns in a player or team, suddenly the game isn't just a game; the writer realizes it's an art.

The Game

Just as some of us may run to our computers after an episode of *Game of Thrones* in search of the latest recaps and commentaries, sports enthusiasts may search for writing that breaks down a game and analyzes its bits and pieces. Students are quick to make broad generalizations about yesterday's match ("This team's defense was stronger" or "That team was outmanned"), but smart mentor texts will help student writers capture richer, more interesting, and more specific ideas about last night's game.

When writers explore the game, they might make discoveries about the following.

STAND-OUT MOMENTS

When the team's six-feet-eleven center, Daniel Ochefu, threw down a two-handed slam over the outstretched arms of a U.N.C.–Asheville Bulldog, thousands of fans exulted, and it was electric. When the forward Jalen Brunson rose to shoot, one could admire the odd, tightly wound mechanics of his shot, with its canon-like release.

—Ian F. Blair, "Enjoying March Without the Madness," *The New Yorker*

[The Gamecocks] needed to shoot a 3 or go for a quick 2. . . .
Guard Rakym Felder dribbled aimlessly for a few seconds
and passed to guard Duane Notice who swung it to SEC
Player of the Year Sindarius Thornwell, who didn't seem
immediately interested in shooting.

> —*Rodger Sherman,* "Gonzaga Made the Foul of the
> Year to Secure a Trip to the Championship," *The Ringer*

The Team

Not surprisingly sportswriters often focus on the team—team dynamics, what a certain pattern of wins and losses reveals about a team, and how teams change over time. When a writer explores the performance of a team, she often mulls over trends in the performance of both coaches and players so that she can make predictions about their future potential, figure out what made them successful, or determine what went wrong.

When writers explore the team, they might make discoveries about the following.

PROBLEMS IN TEAM PERFORMANCE

There were troubling signs for Golden State even before last
night's loss. On Thursday, they barely escaped with a win
at Utah. Their previous three games all were home wins by
smaller margins than our CARM-Elo-based point spread
suggested. And since the All-Star Break, the Warriors have
outscored opponents by an average of 3.6 fewer points per
game than our spreads predicted.

> —*Neil Paine and Carl Bialik,* "How Losing to the Celtics
> Changes the Warriors' Odds of 73 Wins," *FiveThirtyEight*

THE DRAMA OF THE GAME

Looking back, the Warriors' recent losses, some of them
all too avoidable—the Celtics and the Timberwolves come

to mind—are a testament to how completely they have mastered the art of entertainment. The buildup of suspense before their game against the Memphis Grizzlies, their last chance to reach a history-making seventy-three wins, was a masterpiece of its own.

—*Vinson Cunningham, "A Perfect NBA Season," The New Yorker*

A COACH'S TEAM-TRENDS OVER TIME

In previous years, Saban's defense has had trouble with hurry-up, no-huddle offenses led by mobile quarterbacks like Cam Newton and Johnny Manziel—guys like Deshaun Watson. Saban's defenses in the past were anchored by big, deliberate run-stoppers, like Terence Cody at nose tackle, and Trey DePriest at linebacker. Saban has spent the last few years recruiting lighter and faster defenders, and transforming the players already on the team into that mold. This year's defense bore the fruit of those labors—just enough in the title game.

—*Monte Burke, "Win over Clemson Clinches It: Nick Saban Is the Greatest Coach in History," Forbes*

Individual Players

The English teachers in us want to argue that players on teams aren't all that different from characters in a book that change and develop and have a story to tell. This is why sportswriters like Vinson Cunningham often describe players in terms of literature. Sportswriters who focus on players inevitably talk about their contributions to a game, a season, or the sport, while also discussing the development of players' skills.

When writers explore players, they might make discoveries about the following.

Because of the highlight-reel base-running plays, people often forget that Robinson was also an incredible hitter. He topped a .295 batting average eight times, winning the NL batting crown in 1949 with a .342 average. He also had the majors' seventh-highest on-base percentage during the course of his career (1947–1956), drawing a walk on 12.8 percent of his plate appearances in addition to his outstanding ability to hit for average.

—*Neil Paine*, "Advanced Stats Love Jackie Robinson," *FiveThirtyEight*

He takes 17.7 percent of the team's touches in the attacking half of the field. That's fourth in La Liga among players who've played more than 400 minutes, but it's crazy high for a team like Barcelona that are seemingly attacking all the damn time. . . . Unsurprisingly, Messi is similarly dominant with shots, taking a league-high 40 percent of Barcelona's. The club is a solar system and Messi is the sun.

—*Mike L. Goodman*, "No Messi, No Problem: Neymar Becomes a Superstar," *Grantland*

Saban's greatest strength as a coach—and perhaps one of the reasons that he did not excel in the NFL—is recruiting. (It's a skill that's devalued in the pros.) Alabama has become the standard in college football since Saban's second year in 2008 mainly because it almost always fields a team that just simply has better players.

—*Monte Burke*, "Nick Saban and the Triumph of Coaching," *Forbes*

WHAT A PLAYER MEANS TO THE SPORT

The pace at which Curry is setting and breaking his own records—he recently obliterated his own mark of two hundred and eighty-six three-pointers in a single season—suggests that he's either a once-in-a-generation phenomenon or the herald of some basketball evolution. Maybe he's both. He's certainly a new kind of shooter, one who doesn't need to elevate above his opponents to score.

—*Pasha Malla, "How the Jumpshot Brought Individualism to Basketball," The New Yorker*

PROBLEMS IN PERFORMANCE

I haven't watched every match he's played this winter, but I have noticed that, at times, he's stepping inside the baseline early in rallies, trying, it would seem, to shorten points; this taking the ball early, on the rise, can throw off the timing of his mighty forehand and result in his pushing the ball back, leaving it short for his opponent to attack.

—*Gerald Marzorati, "The Twilight of Nadal," The New Yorker*

The Person Behind the Player

Occasionally sportswriters shift their focus away from the person-as-athlete in favor of a different angle. Writer Monte Burke, author of *Saban: The Making of a Coach,* is well known for his profiles of coaches and athletes, but other writers, too, make quick detours away from the game-focused writing of the season to explore a player of interest in more detail.

AN ATHLETE'S INNER DEMONS

The decade separating the cemetery in Kansas and the marina in the Bahamas has seen Tiger lose many of the things most important to him, and the more time passes, the more it's clear he left some essential part of himself there in the ground between Miles and Maude Woods. How did all he'd built come undone so quickly and so completely? That's the question that will shadow him for the rest of his life. The answer is complicated and layered. He fell victim to many things, some well-known and others deeply private: grief, loneliness, desire, freedom, and his fixation with his father's profession, the military. These forces started working in Tiger's life almost as soon as his G-IV landed back in Orange County after he buried his father's ashes.

—*Wright Thompson*, "The Secret History of Tiger Woods," *ESPN*

DIFFERENT SIDES OF A PLAYER'S PERSONA

Sometimes he was a hero. Sometimes he was a villain. Sometimes fans adored him. Sometimes fans couldn't stand him. The only place where Kobe Bryant's HeroVillain never tread was the middle ground, accounting for what is arguably the most memorable twenty-year marriage between an athlete and town in the history of sports.

—*Bill Plaschke*, "As a Hero or Villain, Kobe Bryant Never Took the Middle Ground," *LA Times*

A PLAYER'S CHARACTER

Tebow's former teammates answer one question more often than any other: Is he really that good? This is not a football question. It pertains to his character, his virtuous public image, which inspires both love and hatred. If you want a reason to hate Tebow, the answer to the question doesn't matter. If the answer is no (he is only pretending to be good), then you hate him for being a fraud. If the answer is yes (he really is that virtuous), you hate him even more. When John Oliver said he would shoot Tim Tebow before shooting Osama bin Laden, it was easy to understand why. You know you're better than a terrorist. With Tebow you can't be sure.

—*Thomas Lake*, "The Book of Tebow," *Sports Illustrated*

Impact on the Sport

Sportswriting wouldn't be sportswriting if not for the literature about the sport itself. Some of the more interesting pieces we've found look at how one basketball player's career helps writers track the evolution of the sport over time to how an individual player can change the face of the sport itself.

THE HISTORICAL RESONANCE OF A PLAYER

Bryant's game had its flaws, and he was certainly no Jordan, but he was a player of undeniable historical importance. His résumé speaks enough to the on-court portion of his legacy, but for statheads, Kobe's career helps us track the evolution of basketball analytics over time, both in its reaction to his performance and its ability to capture the meaningfulness of that performance in the first place.

—*Neil Paine*, "Kobe Haters Are Stuck in 2008," *FiveThirtyEight*

As NBA analyses evolve, we have new means to understand how great point guards like Paul change the game. Assists are one thing. But they account only for the shots that teammates make, and that's only part of the playmaking story. Thanks to the league's player tracking system, we can now analyze the origin of every shot in every game. Upon closer inspection, when Paul is creating shots—either for his teammates or for himself—he blends volume and effectiveness as well as anyone in the NBA.

—*Kirk Goldsberry*, "Chris Paul Is a Point God," *FiveThirtyEight*

THE EFFECT OF A NEW REGULATION

The NFL is months away from starting, but even in the midst of March Madness, the league managed to grab headlines. Yesterday, the NFL announced that it would move the touchback to the 25-yard line, inciting a lot of backlash from the media and fans alike. At the surface, this looks like a move to protect kick returners by encouraging more touchbacks and therefore fewer full-speed collisions between players to most people, except perhaps Jerry Jones.

—*Kurt Bullard*, "Kicking Off Spring: The Impact of the New Touchback on Kickback Return Strategy," *Harvard Sports Analysis*

THE STORY BEHIND A SIGNATURE MOVE

The jump shot is basketball's equivalent of a singer's voice: All are variations on a basic theme (aim, liftoff, release), but no two are identical—and some are so distinctive that they become iconic. So when Armstrong replicates Kevin Martin's cockeyed spot-ups or Paul Pierce's splay-legged step-backs, he seems to be not just replicating a signature move but getting at some essence of the man himself.

—*Pasha Malla*, "How the Jumpshot Brought Individualism to Basketball," *The New Yorker*

Where You Find It

Figure 10.1 lists six of our favorite go-to sources for mentor texts in sports commentary and analysis.

Source	Medium	Go to for . . .
HuffPost Sports	Website, blog	*HuffPost Sports* bloggers provide rich, varied, current sports commentary and analysis; ranging from a stay-at-home-dad part-time-sports writer to a history professor, the blog offers a lot of variety.
Harvard Collective	Blog	Smart college students devoted to sports analytics.
Grantland archives	Website archives	Although this ESPN-owned sports and pop-culture blog was shut down in late 2015, the archives will forever provide favorite, relevant (although not current) mentor texts for students.
The Ringer	Digital newsletter, website	Our new favorite! Smart, topical sometimes tongue-in-cheek sports analysis delivered to your inbox every couple of days.
FiveThirtyEight	Website	Uses hard numbers to "tell compelling stories" about sports; copious charts, graphs, and images accompanying the writing.
The New Yorker: Sporting Scene	Website	The Sporting Scene offers profiles of players across all sports, as well as a few newsier pieces about trending topics.

Figure 10.1: Where to Find Sports Analysis

Key Mentors

Vinson Cunningham

Twitter handle: @vcunningham

Known for: A staff writer for the *New Yorker*, Vinson Cunningham is a perfect example of why we love sports writers—they tend to dabble in other things besides sports, bringing vast knowledge and priceless mentorship to our writers. Cunningham's knowledge of pop culture, music, and literature enriches his sports writing, affording him figures of speech and comparisons that are fresh, unique, and transcendent. When Cunningham compared teams in the NBA Finals this year to various trending television shows in his article "A Perfect NBA Season," we were hooked.

Some Mentor Texts to begin with:

- "LeBron James: King of Narrative," *The New Yorker*
- "LeBron James and Steph Curry Remind Us Who They Are," *The New Yorker*
- "A Perfect NBA Season," *The New Yorker*.

Danny Chau

Twitter handle: @dannychau

Known for: After *Grantland* shut down, we were sad to lose writers we had grown to love and depend on in our classrooms. Lucky for us, many of *Grantland*'s original writers moved over to *The Ringer*. Once again we can stalk the writings of Danny Chau. We love Chau's playful witticisms and fresh take on the world of sports. His pieces are full of delightful surprises, like this sentence from a piece about the basketball team, the Atlanta Hawks: "The Hawks' defense is a reflection of their team-first identity: They cluster together like a man-of-war, sealing access to the paint with swarms and traps before allowing their tentacles to jut out at shooters on the perimeter." Did you know sportswriting could be beautiful? Even lukewarm spectators like us become interested in titles like "By Adding Kevin Durant, Golden State Scorches the Earth" and "Golden State's Space Odyssey."

Some Mentor Texts to begin with:

- "LeBron James vs. LeBron James: The Finals MVP Writes His Own Legacy," *The Ringer*
- "Be Like Steph: LeVar Ball and His Three Sons Are Trying to Change Baskeball, One Thirty-Foot Shot at a Time," *The Ringer*
- "Peak Cavs: Why Atlanta Doesn't Stand a Chance Against This Version of Cleveland," *The Ringer*.

Kirk Goldsberry

Twitter handle: @kirkgoldsberry

Known for: A *Grantland* original, Goldsberry is a perennial favorite. Currently a visiting scholar at Harvard, Goldsberry is taking a short hiatus from sportswriting, but his most recent articles from 2015 still ring true and relevant. We admire

Kirk's bold, often contradictory titles—"Kristaps Porzingis Is a Freak—and Potentially a Superstar" and "How the Golden State Warriors Are Breaking the NBA"—chart and image-riddled web articles, and simple, clear prose (even sports newcomers like us feel comfortable digging into a Goldsberry article).

Some Mentor Texts to begin with:

- "How the Golden State Warriors Are Breaking the NBA," *FiveThirtyEight*

- "Outsider Artist: Understanding the Beauty of Steph Curry's Jumper," *Grantland*

- "Chris Paul Is a Point God," *FiveThirtyEight*.

Ideas for Student Writing

Writing what's in our hearts is no cakewalk, even for your biggest sports enthusiasts who know Steph Curry's statistics backward and forward or are eager to share their opinions about this year's Super Bowl contenders. While there may not be a shortage of passion for sports in your classroom, budding sportswriters often have trouble putting their ideas on paper. It can be helpful to have a handful of mentor texts doing the kind of work they want to do at their disposal. Figure 10.2 will help you help those students who have a vague idea of what they want to write about but are struggling to put pen to paper.

Student Wants to . . .	Might Take the Form of . . .	Mentor Texts . . .
Show the value of a player to a team	A piece that looks at how a player's contributions shape the team	"The Bulls' Offense Still Starts and (Especially) Stops with Derrick Rose" (Kirk Goldsberry, *FiveThirtyEight*)
Celebrate a player's contributions	A piece that pays homage to a player in a specific season or throughout his/her career	"God Bless Russell Westbrook, May He Never Change" (Bethlehem Shoals, *GQ*)

Figure 10.2: Ideas for Student Writing in Sports Analysis

Student Wants to . . .	Might Take the Form of . . .	Mentor Texts . . .
Analyze a player's performance	A piece that breaks down a player's performance in a specific game	"Superhero Ball—Breaking Down Lebron's Historic NBA Finals Performance" (Kirk Goldsberry, *Grantland*)
Comment on a game	A piece that comments on a single game and looks forward to the next one	"Lebron James: King of Narrative" (Vinson Cunningham, *The New Yorker*)
Discuss sports teams' dynamics	A piece that looks at the on-court relationships between players	"True Browmance: How Tyreke, Jrue, and Gentry Can Help Anthony Davis" (Kirk Goldsberry, *Grantland*)
Analyze a player's season or career	A piece that explores and evaluates a player's performance	"Russell, the Creator" (Kirk Goldsberry, *Grantland*)
Look at how a player has changed over time	A comparative piece about one player	"God Bless Russell Westbrook" (Bethlehem Shoals, *GQ*)
Analyze a new trend	An exploratory piece about a new trend or pattern	"World's Top Professional Golfers Prove That Champions Need a Rest and Recovery Strategy" (Steve Siebold, *Huffington Post*)
Explore a technique or play	A piece that explores the effects of a technique on the game	"How the Jumpshot Brought Individualism to Basketball" (Pasha Malla, *New Yorker*)

Figure 10.2: Continued

CHAPTER ELEVEN

video game analysis

A lthough not as ubiquitous as film, music, or sports analysis, video game analysis is like oxygen for some of our students. Is this game worth my allowance? How can I convince my parents to let me play this game? Have the mechanics been updated in this new version—are the weapons actually better? These are some of the questions that bring our students to video game literature time and time again.

We all teach students whose favorite pastime is video gaming. It's not uncommon to find these students hunched over a computer during a study hall, clicking their way through a game—or worse, playing their way through your class. They often come to class bone-weary and red-eyed from gaming into the wee hours of the morning. So consumed by their video game worlds, these students may be distracted, disengaged, or bored in class. But ask any of these students about the latest video game release, and they come alive. Ask any of these students what's keeping them up at night, and they'll tell you about the level they're trying to finish. Ask any of these students what the critics are saying, and they'll have their own insights to share. And it's this passion that we want to capture in class. If video games are the thing that spark joy in your students, then video game analysis must be a choice in your writing classroom.

What Writers Explore

It's no wonder that video game writers are a passionate bunch—while a video game has a lot in common with a movie (characters, setting, plot), it's also infinitely more layered and personal. A video game isn't just something you watch and appreciate; it's an entire world. A different universe in which the player lives and breathes and dies. A place players spend hours, weeks, months of their lives.

So, the stakes are high for video game writers. They are doing more than simply exploring whether the story is interesting and the graphics are realistic. They are evaluating reality itself and considering whether players should invest themselves in this world.

We ought to mention that in the world of video game analysis, the vast majority of writing takes the form of a review; you can bet that this is what your student writers will probably be writing themselves. Still, these reviews have a more expansive quality than most, zooming out broadly at points to illuminate what the game says about the world. Video game analysis is a way for some of our student writers to truly show their expert content knowledge. They shift into their own language as they delve into gameplay, modes, and theming. We often see a very different level of writing from our students when they bring the world of video games into their writing. You're going to be amazed.

The Game World

Like screenwriters, video game designers are in the business of world building. Every game is a world unto itself, complete with characters, a setting, and laws. Graphics, colors, sounds, lighting—these are the materials of the designer, as well as fodder for people who study and write about video games. These elements in a video game are so nuanced (and so new to those of us outside the gaming world) that we are going to consider each one individually to show you the language writers use and the myriad ways they consider these important game features.

GRAPHICS

Graphics are what you see on the screen—the picture. And while graphics don't necessarily make a great game, they greatly influence the player's experience. Graphics are more than how pretty things look; they're about the level of complexity the programmers put into the overall world.

When writers explore graphics, they might make discoveries about the following.

Visual Limitations

> Even though the art isn't always pretty—it's often ugly, even— *Undertale* is an incredibly expressive game from start to finish, making up for visual limitations with excellent music and charming animations.
>
> —Kallie Plagge, "Undertale Review," IGN

How Visuals Are Created

> The developers behind [*Star Wars Battlefront*] were so concerned with making it look like *Star Wars* that they actually went to Lucasfilm and got their hands on the real props and models that were used in the original trilogy, scanned them, and then made virtual recreations. That means when you see an X-Wing fly above your head in the middle of a multiplayer match, it's not just a digital version of the iconic ship, it's a digital version of the *actual* ship from the film. Does that really mean anything? No, but it's cool and it goes a long way toward making the game look like *Star Wars*.
>
> —Anthony John Agnello, Sam Barsanti, Matt Gerardi, Zack Handlen, William Hughes, and Joe Keise, "Our Favorite Games of 2015, Part One," A.V. Club

How Visuals Set a Tone

> In our age of slick aesthetics and complex game design, *Devil Daggers* feels like a dispassionate, brutalist counterpoint. . . . The horrors that you face look like they've been stripped straight from a grimy, heavy-metal-loving PlayStation 1 game, all nondescript skulls and bugs and

tentacled demon-spawning obelisks shrouded against a
backdrop of pure darkness.

—*Matt Gerardi, "Devil Daggers Is an Irresistible Sisyphean Nightmare," A.V. Club*

What the World of the Game Looks Like

The story takes place over the course of an entire summer,
with different "days"—which are treated as chapters of
the story—playing out at different hours of the day and
night. That allows bold reds, yellows, and oranges to color
this fictional Wyoming forest's beautifully painted scenery
(a contribution by renowned illustrator Olly Moss)—all in
a comfortable and immersive first-person perspective. . . .
The Two Forks Woods sticks in my mind like a real place: the
narrow passage through Thunder Canyon, the serene calm
of Jonesy Lake, the comically small size of Pork Pond, and
the unexplained mystery of the Medicine Wheel.

—*Ryan McCaffrey, "Firewatch Review: A Controlled Burn of Brilliance," IGN*

VOICEOVERS, MUSICAL SCORE, AND SOUND EFFECTS

Together, graphics and sound work to create rich imaginative worlds through
which the player navigates. Voiceovers, musical score, and sound effects add di-
mensionality to the game and can heighten a game's immersive quality. But a
poorly chosen voice actor or a subpar soundtrack can grate on players' ears. Just
like in film, the sounds should match the feel and mood of a game.

When writers explore voiceovers, musical score, and sound effects, they
might make discoveries about the following.

How Music Sets a Mood

The old-school Warp Records–style ambient electronic music,
the customizable color palette, and the quiet naming of
each stage all add texture and depth to its contained tales.

—*Anthony John Agnello, Sam Barsanti, Matt Gerardi, Zack Handlen, William Hughes,
and Joe Keise, "Our Favorite Games of 2015, Part One," A.V. Club*

Unravel is more concerned with mood than specifics, and the combination of its haunting yet soothing music with occasional images of families engaged in familiar activities is evocative without ever being entirely coherent.

—Zack Handlen, "*Unravel* Stays Tied to a Single Thread," *A.V. Club*

Sound Effects

For one thing, splash screens, text, sound effects, and music are delivered with old-school charm, while the players and animations are still current gen. And as good as the current gameplay is, it doesn't quite fit in with the loose arcade setting of the past.

—Caley Roark, "*MLB The Show 17* Review," *IGN*

Voice Performances

There is no fast-paced action or head-scratching puzzles, so the dialogue needs to carry a lot of *Firewatch's* weight. Thankfully, the nuanced and intimate performances led by *Mad Men's* Rich Sommer and Cissy Jones, of Telltale's *The Walking Dead*, are more than up to the task.

—Derrick Sanskrit, "*Firewatch* Sees Relationships Rise from the Ashes of Loss," *A.V. Club*

The Story

Stories are how we express ourselves and make sense of the world—even in the imaginative worlds of video games. While not all games have a narrative, games that integrate gameplay with storytelling are compelling in their own way. Video game writers look at all the things people writing about books, TV, and film look at: characters, setting, point of view, and genre.

When writers explore the story in a video game, they might make discoveries about the following.

CHARACTERS

Experiencing the depth of the monsters' hopes and dreams is crucial to *Undertale*'s exploration of morality, personhood, and conflict. . . . Most of the main characters are also very well developed with consistent personalities across different dialogue and story routes.

—*Kallie Plagge, "Undertale* Review," *IGN*

SETTING

The labyrinthine house will sometimes transform from a road of trials into a dungeon, trapping the artist in rooms with no exits or offering doors that open to brick walls. Paintings themselves frequently behave antagonistically, and the game wrings several scares out of images transforming, flying off walls, or sneaking up on the player. It's a world where art is uncooperative and incomprehensible, both physically and in the mind of the artist.

—*Patrick Lee, "Layers of Fear* Aims for Arty Horror, but Its Strength Is Simple Scares," *A.V. Club*

PLOT

The only thing slowing you down is *Superhot*'s story. Primarily told through text chats outside the action scenes and the occasional moment of in-game subversion, it provides a sort of meta-narrative for the game, suggesting that you're playing a game you shouldn't be and there's something far more sinister going on.

—*Matt Gerardi, "Superhot* Emulates Hollywood Fight Scenes by Letting You Make Your Own," *A.V. Club*

Pokémon's narrative echoes this philosophy as well. The beginning stages of the world are peppered with dead ends—a gym with a locked door, inaccessible islands, bushes and boulders blocking your path. Encountering these impasses early on makes it more rewarding when you return to overcome them. Similarly, your journey begins and ends with your mentor Professor Oak and a battle against your childhood rival, giving the game a pleasant circularity. Much as the Pokémon you train increase in value the longer you stay with them, the world of Pokémon is full of potential.

—Matt Crowley, "Pokémon Created a Phenomenon by Delaying Gratification," A.V. Club

Originality

Is this a rehashing of a tried and true formula? Is the new story a welcome addition to the "canon," or is this a game that is new in every aspect? These are the questions video game writers ask when considering the freshness, or originality, of a game.

When writers explore the freshness of a game, they might make discoveries about the following.

CONNECTIONS AND CALLBACKS

Devil Daggers grounds itself in the look and feel of old-school PC shooters of the '90s like DOOM and Quake, then strips the experience down into its purest elements and drops you in without explanation.

—Chloi Rad, "Devil Daggers Review," IGN

PREDICTABILITY

Walking through the same predictable hallways just doesn't make for a scary experience, especially when paired with boring clichés like creepy dolls and angsty wall scribbles. It isn't even a problem that *Layers of Fear* features traditional horror tropes to begin with—the bigger issue is that it doesn't bother to play around with these elements or repackage them as something fresh.

—*Chloi Rad*, "*Layers of Fear* Review," IGN

EVOLUTION OF GAMING

Similarly, *Titanfall* abides by the familiar core tenets of the modern military shooter, but the game's breathtaking speed and scale sets it apart as an evolutionary leap forward. There's a logical reason that *Titanfall* borrows a lot of DNA from its first-person shooter forebears. It's the first game from Respawn Entertainment, a studio that rose from the ashes of a messy divorce between Activision and some of the higher-ups at the *Call of Duty* studio, Infinity Ward. The pedigree is evident from the start. A game of *Titanfall* begins like any recent *Call of Duty* multiplayer battle might—with a deathmatch or an objective-based round between two teams of six players who are armed to the teeth.

—*Ryan Smith*, "*Titanfall* Supplants Its Ancestors with Speed and Scale," A.V. Club

Gameplay

Gameplay is hard to pinpoint with a single definition. It's the overall experience of playing a game. It's big. And it's a term you will encounter a lot in video game writing.

Gameplay encompasses everything a player does, from start to finish. It includes the rules, the obstacles, the degree of challenge, the number of player modes, the immersive experience of the game. Gameplay combines story and the mechanics of the game to create a unified experience.

When writers explore gameplay, they might make discoveries about the following.

EASE OF PLAY

> Wait a few seconds in the game's lush natural environments, and spontaneous "events" will pop up nearby, offering a chance to run a hundred feet south to fulfill one of a small handful of randomly generated beats for a few experience points. It's an unnecessary distraction that grows more annoying over time—after a few hours you've seen everything those events have to offer, and the rewards for completing them aren't worth taking the time away from other, more interesting missions.
>
> —Zack Handlen, "Beasts Are the Beauty of the Frantic, Overstuffed *Far Cry Primal*," *A.V. Club*

DETAILS IN THE GAME

> Sharp design choices permeate even tiny details of gameplay, like scene changes that vary based upon your mode of transportation as you leave each area, or a free-flowing results screen after victory in battle.
>
> —Andrew Goldfarb, "*Persona 5* Review," *IGN*

PLAYER MODES

> The dismissal of any meaningful single-player modes is disappointing and, ultimately, a wrongheaded decision. They are an invaluable training ground for players who don't care about cutthroat competition or are looking to familiarize themselves with the game's basics, and their absence is another blow to the series' already-low accessibility. Survival is the ostensible

stand-in for the more traditional modes *SF5* lacks, but its difficulty is so poorly paced and its AI opponents so inhuman that it's nowhere near an equally effective replacement.

> —*Matt Gerardi,* "No Matter What Character You Play,
> in *Street Fighter V,* We're All Ryu," *A.V. Club*

A lone player can control all four busters and take the game on solo, but it encourages play with a group of four. The fight is collaborative and demands communication. There are so few moves you can make and so many ghosts on the board that being on the same page as your teammates is key.

> —*Steve Heisler,* "*Ghostbusters: The Board Game* Channels
> the Camaraderie and Frenzy of the Films," *A.V. Club*

DEGREE OF CHALLENGE

But these light-up labyrinths quickly became more sophisticated, adding new rules and constraints to the basic maze-like structure and thus allowing for the real tough, yet fulfilling challenges to emerge.

> —*Chloi Rad,* "*The Witness* Review: A Labyrinthine Mystery
> Through a Brilliantly Designed World," *IGN*

Those first several hours are a psyche-crushing test of will. You will lose, and you will lose a lot. How you react to that adversity is what will determine whether you get anything out of *Street Fighter V.*

> —*Matt Gerardi,* "No Matter What Character You Play,
> in *Street Fighter V,* We're All Ryu," *A.V. Club*

I estimate it would take 80 to 100 hours to fully do and see everything here, but there's a satisfying amount of thematic weight and contextual clues that I was able to reach the ending the first time without feeling like *The Witness* owed me a greater answer to its riddles. Story doesn't drive *The Witness* as much as its mystery, nor does it treat story as an arbitrary reward for your efforts; what's there only enriches an already fulfilling experience.

—Chloi Rad, "*The Witness* Review: A Labyrinthine Mystery
   Through a Brilliantly Designed World," *IGN*

Both the best, and the worst, aspects of *Xenoblade Chronicles X* can be summed up in the game's most triumphant moment. After roughly 40 hours, your character finally unlocks the ability to fly. Zooming through the sky in a giant robot, blazing across territory that was once a perilous (if beautiful) slog to traverse, there's a giddy sensation of freedom that has its roots in all the hoops the game has made you jump through to finally get to this point.

—William Hughes, "You'll Have to Fight *Xenoblade Chronicles X*
   to Get at the Fun It's Hiding," *A.V. Club*

Theme/Purpose

There is more to video games than meets the eye. Behind the colorful interface and loud noises lies something deeper: a message, a purpose, a reason the game was written.

When writers explore the theme or purpose of a game, they might make discoveries about the following.

A CONNECTION TO UNIVERSAL HUMAN EXPERIENCES

Loss doesn't make people stronger. The way we cope with loss, that's where we see true character growth. The loss of a loved one, of a relationship, of a job, of trust, of sanity—these are challenges that reveal what type of person we truly are, what we'd like to be, and how hard we're willing to work to get there. Everybody in *Firewatch* is coping with loss in one manner or another.

—Derrick Sanskrit, "*Firewatch* Sees Relationships Rise from the Ashes of Loss," *A.V. Club*

Amplitude looks inward, exploring just how deeply we allow music to burrow into us and what effect it has on us once it's there. It's a music game more interested in getting you to scratch your head than shake your hips.

—Patrick Lee, "*Amplitude* Presents Music Not Just as a Reason to Live but as Life Itself," *A.V. Club*

HOW THE PLAYER HELPS SHAPE THE GAME'S MEANING

When you're not being menaced by mysterious figures, you'll spend most of your time with it following a clearly laid out story, wandering through lush backgrounds, swapping jokes with friends, and occasionally staring at a radio dial. But it's very good at what it sets out to do: Hand players the reins of an engaging horror story, and give them the tools to craft one believable teenage girl's reaction to its extraordinary events.

—William Hughes, "*Oxenfree* Tells a Great Horror Story by Taking Its Teenage Heroes Seriously," *A.V. Club*

Where You Find It

Figure 11.1 lists five of our favorite go-to sources for mentor texts in video game analysis.

Source	Medium	Go to for . . .
Gameological (*A.V. Club*)	Website	Picked up by *A.V. Club* in 2013, *Gameological* is our top pick for video game reviews; the writing here takes reviews to the next level. This website also offers some informal video game writing in columns like "What Are You Playing This Weekend?" and "Keyboard Geniuses."
IGN	Website	The reviews here are formatted in easy-to-navigate sections, which can be helpful for students new to video game writing.
Gamespot	Website	A general video gaming go-to source with news, reviews, and previews of games
Polygon	Website	*Polygon* prides itself on its ability to "bridge the gap between criticism and buying reviews." They specialize in video game reviews and video game culture writing.
Cane and Rinse	Podcast	Fully dissected video game reviews in podcast form

Figure 11.1: Where to Find Video Game Analysis

Key Mentors

We think the talented writers below could make even the most video-game-averse person want to play. Chloi Rad, Matt Ryan Smith, and Matt Gerardi are three writers who surprised us and ignited a curiosity about video games we didn't know we had.

Chloi Rad

Twitter handle: @_chloi

Known for: Video game reviews

After reading Chloi Rad's review of *Witness*, we wanted to get our hands on her entire oeuvre. A staff writer at IGN, Rad does double-duty when it comes to mentoring. Not only does she write thoughtful commentary on video games marked by double-entendre and gorgeous writing, she is a strong female voice in a male-dominated industry.

Some Mentor Texts to begin with:

- "The *Witness* Review: A Labyrinthine Mystery Through a Brilliantly Designed World," *IGN*
- "*Devil Dagger*'s Review: An Intense Arena Shooter Where Every Second Counts," *IGN*
- "*Layers of Fear* Review: A Paint-by-Numbers Horror Game That Can't Capitalize on Its Concept," *IGN*.

Ryan Smith

Twitter handle: @ryansmithwriter
Known for: Sports and video game writing

Smith isn't a one-trick pony—he also writes for *The Chicago Reader*, a Chicago news, culture, and film website, and *The Onion*, our favorite resource for satire. Our students love his sharp analogies—many of them dealing with sports—and in-your-face humor. With an active Twitter profile and the word "writer" in his handle, we choose Smith to mentor our writers into better analysis.

Some Mentor Texts to begin with:

- "Try as It Might, *Black Ops III* Can't Transcend *Call of Duty*'s Limits," *A. V. Club*
- "Video Game Culture Needs Something More Than Backward Compatibility," *A.V. Club*
- "In *Evolve*, It's Either One-for-All or One-for-Naught," *A.V. Club*.

Matt Gerardi

Twitter handle: @gerardi
Known for: Game reviews, pop culture writing

Gerardi is the editor of *Gameological*, a partner site of *The A.V. Club*. Gerardi writes notable reviews, but even cooler is the work he does in "Keyboard Geniuses," a column that smartly synthesizes the informal analysis of "keyboard geniuses," or ordinary video gamers who don't write for a living.

Some Mentor Texts to begin with:

- "*Halo 5* Is a Step Backward, but It's a Step in the Right Direction," *A.V. Club*

- "*Superhot* Emulates Hollywood Fight Scenes by Letting You Make Your Own," *A.V. Club*

- "World Warrior Music: Ranking Every *Street Fighter V* Character Theme," *A.V. Club*.

Ideas for Student Writing

Often students' ideas about video games are all over the place. They're excited about this and picky about that, and they don't know where to begin.

It can be really helpful to study a handful of mentor texts to get a feel for possible structures, focal points, and ways in. In Figure 11.2 we've matched mentor texts to "seeds"—those vague ideas students begin with that need some honing.

Student Wants to Write About ...	Might Take the Form of ...	Mentor Texts ...
How two games compare	A piece that shows how a newer game borrows from, supplants, or pales in comparison to its predecessor	"*Titanfall* Supplants Its Ancestors with Speed and Scale" (Ryan Smith, *A.V. Club*)
Theme	A piece that explores and emphasizes the underlying message of a game	"*Firewatch* Sees Relationships Rise from the Ashes of Loss" (Derrick Sanskrit, *A.V. Club*)
The occasion/story behind a game	A piece that explores the emotional significance of a game	"*That Dragon, Cancer* Review" (Lucy O'Brien, *IGN*)

Figure 11.2: Ideas for Student Writing in Video Game Analysis

Student Wants to Write About ...	Might Take the Form of ...	Mentor Texts ...
Music	Listicle in which writer ranks the theme songs of different characters	"World Warrior Music: Ranking Every *Street Fighter V* Character Theme" (Matt Gerardi, *A.V. Club*)
Video game culture	A piece about a new concept in the video game world	"Video Game Culture Needs More Than Backward Compatibility" (Ryan Smith, *A.V. Club*)
Space	A review that focuses on the effects of setting on theme	"*The Witness* Review" (Chloi Rad, *IGN*)

Figure 11.2: Ideas for Student Writing in Video Game Analysis

CHAPTER TWELVE

literary analysis

H here's the thing about analytical writing on literature: It's nowhere, and it's everywhere.

The "literary analysis" you wrote on *Of Mice and Men* when you were a high school sophomore—and may be having students write right now—doesn't exist in the real world of writers, and formal, academic analysis can be found only in academic journals. Which are read by academics. When you open *The New York Times Book Review* to find your next great read, you will not find the trappings of high school literary analysis.

But when we look past "literary analysis" to the broader, wilder, authentic world of writing, literary analysis is everywhere. It's in a retrospective looking at the significance of a writer in our culture. It's in an essay discussing how a book changed an author's relationship with her mother. It's in a review of the new must-read Jonathan Franzen novel. In nearly every digital periodical, we can find myriads about novels, nonfiction, poetry, the writers who create it, and the way it shapes our lives.

Some of our students are, in fact, passionate experts on the books and writers they love. They *want* to write about literature. Though they are at first uncomfortable breaking out of the ways they have been required to talk about literary texts in the past, they are longing to join this conversation—to break out of their familiar confines and connect the reading they love with the world they live in. These students long to write real literary analysis.

Then there are students you would never guess would *ever* choose to write about literature. But when given choice about what they read, these students discover and come to love books and writers and have thoughts and opinions they, too, want to share with the world.

Often the writing we assign students about their reading dampens and even destroys their love of it. Showing all of these students—the born-to-read and the late bloomers—what's real in the world of literary analysis can be a game changer.

What Writers Explore

The raw material for the academic literary analysis you are used to and the more authentic literary analysis your students will be writing now are essentially the same. Writers of literary analysis still consider these familiar elements—author, character, language, setting, theme—but they write about them in different ways. Instead of staying firmly anchored within the text itself, literary analysis shifts the focus, making space for the personal.

Writers of authentic literary analysis explore not only why characters behave the way they do but how their behavior illuminates and holds a mirror up to our own lives. They explore the symbolism in a novel as a way to uncover the deeper meanings in the commonplace objects of our lives. They tease out the underlying meanings in a book to turn their own lives upside down in search of meaning. These writers inherently know that a book is so much more than what happens between the front and back covers; a book is a voyage of self-discovery.

Aren't you interested in knowing how your students see themselves in the literature they read? Aren't you excited now to invite your students to this better, truer way of writing about their reading? The writing and writers you meet below will show you and your students the way to analysis that smartly probes the words on the page *and* the feelings of the reader—writing that does the intellectually and emotionally rigorous work of excavating the text and the self.

Elements of Literature

Most students will begin any literary analysis with the fundamental elements of literature that they have been studying since elementary school. Because students have likely had oodles of worksheet-riddled experiences with these concepts, they need well-chosen mentor sentences to model the difference between observing these elements in a text and elevating that observation to the point of true analysis.

SETTING

Writers consider the setting's impact on the imagery and the tone of the text. Often, a significant setting serves as a metaphor for the story itself.

Writers who explore setting might make discoveries about the following.

The Relationship Between Setting and Genre

> Landscape matters: Britain's antique countryside, strewn with moldering castles and cozy farms, lends itself to fairy-tale invention.
>
> —Colleen Gillard, "Why the British Tell Better Children's Stories," *The Atlantic*

A Writer's Jaunt into New Territory

> Atmospherically, Chevalier is a gifted conjurer of, say, the sweaty, unwashed bedding of 19th-century America. But *At the Edge of the Orchard* is a bumpy wagon ride, a slog through mud followed by a mad gallop, including some ludicrous trips up and down a mountainside.
>
> —Mary Pols, "Tracy Chevalier's *At the Edge of the Orchard* and Jane Hamilton's *The Excellent Lombards*," *The New York Times*

PLOT

Writing analytically about plot is a minefield for student writers who often wind up writing plot summary or simply naming elements of the plot pyramid ("In the rising action . . .", "The climax happens when . . ."). When students' previous experience has largely been about identifying the parts of plot, they don't have a lot of language for analyzing a plot's effectiveness. Enter mentor texts.

Writers who explore plot might make discoveries about the following.

Repurposed and Remixed Storylines

Helen Fielding's 1996 novel, *Bridget Jones's Diary*, showed that it was possible to lift Austen's story line and create a funny contemporary novel about a spirited young woman in search of love, while reminding us that *Pride and Prejudice* was one of the original screwball comedy/romcom templates.

—*Michiko Kakutani,* "Curtis Sittenfeld's *Eligible* Updates Austen's *Pride and Prejudice*," *The New York Times*

The Psychological Implications

He's also a master of slow-burning action. The plot of *Victory* moves with ruthless inevitability. . . . [t]his is a book that you read as much for the sake of the adventure story as the psychology.

—*Sam Jordison,* "How Reading Joseph Conrad Has Changed with the Times," *The Guardian*

Plot Holes and Believability

However, first we must undergo the setup, which at times feels oddly false and disconnected. As the girls make fun of Kammie for falling in the well, then take their sweet time before getting help, it's hard to believe that even the meanest of mean girls wouldn't recognize the gravity of the situation right away.

—*G. Neri,* "Book Review: *The Girl in the Well Is Me* by Karen Rivers," *The New York Times*

Plots That Fall Flat

But the novel isn't "about" anything—it's just plot, reheated from stories we already know but can't quite remember.

—*Katy Waldman,* "The Borrowed Light of the Real," *Slate*

CHARACTER

We've never read an article in the real world that describes characters as round, flat, static, or dynamic. So, how *do* writers discuss the characters that populate the stories we read? Mentors show us ways to describe, name, and evaluate characters.

Round, Rich Characters

> But Cleary's supposedly ordinary girls are complex: resentful of their mothers one moment and sympathetic toward them the next, willing to do anything for one special boy but indignant when they're taken for granted.
>
> —*Ruth Graham, "Stories for the Square Girls," Slate*

Personal Heroes

> Galt—like the boy heroes of the science fiction that I also loved—was the perfect adolescent savior, a comic-book supervillain cast as a superhero. "I will stop the engine of the world," he bragged.
>
> —*Jacob Bacharach, "Ayn Rand Made Me a Communist," The New Republic*

Characters That Fall Flat

> His characters are flat on the page, with none of the interiority and richness that would give them depth and make them live and breathe.
>
> —*Esther Wang, "Moving Beyond 'Crazy Rich Asians' in the Stories We Tell About China," Buzzfeed*

Contrasting Characters

> The swooniest parts of *Jane Eyre* are obviously those which deal with the Byronic, unhandsome, guilt-ridden, manipulative, abrasive, brooding, lying, charming, inconsolable, irresistible Mr. Rochester (who is a very

different sort than Austen's shy, prickly, snobbish, overwhelmed Mr. Darcy).

—*Lyndsay Faye, "If Jane Eyre Came out Today, Would It Be Marketed as Genre?" LitHub*

Characters Who Become Types

Hamlet gave us Claudius, the stepfather from hell; while Othello's Iago, with his ferocious intellect and charisma, is a kind of Elizabethan Hannibal Lecter. The name of the wickedly manipulative Lady Macbeth has become synonymous with female evil.

—*Peter James, "If Shakespeare Was Writing Today, He'd Be a Crime Writer," The Guardian.*

THEME

Theme is the Big Kahuna of classroom discussion and writing on literature. It's the end zone toward which we are always trying to move our students. Real writers of analysis also often uncover the theme of a text: What is the big idea of the text? What does the author want the reader to understand? What does this text mean to me?

When writers explore the theme, they might make discoveries about the following.

A Theme That Crosses Multiple Books

This is a running theme in all four books: Better to like an interesting boy who actually likes you back than to waste time pining after one who, like Johnny, is both too good and not good enough.

—*Ruth Graham, "Stories for the Square Girls," Slate*

Themes Specific to a Culture

If British children gathered in the glow of the kitchen hearth to hear stories about magic swords and talking bears, American children sat at their mother's knee listening to tales larded with moral messages about a world where life was hard, obedience emphasized, and Christian morality valued.

—*Colleen Gillard*, "Why the British Tell Better Children's Stories," *The Atlantic*

The Big Idea of a Single Text

The more you consider this strange little masterpiece, the more suggestive it becomes, shifting from a single incident at a beach to a tiny allegory of loneliness and the desire for human connection.

—*Michael Dirda*, "Michael Dirda on the Misunderstood Poet Stevie Smith," *The Washington Post*

If this book were a PowerPoint presentation, as it surely has been, the best slide would be the two equations that offer a simple proof for why grit trumps talent: Talent × effort = skill. Skill × effort = achievement. In other words, "Effort counts twice."

—*Judith Shulevitz*, "*Grit* by Angela Duckworth," *The New York Times*

Author

While sometimes considered outside the scope of serious literary analysis, analysis of the author is close reading of a different kind. A writer might bring the author into the scope of his analysis for a number of different reasons. He might be examining patterns across an author's work, arguing for the author's place within the genre, the culture, or the literary pantheon. Or the writer might be closely reading the author's biography, considering how the author's experiences can be read in her craft.

When writers explore the author, they might make discoveries about the following.

AN AUTHOR'S PLACE IN THE LITERARY WORLD

His first book, *Harmonium*, published in 1923, established Stevens as the patron saint of the inner life held captive by the outer life—a peculiarly American condition.

—*Adam Kirsch, "The Patron Saint of Inner Lives," The Atlantic*

Different as the two novels are, they both attest to Ms. Lee's professed ambition to be "the Jane Austen of South Alabama"—her eye for small, telling details; her ear for small-town chatter (and the emotional subtext beneath), and her natural storytelling instincts.

—*Michiko Kakutani, "In Harper Lee's Novels, A Loss of Innocence as Children and Again as Adults," The New York Times*

HOW THE AUTHOR'S LIFE CONTRIBUTED TO HER WORK

Bronte truly suffered through the boarding school child abuse she describes in *Jane Eyre*, which ruined the health and probably took the lives of two of her sisters. But did she embroider a sonnet about it to hang on the wall? No: she wrote a massive blockbuster barnburner about it, following in the footsteps of other successful female commercial authors like Aphra Behn, Jane Austen, and Mary Shelley.

—*Lyndsay Faye, "If Jane Eyre Came out Today, Would It Be Marketed as Genre?" LitHub*

It's easy to see her books as a reaction to this difficult early relationship with reading. Cleary understands that, unlike the characters in her school primers, children are not only concerned with "spinning tops, swinging high, and riding their stupid pretty ponies." They are worried about the world around them, concerned that they are not feeling the right feelings, or that an adult will be able to see into their thoughts.

—*Gwyneth Kelly*, "Beverly Cleary is 100. Ramona Quimby Is Timeless." *The New Republic*

Style

When analyzing a work of literature, writers must address the actual words on the page—the way the author weaves together images and phrases, plays with language, crafts sentences. Describing an author's style is often difficult for students. Mentor texts can be especially helpful in giving students models for using language—often fanciful and figurative—to characterize an author's language and voice.

When writers explore style, they might make discoveries about the following.

THE AUTHOR'S LANGUAGE

Her dense but light-fingered language holds a dozen wiggling and contradictory ideas in suspension.

—*Katy Waldman*, "Licked by Fire," *Slate*

The novel's source, no doubt, imbues it with authority, but its literary power derives from Bock's elastic language, stretching from his detailed inventories of extreme medical procedures to the lyric melancholy of his descriptions of mood and place.

—*Maureen Corrigan*, "This Novel Doesn't Find Meaning in Cancer, It Gives Malevolence Its Full Due," NPR

LENGTH OF SENTENCES

In the novel, Proust accomplishes this moment of ecstatic transport with soaring, elevated prose: his long, loopy sentences grow still longer and loopier, and we feel his narrator's yearning, his soft ache, for, well . . . things past. For lost time.

—*Glen Weldon*, "French, English, Comics: Proust on Memory, in Any Language," NPR

THE AUTHOR'S VOICE

> Then there's the utter confidence of Oyeyemi's voice and the way it dips into a conversational mode every now and then to make you feel as if you've been waved into a gossipy circle to get the real lowdown.
>
> —*Laura Miller, "I Want to Read Everything," Slate*

Literary Connections

One way that writers describe authors and their art is by comparing them to other texts and to other authors, setting the author into a bigger context as a way to build a connection for the reader. Writers use these connections to draw surprising parallels, sharp contrasts, and to situate an author in his proper literary place.

When writers explore a text's connections to other texts and authors, they might make discoveries about the following.

INFLUENCES ON THE AUTHOR

> No poet is more formally precise than Walt Whitman at his most expansive, no poet more wildly extravagant than Emily Dickinson at her most curtailed; freedom is not sloppiness, structure is not constriction. But perhaps more clearly than any other poet of the 20th century, Moore allows us to see why this is the case.
>
> —*James Longenbach, "Less Is Moore," The Nation*

CONNECTIONS BETWEEN TEXTS

> For though Franzen would no doubt bristle at the connection I'm making here between his novel and Wharton's, *Purity* is, in many ways, a rewrite of *The Children*, albeit a strikingly less sympathetic one.
>
> —*Sheila Liming, "The Puerility of Purity: How Franzen's Latest Novel Rewrites an Edith Wharton Novel You've Probably Never Heard Of," L.A. Review of Books*

QUALITIES SHARED AMONG AUTHORS

These authors have very little in common, by the way such things are typically measured: they share neither genre, style, gender, race, nor nationality. What they do share is the sense of personal urgency, the hunger, they've created in readers.

—Jedediah Purdy, "Maybe Connect," *L.A. Review of Books*

Diction and Symbolism

In literature, every word counts. Our understanding of a character's behavior or a plot development can sometimes hinge on a specific noun, verb, adjective, or even an article.

Writers of literary analysis can spend multiple sentences—or even paragraphs—exploring the denotation and connotation of a single word to understand its effect on the scene or work as a whole. Sometimes the words they probe are symbols that appear across a text, and writers study the multiple occurrences of these words throughout a text.

When writers explore diction and symbolism, they might make discoveries about the following.

THE SIGNIFICANCE OF A SINGLE WORD

Moore throws immense weight on the word "if" by dangling it at the end of two lines, and as a result, the poem asks us to hear the sentence's intonation in one particular way and not another: "*if* one is afraid"—"*if* one approaches it familiarly."

—James Longenbach, "Less Is Moore," *The Nation*

THE MEANING OF A SYMBOL

If birds assume such a central role in Thoreau, it is because they are for him undying repositories of memory. Some readers have noted that his writing employs birds as metaphors of elegiac recollection. . .

—Branka Arsic, "Henry David Thoreau's Magical Thinking," *The New Republic*

THE CONNOTATION OF THE LANGUAGE

> The language he uses regarding his new wife and their circumstances is steeped in transactional terms, though he isn't sure who exactly is in power between the two of them: "I have not bought her, she has bought me, or so she thinks."
>
> —*Bridget Read*, "Charlotte Bronte May Have Started the Fire, But Jean Rhys Burned the House Down," *LitHub*

Cultural Connections

When writers closely examine a work of literature, they don't just stop at the text itself. If they did, they would have a very limited (very scholarly) readership. Rather, writers often zoom out and consider how the text is significant in our culture, how it speaks to contemporary issues. This is another technique that can challenge students who have had limited experiences in life. These mentor sentences can show student writers how simple this zoom-out can be.

When writers explore a text's connection to the culture, they might make discoveries about the following.

HOW A TEXT SPEAKS TO A CONTEMPORARY TREND

> It's pretty clear to me why the KonMari Method has caught on in the U.S. A recurring emphasis on self-improvement and an obsession with restriction can be found in everything from diet trends (where we learn to cut calories in order to be smaller and less encumbered by literal weight), to the consumer culture fixation with replacing old things that no longer provide joy with new, "improved" things that will.
>
> —*Arielle Bernstein*, "Marie Kondo and the Privilege of Clutter," *The Atlantic*

HOW A TEXT SPEAKS TO A PROBLEM IN SOCIETY

> But books like *Knock Knock, Visiting Day,* and *The Girl in the Well Is Me* have the power to reassure millions of children that they are not alone. For young readers who are not coping with losing a parent to incarceration, these

books can provide something just as meaningful. They can help them grow into adults who see America's inmates as human beings.

—*Sarah Marshall,* "Bedtime Stories About Jail," *The New Republic*

Ms. Lee's two novels both concern the loss of illusions, and public reaction to her books provide a window on America's slow, stumbling efforts to grapple with racial inequality. They also raise important questions about the dynamic between fiction and history, and how we assess works of art from earlier eras—whether by the standards of the times in which they were written or through the prism of our values today.

—*Michiko Kakutani,* "In Harper Lee's Novels, A Loss of Innocence as Children and Again as Adults," *The New York Times*

A Text's Impact on the Reader

One of the most common explorations in literary analysis is considering how a text impacts the individual. Writers don't just record their emotions and reactions, though. They analyze their personal experiences with literature to account for its impact. Students, who, in many cases, have been conditioned to never connect the self with literature in writing particularly need models of this kind of analytical thinking.

When writers explore the text's impact on the reader, they might make discoveries about the following.

THE TEXT'S APPEAL TO THE READER

The Fountainhead was a fable for children; *Atlas* was the Word. And though I didn't actually read it until the following school year, I found it, even in the abstract, immensely appealing.

—*Jacob Bacharach,* "Ayn Rand Made Me a Communist," *The New Republic*

THE READER'S REACTION TO THE TEXT

Her cadence, her rhythm—they pulled me outside of my skin so that I was yet again more than the quicksand in my stomach.

—*S. J. Sindu,* "Sanctuary: Jeanette Winterson Saved My Life," *L.A. Review of Books*

HOW THE TEXT CONNECTS TO THE READER'S EMOTIONS

That was the winter I reread Charlotte Brontë's *Villette*, one of my favorite novels, and the one that makes me most lonely. I have always revisited it lovingly, but with trepidation. . . . For I am, admittedly, a hungry-hearted creature; I crave protagonists who seem to welcome my company, whose narration pulsates with our mutual desire: see me, hear me, witness me.

—*Rachel Vorona Cote,* "Searching for Salvation in Charlotte Bronte's *Villette*," *LitHub*

Where You Find It

Figure 12.1 lists six of our favorite go-to sources for mentor texts for literary analysis.

Source	Medium	Go to for . . .
The Atlantic	Website/magazine	Interesting and different perspectives on books old and recent—the essays here tend toward looking at how texts exist in our culture and/or impact the individual.
L.A. Review of Books	Website	Thoughtful essays on contemporary literature and writers; features an entire section of "literary criticism."
NPR Books	Website	Short but sweet book reviews and other writing about literature that students can easily digest; they also frequently have wonderful series of articles on favorite books, favorite poems, favorite characters, and so on.

Figure 12.1: Where to Find Literary Analysis

continues

Source	Medium	Go to for ...
The Guardian	Website	Weekly poem analysis, best books series, literary listicles, thoughtful book reviews, writing about global literature, writing about classic literature; they also have a weekly Guardian Books podcast.
LitHub Daily	Digital Newsletter	Chronicle of the best literary writing on the Internet; while not all of it is strictly analytical, you can get a regular stream of amazing analytical pieces you might not see in your regular haunts.
Slate Audio Book Club	Podcast	Detailed, collaborative analysis of a single text

Figure 12.1: Continued

Key Mentors

From Pulitzer Prize–winning journalists to literary podcasters, these three mentors can serve as a rich starting point for student writers' look at the literary analysis in the real world.

Michiko Kakutani

Twitter handle: @michikokakutani

Known for: As the Pulitzer Prize–winning chief book critic for *The New York Times* for the last thirty years, Michiko Kakutani is pretty much *the* book critic to read. According to her Pulitzer Prize citation, Kakutani is known for her "passionate, intelligent writing on books and contemporary literature." She is exhaustive in her research and exacting in her reading; she can also be controversial. Kakutani is particularly accessible for students because while writing beautifully, she usually writes simply and focuses on supporting her evaluation. As a long-time veteran of the *Times*, there is also a lot of writing about her writing, which is interesting for students to study.

Some Mentor Texts to begin with:

- "Curtis Sittenfeld's *Eligible* Updates Austen's *Pride and Prejudice*," *The New York Times*

- "In Harper Lee's Novels, A Loss of Innocence as Children and Again as Adults," *The New York Times*

- "Review: *Purity* Is Jonathan Franzen's Most Intimate Novel Yet," *The New York Times*.

Katy Waldman

Twitter handle: @xwaldie

Known for: Katy Waldman's writing is some of the most beautifully crafted writing in journalism. Her writing shows students that analysis can be as beautiful as it is smart. As *Slate*'s "words correspondent," Waldman writes about language in film, in television, in podcasts, and in books. Her versatility makes her a mentor students will come back to again and again for all kinds of analytical writing. While Waldman does write reviews, her writing usually has a wider scope, zooming out to look at books' impact in our culture. You can also find Waldman on *Slate*'s *Audio Book Club* podcast, discussing single texts at length.

Some Mentor Texts to begin with:

- "The Surreal, Dionysian Poetry of Prince's Lyrics," *Slate*

- "All Desserts Look Alike," *Slate*

- "There Once Was a Girl: Against the False Narratives of Anorexia," *Slate*.

Rachel Vorona Cote

Twitter handle: @RVoronaCote

Known for: Rachel Vorona Cote is a contributer to *Jezebel* as well as the *L.A. Review of Books* and *The New Republic*. She specializes in writing about classic literature in fresh ways and often features first-person anecdote and storytelling. Her funny, relatable voice is one students will instantly recognize and relate to as she pulls old-school literature into modern-day relevance.

Some Mentor Texts to begin with:

- "Are You an Anne Shirley or an Emily Starr?" *LitHub*
- "Searching for Salvation in Charlotte Bronte's *Villette*," *LitHub*
- "Virginia Woolf's Philosopher of Novelty," *Hazlitt*.

Ideas for Student Writing

While many of your students will have experience writing some kind of literary analysis, that doesn't necessarily mean they will be any more prepared to write it than they are any other type of analysis. Many students writing literary analysis will have broad understandings of the ideas that interest them but no clear sense of what form their wonderings should take. In fact, these writers might have even more trouble concretizing their concept as something *other* than a traditional five-paragraph essay they've come to know.

Figure 12.2 illustrates ideas and mentor texts to help grow the seeds of your students' interests into publishable writing.

Student Wants to Write About . . .	Might Take the Form of . . .	Mentor Text . . .
Personal connection to a book	A piece detailing how reading a book changed the reader's political views	"Ayn Rand Made Me a Communist" (Jacob Bacharach, *The New Republic*)
A poem	Poem of the week essay (à la *The Guardian*)	"Poem of the Week: 'Sonnet XIII' by William Shakespeare" (Carol Rumens, *The Guardian*)
Multiple works by a single author	A profile of an author's oeuvre	"Less Is Moore" (James Longenbach, *The Nation*)
An author	A piece providing a unique take on his/her work	"Henry David Thoreau's Magical Thinking" (Branka Arsic, *The New Republic*)

Figure 12.2: Ideas for Student Writing in Literary Analysis

Student Wants to Write About . . .	Might Take the Form of . . .	Mentor Text . . .
An opinion about a book	A savvy book review	"*The Rest of Us* Is Apocalypse Adjacent" (Tasha Robinson, NPR)
A character	A character study	"In Character" series (NPR)
A pattern they notice in the text	A literary infographic showing the relationships among characters in a play	"Shakespearean Tragedies Visualized Through Character Interactions" (*EBookFriendly*)
A small part of a text	A piece that closely reads a significant passage	"By Heart" series (*The Atlantic*)
A book's connection to society at large	A piece detailing how a text speaks to a current event	"This Week's Must Read" series (NPR)

Figure 12.2: Continued

CHAPTER THIRTEEN

gathering your own resources

A bby is a professional ballerina and a full-time high school student. She wants to write a commentary analyzing two different dancers' performances of the part of Juliet in single production of *Romeo and Juliet*. Jake is obsessed with robotics, and he wants to analyze the strength of each local school's robotics team ahead of the state competition. These are their passions. This is exactly what they should be writing about.

But where are the chapters on dance analysis? Robotics analysis? The myriad, endless kinds of analysis that are not explored in this book?

If nearly all writing is, at its core, analytical, and if students should be writing analysis that follows their passions, their interests, and their curiosities, then it stands to reason the possibilities for subgenres of analytical writing are as vast and limitless as the students sitting in our classrooms. And there just isn't room in this book to dive into every subgenre of analysis one student in one of your classes one year might choose to write.

This chapter is your how-to guide to pulling together your own resources for any and every kind of analysis under the sun—and for inviting *your students to join you* in the process. When you invite your students to join you in the process, you will be giving them a gift that reaches far beyond the scope of the writing they are doing in your class. Throughout their lives, if there is a kind of writing your students want to do, they will be able to find it and use what they find to guide and inspire their work.

Topic Expertise Meets Writing Expertise

When students have expert knowledge of a topic, it can be tempting to conclude that they don't really need us and that it's safe for us to let them hold the reins entirely. But while students might have topic expertise, they're not necessarily expert writers (yet). We still have a crucial role to play, and that's why we need resources—an overview of writing in the subgenre, highlights from the best writing, go-to mentors. These resources give us the expertise we need so we can facilitate the movement of a student's topical knowledge into sophisticated, publishable writing.

In many cases, this resource-gathering will be collaborative. Chances are good that students' writing will be sparked by their reading, so they will typically be able to get us started on our hunt. When Jake wanted to write a commentary on why a particular deck of cards should be banned in a card game, Rebekah asked him to point her in the direction of some websites that would educate her. When Robbie wanted to write how the 1969 Stingray is superior to the 1969 Mustang, Rebekah asked him to show her a mentor text in his favorite car magazine that makes a similar comparison. When Erika wanted to write a sports commentary about lacrosse sticks, Rebekah wasn't convinced her position was fresh and debatable. So, Erika went in search of articles making different arguments about the importance of lacrosse sticks to show that her claim was unique. (Believe it or not, these exist!) These mentor texts led to others as well as to key mentors and top websites for analytical writing about card games, cars, and lacrosse.

Students' expertise led the way and pointed Rebekah in the right direction. It helped her get started so that she could then add to their resources, talk with them more intelligently in writing conferences, and begin to ask questions and make suggestions that would take their writing to the next level.

How to Use What You Find

Ultimately, you will use your newly gathered resources in the same way you used those provided for you in the other Section 3 chapters. The biggest difference will be that these resources will be used with a single student (perhaps two or three if that student is persuasive and gathers followers) rather than a small group of like-minded writers. In addition to getting a feel for the topic yourself, these resources might help an individual student:

- Hone and polish her idea.
- Move beyond the basics and explore the breadth of the topic in her writing to meet her reader's expectations.
- Increase the sophistication of her writing on the sentence level by providing mentor sentences for individual study.
- Branch out and explore a variety of sources known for writing in this subgenre and find her own mentor texts.
- Identify personal mentor writers.

Of course, you know your students best. In some cases, you might be able to hand him or her a mentor text and simply say, "Give this a read, see what you think, and consider how you might use this in your piece. I'll check back in with you later." Another student will need considerably more one-on-one work time in writing conferences, moving through whole articles or mini mentor texts with you and discussing the implications for the work step by step. Most students will need a balance of both.

How to Gather Your Own Resources

In *Writing with Mentors*, we urged teachers to use their regularly scheduled, daily reading lives to propel their search for mentor texts. Finding mentor texts doesn't have to be difficult, we argued, because great writing that can guide and inspire students' lives everywhere.

But, that's the rub, isn't it? Many of these subgenre outliers won't be in your regular reading diet. Your students may be introducing you to writing you didn't even know existed. But that doesn't mean you need to revert to spending endless hours randomly searching for texts that might work. Here are some methods we've found to get us to the best resources faster.

Start with a Go-To Source

When feeling shaky about culling resources for an unfamiliar topic, start with your trusted, go-to sources. You have seen many of ours throughout Section 3 in the "Where to Find It" section of each chapter. Feel free to adopt them as your own! While they may not yield exactly what you are looking for, working with a publication you know has solid writing will make you feel more comfortable as you navigate a new topic.

For example, when Rebekah conferred with Mary Kate, she revealed that while she did not yet have a narrowed topic or specific claim, she wanted to write a piece of analysis on dogs. Mary Kate did not have a regular diet of pet-centric reading, so she wasn't able to kick off Rebekah's search with a great recommendation. Utterly lost, Rebekah headed straight to some of her favorite sites for smart analytical writing.

We've learned that before we launch into a search, we should consider which of our go-to sources is most likely to address the student's chosen topic. This might seem like a no-brainer, but taking a moment to breathe and really think through the best option gets us to the finish line faster than haphazard googling and random searching.

In this case, Rebekah knew that she would need to use the best sources for general writing that covers a wide variety of topics. She could rule out sites that specialize in analysis of pop culture, sports, or music. She chose *The New York Times*, NPR, *The Atlantic,* and *The Guardian.*

You might also consider special interest magazines and publications that may contain the kind of writing your students are looking for. One trick is to search the magazine subscriptions at amazon.com. Amazon offers over twenty-five different categories of magazines, ranging from news and political commentary to animal care and pets to literary, sci-fi, and mystery. Enter your search terms, and discover a plethora of magazines and journals that exist on your topic. For example, the keyword "dog" yielded more than half a dozen magazines devoted specifically to writing about dogs. From there, you might decide to purchase a magazine or see if your local library carries it. The bottom line is: If there is even a small group of people in the world who share a similar interest, there is a gazine (online or print) devoted to writing about that interest.

ASK: WHAT KIND OF ANALYTICAL WRITING EXISTS ON THIS TOPIC?

It's important to focus on the word "analytical" here since a search of *The New York Times* might bring up myriad articles on medical advancements in the care of dogs or profiles of soldiers who use therapy dogs, but these are not necessarily analysis. We need to be vigilant about making sure that the resources we pull will help students write analysis. (And we need to help students be vigilant about this in their own searches, too!) It's easy to get excited about an interesting article that isn't analytical and forget that goal.

Figure 13.1 shows what Rebekah found in thirty minutes of searching to find resources for Mary Kate's dog analysis.

DO SOME READING

Or, at least do a lot of skimming, looking for pieces that have potential to help your student. It goes without saying that you are looking for pieces that are well-written. That's why you have started with a trusted source that you know will feature writing full of notable craft. So, beyond that, you are looking for pieces that:

- Are accessible to your student.
- Represent a range of perspectives, claims, and writing techniques.
- Have tangible text and craft features that can guide student writing.

As you are reading, you might find articles and essays that just won't work as a whole text for one reason or another—content, length, difficulty—but they *do* have brilliant moments you could share with your students. Go ahead and pull

The New York Times	NPR	*The Atlantic*	*The Guardian*
Analysis of the ethics of getting a dog from a breeder versus a shelter	Film analysis of a movie about a dog	Essay analyzing the relationship between humans and dogs in light of new genetic research	Personal essay arguing that there has never been a better time to rescue a dog
An op-ed about the harm caused by leaving dogs alone for too long		Commentary on what practices of eating dog meat reveal about cultural taboos	Op-ed on why allowing dogs in the office is a good idea
A few reviews of nonfiction books about dogs		Essay on why we love dogs in spite of the pitfalls of dog ownership	Essay on why workplaces should give paid leave to care for pets
Analysis of the Westminster Dog Show		Essay arguing that dogs are the "single greatest force" protecting US soldiers	
Personal essay analyzing the places people (illegally) take their dogs			

Figure 13.1: Analytical Writing About Dogs in Four Go-To Sources

these excerpts to include as mini mentor texts or for individual sentence study. These smaller bites of inspiration can often make seeing a writer's moves easier for student writers, particularly for struggling writers.

Your big goal here, though, is to observe the ways writers analyze the given topic and to hopefully find one (or two) great mentor texts to help you begin moving forward. In Rebekah's hunt, she honed in on two pieces that she thought might be especially useful: "Is Your Pet Lonely and Bored?" from *The New York Times* and "We Need War Dogs, More Than Ever" from *The Atlantic*. These pieces had clear, strong claims and featured structures and craft that Rebekah thought could help Mary Kate shape her ideas.

Locate the Experts

When our students write wholehearted analysis, the expertise in the classroom shifts. Students become content experts, and teachers become experts on writing and on their students. The *other* experts who guide students' work, of course, are the mentor writers students will apprentice themselves to as they study mentor texts.

After learning a bit about analysis in the subgenre and having located a couple of strong mentor texts, we begin to look to the expert mentors to help us flesh out a broader mentor text cluster.

ASK: WHAT ELSE HAS THIS MENTOR WRITTEN?

We move forward by researching the writers of our key mentor texts: Do they regularly write on this topic? If so, what else have they written recently? Could those pieces also be useful resources to show how to write analysis on this topic?

In many publications, you can simply click on the writer's name to see what else he or she has written on that site. And just a minute or two on Twitter will connect you with the writer's feed, full of links to his or her recent writing.

ASK: WHAT ELSE IS THIS MENTOR READING?

One of the best things about finding a great mentor writer in a student's chosen subgenre is that he or she can introduce you (virtually, of course) to a host of other mentor texts and writers. Chances are good that if the mentor is well-known for his writing on a particular topic, he is doing a lot of reading (and tweeting and retweeting) on that topic, too. And these new discoveries can help flesh out a group of mentor texts, adding a variety of perspectives and writing styles to the resources we share.

Take Rebecca Frankel (@becksfrankel), for example. She is the author of "We Need War Dogs, More Than Ever" and a weekly article in *Foreign Policy*, "Rebecca's War Dog of the Week." In this column, Frankel writes about the role of dogs in the US military. Some of it is news and some articles are profiles of heroic war dogs, but there are also handfuls of articles analyzing the issues that surround animals in combat. While these would also be helpful resources for Mary Kate, a scan of her Twitter feed reveals links to articles by other writers analyzing the role of combat dogs in history, an essay analyzing the similarities between the way people feel about children and they way they feel about their dogs, and more! Each of these could also serve as a helpful resource for Mary Kate.

Crowdsource

When all else fails, a personal learning network of like-minded teachers on Twitter can be the very best place to connect with expert writers and great writing on any topic. Allison has tweeted writers asking them specifically for recommendations. Writers who specialize in a topic can lead you to other interesting articles and writers.

So can our personal learning network. On any given day, we will sound a call to our teacher colleagues, like, "What are your favorite pieces of nonfiction writing about dogs?" and suggestions will roll in. You will also be able to tap into the individual reading preferences of the users you follow. We go directly to our friend Jay Nickerson (@doodlinmunkeyboy) for writing on comics and nerd culture. Karla Hilliard (@karlahilliard) is our girl for smart cultural analysis. Never underestimate the power of a think tank. That's what you have on Twitter.

You might also consider sharing the workload with a colleague who is also opening the doors to her students for wholehearted, authentic analysis. Search for and contribute resources to the *Moving Writers* mentor text dropbox (https://movingwriters.org/mentor-text-dropbox-project/).

Study and Organize Your Findings

Once you have assembled a group of mentor texts for a specific kind of analysis, you can study the texts more carefully, look for patterns in the writing, and figure out:

- The essential components of writing in this subgenre (What Writers Explore)
- Best sources for finding analysis on this topic (Where to Find It)
- A few of the best writers on this topic (Key Mentors)
- A few full-length mentor texts that might help students refine their ideas and develop a plan for writing (Ideas for Student Writing).

We find that these categories are a good way to organize our notes as we study, but there is no need to flesh out each section to the extent that we have in the previous chapters. Writing down bits and pieces of what you have found and why it works will help you down the road as you work with students. And don't underestimate the power of sharing the behind-the-scenes work you're doing with students. When Kiera tells you she wants to write a piece of fashion analysis, be honest with her. Tell her that you don't know much about it, but you're going to go in search of it, and together you'll figure out how it's written. And then, later, when you have a much clearer sense of the work that fashion writers do, show her how you came to this understanding—share your chicken-scratch notes and walk her through the process.

In the end, remember that you can always support students with mentor texts you've already found for other purposes. Even if you don't have any writing on hand about a student's specific topic, you might have different analytical pieces whose structure, tone, or use of evidence can help that writer think about his topic.

Let's Be Honest

OK. Yes. This *is* a considerable amount of work for that singular student who has an unusual passion and a wild idea. So why not steer him away from the go-kart analysis he dreams of writing and instead encourage some good old film analysis? Because while he might love his favorite movie, his heart—his *whole* heart—is invested in something else. That's what you want him to write about.

When we give our time and extra effort to pull resources for a single inspired student, we validate his vision. We say, "Your idea is important, and I am going to give you my full attention to help see it to fruition." That validation pushes beyond the single piece of writing—it validates the student's identity as a writer.

Over time, you will develop resources for all sorts of topics that other, future students might need as well. (Mary Kate probably won't be the last student we ever have who's interested in writing about dogs!) But even if you don't, gathering the resources to help a student become the writer he *wants* to be is always worth it.

References

Abad-Santos, Alex. 2017. "Review: *Guardians of the Galaxy, Volume 2* is Marvel's Funniest Film, and Much Braver Than the Original." *Vox,* May 5. Accessed May 31, 2017. www.vox.com/culture /2017/4/26/15414840/guardians-of-the-galaxy-vol-2-review.

Adamcyzk, Laura. 2016. "*My Girl* Delivered Death in an Unbearably Precocious Package." *A.V. Club*, November 28. Accessed May 31, 2017. www.avclub.com/article/25-years-ago-my-girl -delivered-death-unbearably-pr-245967?scrlybrkr=5d68ca22.

Agnello, Anthony John, Sam Barsanti, Matt Gerardi, Zack Handlen, William Hughes, and Joe Keiser. 2015. "Our Favorite Games of 2015, Part One." *A.V. Club*, December 21. Accessed June 1, 2017. www.avclub.com/article/our-favorite-games-2015-part-one-229608?scrlybrkr=5d68ca22.

Als, Hilton. 2016. "Beywatch." *New Yorker*, May 30. Accessed June 1, 2017. www.newyorker.com /magazine/2016/05/30/beyonces-lemonade?scrlybrkr=f59cd3c9.

Arsic, Branka. 2016. "Henry David Thoreau's Magical Thinking." *New Republic*, February 8. Accessed June 1, 2017. https://newrepublic.com/article/129218/henry-david-thoreaus-magical -thinking.

Bacharach, Jacob. 2016. "Ayn Rand Made Me a Communist." *New Republic*, January 27. Accessed June 1, 2017. https://newrepublic.com/article/128441/ayn-rand-made-communist.

Bastien, Angelica Jade. 2016. "*Legends of Tomorrow* Recap: Fire and Ice." *Vulture*, March 4. Accessed May 31, 2017. www.vulture.com/2016/03/legends-of-tomorrow-recap-season-1 -episode-7.html.

Baumann, Michael. 2017. "A Good Man Behind the Plate Is Hard to Find." *The Ringer*, April 5. Accessed May 31, 2017. https://theringer.com/2017-mlb-best-catchers-gary-sanchez-buster -posey-3ef28e28252d.

Baumann, Michael. 2017. "*The Expanse* Steals Gracefully from All Your Favorite Shows." *The Ringer*, April 13. Accessed May 31, 2017. https://theringer.com/the-expanse-syfy-tv-game-of -thrones-battlestar-galactica-bb64d5169dec.

———. 2017. "Andrelton Simmons Is Peerless." *The Ringer*, April 27. Accessed May 31, 2017. https://theringer.com/mlb-shortstops-los-angeles-angels-andrelton-simmons-119c55e84657.

Bergreen, Laurence. 2003. *Over the Edge of the World*. New York: Harper Collins.

Bernstein, Arielle. 2016. "Marie Kondo and the Privilege of Clutter." *The Atlantic*, March 25. Accessed June 1, 2017. www.theatlantic.com/entertainment/archive/2016/03/marie-kondo-and-the-privilege-of-clutter/475266/.

Blair, Elizabeth. 2008. "Henry Fleming: Reluctantly Wearing 'The Red Badge." NPR, July 20. Accessed May 31, 2017. www.npr.org/templates/story/story.php?storyId=92469448&scrlybrkr=ef910d1a.

Blair, Ian F. 2016. "Enjoying March Without the Madness." *New Yorker,* April 4. Accessed June 1, 2017. www.newyorker.com/news/sporting-scene/enjoying-march-without-the-madness?scrlybrkr=f59cd3c9.

Blau, Sheridan. 2003. *The Literature Workshop*. Portsmouth: Heinemann.

Bomer, Katherine. 2016. *The Journey Is Everything*. Portsmouth: Heinemann.

Breihan, Tom. 2017. "America Had Never Seen Anything Like *Crouching Tiger, Hidden Dragon*." *A.V. Club*, May 5, 2017. Accessed May 31, 2017. www.avclub.com/article/america-had-never-seen-anything-crouching-tiger-hi-254611?scrlybrkr=5d68ca22.

Brogan, Jacob. 2017. "Why *Frankenstein* Is Still Relevant, Almost 200 Years After It Was Published." *Slate*, January 3. Accessed May 31, 2017. www.slate.com/articles/technology/future_tense/2017/01/why_frankenstein_is_still_relevant_almost_200_years_after_it_was_published.html?scrlybrkr=7027ae7e.

Brooks, David. 2017. "The Home-Buying Decision." *New York Times*, January 6. Accessed May 31, 2017. www.nytimes.com/2017/01/06/opinion/the-home-buying-decision.html?_r=0.

Brusie, David. 2016. "Tom Petty's *Greatest Hits* Record Remains the Best of Best-Ofs." *A.V. Club*, July 26. Accessed June 1, 2017. www.avclub.com/article/tom-pettys-greatest-hits-record-remains-best-best--239423?scrlybrkr=5d68ca22.

Bullard, Kurt. 2016. "Kicking Off Spring: The Impact of the New Touchback on Kickoff Return Strategy." *Harvard Sports Analysis*, March 24. Accessed June 1, 2017. http://harvardsportsanalysis.org/2016/03/6580/.

Burke, Monte. 2016. "Win over Clemson Clinches It: Nick Saban Is the Greatest College Coach Ever." *Forbes*, January 12. Accessed June 1, 2017. www.forbes.com/sites/monteburke/2016/01/12/nick-saban-is-the-greatest-college-football-coach-of-all-time/#453e4e0818f9.

———. 2016. "Nick Saban and the Triumph of Coaching." *Forbes*, January 13. Accessed June 1, 2017. www.forbes.com/sites/monteburke/2016/01/13/nick-saban-and-the-triumph-of-coaching/#49e0a8c9669c.

Business of Fashion.com. 2017. "Why Edward Enninful Will Be Good for British Vogue." April 11. Accessed May 31, 2017. www.businessoffashion.com/articles/bof-comment/why-edward-enninful-will-be-good-for-british-vogue.

Caramanica, Jon. 2017. "What Happened to J. Crew?" *New York Times*, May 25. Accessed July 15, 2017. www.nytimes.com/2017/05/24/fashion/what-happened-to-jcrew.html.

Chaney, Jen. 2017. "How *13 Reasons Why* Compares to '80s Pop Culture About Suicide." *Vulture*, May 4. Accessed May 31, 2017. www.vulture.com/2017/05/13-reasons-why-and-pop-culture-about-teen-suicide.html?scrlybrkr=b97276da.

Chau, Danny. 2016. "Peak Cavs: Why Atlanta Doesn't Stand a Chance Against This Version of Cleveland. *The Ringer*, May 4. www.theringer.com/2016/5/6/16037852/peak-cavs-why-atlanta-doesnt-stand-a-chance-against-this-version-of-cleveland-3af138b4ebe.

Clark, Kevin. 2017. "The NFL Game of the Year: Packers–Cowboys Finally Delivers a Playoff Classic." *The Ringer*, January 15. Accessed May 31, 2017. https://theringer.com/packers-cowboys-rodgers-classic-playoffs-ccf8911cb5d4.

Cliff, Aimee. 2017. "Why Lorde Is a Great Dancer." *Fader*, April 25. Accessed May 31, 2017. www.thefader.com/2017/04/25/lorde-dancing-green-light-snl-coachella.

Coerner, Brendan I. 2014. "Reading Peyton Manning." *The New Yorker*, January 19. Accessed May 31, 2017. www.newyorker.com/news/sporting-scene/reading-peyton-manning?scrlybrkr=f59cd3c9.

Collins, K. Austin. 2017. "Chris Pratt Is Not a Movie Star." *The Ringer*, May 4. Accessed May 31, 2017. https://theringer.com/chris-pratt-movie-star-leading-man-guardians-of-the-galaxy-99a6cb775e8c.

Concepcion, Jason. 2017. "No Layups '90s Basketball Is Alive and Well in Celts–Wizards." *The Ringer*, May 5. Accessed May 31, 2017. https://theringer.com/2017-nba-playoffs-boston-celtics-washington-wizards-fighting-fouling-trash-talking-330e8274860a.

Corrigan, Maureen. 2016. "This Novel Doesn't Find Meaning in Cancer, It Gives Its Malevolence Full Due." NPR, April 5. Accessed June 1, 2017. www.npr.org/2016/04/05/473099735/this-novel-doesnt-find-meaning-in-cancer-it-gives-its-malevolence-full-due?scrlybrkr=ef910d1a#.

Cote, Rachel Vorona. 2016. "Searching for Salvation in Charlotte Bronte's *Villette*." *LitHub*, April 21. Accessed June 1, 2017. http://lithub.com/searching-for-salvation-in-charlotte-brontes-villette/.

———. 2016. "Are You an Anne Shirley or an Emily Starr?" *LitHub*, October 27. Accessed May 31, 2017. http://lithub.com/are-you-an-anne-shirley-or-an-emily-starr/.

Crowley, Matt. 2016. "*Pokemon* Created a Phenomenon by Delaying Gratification." *A.V. Club*, February 26. Accessed June 1, 2017. www.avclub.com/article/pokemon-created-phenomenon-delaying-gratification-232056?scrlybrkr=5d68ca22.

Cruz, Colleen. 2015. *The Unstoppable Writing Teacher*. Portsmouth: Heinemann.

Culham, Ruth. 2003. *6 + 1 Traits of Writing: The Complete Guide, Grades 3 and Up*. New York: Scholastic.

Cunningham, Vinson. 2016. "The Perfect NBA Season." *New Yorker*, April 15. Accessed June 1, 2017. www.newyorker.com/news/sporting-scene/a-perfect-n-b-a-season?scrlybrkr=f59cd3c9.

Dargis, Manohla. 2016. "Review: *The Wave* Is a Disaster Movie Making a Big Splash." *New York Times*, March 3. Accessed May 31, 2017. www.nytimes.com/2016/03/04/movies/the-wave-review.html?ref=movies.

Delahoyde, Michael. 2011. "New Criticism," *Introduction to Literature*, January 6. Accessed May 16, 2017. https://public.wsu.edu/~delahoyd/new.crit.html.

Dirda, Michael. 2016. "Michael Dirda on the Misunderstood Poet Stevie Smith." *The Washington Post*, March 16. Accessed May 31, 2017. www.washingtonpost.com/entertainment/books/michael-dirda-on-the-misunderstood-poet-stevie-smith/2016/03/16/e623b074-e62b-11e5-a6f3-21ccdbc5f74e_story.html?utm_term=.9ecb6ab4f6df.

Dowd, A. A. 2017. "*Life* Comes at You Fast When You're Being Hunted by a Hostile Space Octopus." *A.V. Club*, March 23. Accessed June 1, 2017. www.avclub.com/review/life-comes-you-fast-when-youre-being-hunted-hostil-252580?scrlybrkr=5d68ca22#.

Edelstein, David. 2016. "*Whiskey Tango Foxtrot* Plays It Safe and Suffers for It." *Vulture*, March 3. Accessed May 31, 2017. www.vulture.com/2016/03/review-whiskey-tango-foxtrot-takes-norisks .html?scrlybrkr=b97276da.

———. 2017. "When It Comes to Tech Thrillers, *The Circle* Is Pretty Square." *Vulture*, April 28. Accessed May 31, 2017. www.vulture.com/2017/04/the-circle-movie-review.html?scrlybrkr =b97276da#.

Eliot, Joanna. 2014. *Infographic Guide to Literature*. New York: Cassell.

Erlewine, Stephen Thomas. 2016. "Why Merle Haggard Was a Country Music Game-Changer." *Pitchfork*, April 7. Accessed June 1, 2017. http://pitchfork.com/thepitch/1089-why-merle-haggard -was-a-country-game-changer/?scrlybrkr=a8530c61.

———. 2016. "Why the Death of Greatest Hits Albums and Reissues Is Worth Mourning." *Pitchfork*, May 2. Accessed June 1, 2017. http://pitchfork.com/features/article/9887-why-the -death-of-greatest-hits-albums-and-reissues-is-worth-mourning/?scrlybrkr=a8530c61.

Faye, Lyndsay. 2016. "If *Jane Eyre* Came out Today Would It Be Marketed as Genre?" *LitHub*, April 21. Accessed June 1, 2017. http://lithub.com/if-jane-eyre-came-out-today-would-it-be -marketed-as-genre/.

Fitzgerald, Helena. 2016. "The Presumptions of Boyfriend Clothes." *Racked*, September 26. Accessed May 31, 2017. www.racked.com/2016/9/26/12907446/boyfriend-jeans-shirts -heteronormativity-expectation.

Flaherty, Colleen. 2015. "Major Exodus." *Inside Higher Ed,* January 26. Accessed August 26, 2016. www.insidehighered.com/news/2015/01/26/where-have-all-english-majors-gone.

Franich, Darren. 2017. "The Crucial Importance and Splendid Madness of *Friday Night Lights* Season 2." *Entertainment Weekly*. February 7.

Garber, Megan. 2016. "The Spin Zone." *The Atlantic*, May 10. Accessed May 31, 2017. www.the atlantic.com/entertainment/archive/2016/05/the-spin-zone/482133/.

Gerardi, Matt. 2016. "No Matter What Character You Play, in *Street Fighter V*, We're All Ryu." *A.V. Club*, February 24. Accessed June 1, 2017. www.avclub.com/review/no-matter-what-character -you-play-street-fighter-v-232713?scrlybrkr=5d68ca22.

———. 2016. "*Devil Daggers* Is an Irresistible Sisyphean Nightmare." *A.V.Club*, February 26. Accessed June 1, 2017. www.avclub.com/article/devil-daggers-irresistible-sisyphean-nightmare -232853?scrlybrkr=5d68ca22.

———. 2016. "*Superhot* Emulates Hollywood Fight Scenes by Letting You Make Your Own." *A.V. Club*, March 3. Accessed June 1, 2017. www.avclub.com/review/superhot-emulates-hollywood -fight-scenes-letting-y-233122?scrlybrkr=5d68ca22.

Gilbert, Sophie. 2017. "'The Body': The Radical Empathy of *Buffy*'s Best Episode." *The Atlantic*, March 9. Accessed May 31, 2017. www.theatlantic.com/entertainment/archive/2017/03/the -body-the-radical-empathy-of-buffys-best-episode/519051/.

Gillard, Colleen. 2016. "Why the British Tell Better Children's Stories." *The Atlantic*, January 6. Accessed May 31, 2017. www.theatlantic.com/entertainment/archive/2016/01/why-the-british -tell-better-childrens-stories/422859/.

Giorgis, Hannah. 2017. "*Dear White People* Doesn't Know How to Reckon with 2017." *The Ringer*, May 3. Accessed May 31, 2017. https://theringer.com/dear-white-people-netflix-tv-show-2017 -473a56842803.

Goldfarb, Andrew. 2017. "*Persona 5* Review." *IGN*, March 29. Accessed June 1, 2017. www.ign.com /articles/2017/03/29/persona-5-review?watch&scrlybrkr=c2c63e1c.

Goldsberry, Kirk. 2015. "Chris Paul Is a Point God." *FiveThirtyEight*, November 18. Accessed June 1, 2017. https://fivethirtyeight.com/features/chris-paul-is-a-point-god/.

Gonzalez, John. 2017. "Mike Brown Has the Best Job in the World." *The Ringer*, May 5. Accessed May 31, 2017. https://theringer.com/2017-nba-playoffs-mike-brown-golden-state-warriors -steve-kerr-6d139d1b6458.

Goodman, Mike L. 2015. "No Messi, No Problem: Neymar Becomes a Superstar." *Grantland*, October 30. Accessed May 31, 2017. http://grantland.com/the-triangle/la-liga-fc-barcelona -neymar-superstar-messi-injury/.

Gopnik, Adam. 2016. "Long Play." *New Yorker*, April 25. Accessed June 1,2017. www.newyorker .com/magazine/2016/04/25/paul-mccartneys-magnificent-melodic-gift?scrlybrkr=f59cd3c9.

Grady, Constance. 2017. "Lorde Is the Celebrity Avatar of Pop Culture's Witch Obsession." *Vox*, May 4. May 31, 2017. www.vox.com/culture/2017/5/4/15340512/lorde-witch-vibes-aesthetic.

Graff, Gerald, and Cathy Birkenstein. 2014. *They Say, I Say*. New York: W. W. Norton & Co.

Graham, Ruth. 2016. "Stories for the Square Girls." *Slate*, April 12. Accessed June 1, 2017. www .slate.com/articles/arts/books/2016/04/beverly_cleary_s_novels_about_teenage_girls _fifteen_the_luckiest_girl_jean.html?scrlybrkr=7027ae7e.

Handlen, Zack. 2016. "*Unravel* Stays Tied to a Single Thread." *A.V. Club*, February 9. Accessed June 1,2017. www.games.avclub.com/unravel-stays-tied-to-a-single-thread-1798188552.

———. 2016. "Beasts Are the Beauty of the Frantic, Overstuffed *Far Cry Primal*." *A.V. Club*, February 25. Accessed June 1, 2017. www.avclub.com/article/titanfall-supplants-its-ancestors -speed-and-scale-202272?scrlybrkr=5d68ca22.

Hassenger, Jesse. 2016. "Clever Subtext Often Trumps Jokes in Disney's *Zootopia*." *A.V. Club*, March 2. Accessed May 31, 2017. www.avclub.com/review/clever-subtext-often-trumps-jokes -disneys-zootopia-232930?scrlybrkr=5d68ca22.

Heard, Georgia. 1999. *Awakening the Heart: Exploring Poetry in Elementary and Middle School*. Portsmouth: Heinemann.

———. 2014. *The Revision Toolbox*, 2nd edition. Portsmouth: Heinemann.

———. 2016. *Heart Maps: Helping Students Create and Craft Authentic Writing*. Portsmouth: Heinemann.

Heer, Jeet. 2015. "Star Wars Films Are Not About Good vs. Evil. They're About Bad Parenting." *New Republic*, December 30. Accessed May 31, 2017. https://newrepublic.com/article/126798 /star-wars-films-not-good-vs-evil-theyre-bad-parenting.

Heisler, Steve. 2015. *Ghostbusters: The Board Game* Channels the Camaraderie and Frenzy of the Films." *A.V. Club*, December 15. Accessed June 1, 2017. www.avclub.com/review /ghostbusters-board-game-channels-camaraderie-and-f-229642?scrlybrkr=5d68ca22.

Herman, Alison. 2017. "ABC Experiments with the Network Miniseries." *The Ringer*, March 13. Accessed May 31, 2017. https://theringer.com/abc-miniseries-when-we-rise-american-crime -b1318c140d1e.

———. "Netflix's Extremely Busy April." *The Ringer*, May 2. Accessed May 31, 2017. https://theringer .com/netflix-april-2017-adam-sandler-chelsea-handler-dear-white-people-4c4b9b0b418d.

Holmes, Linda. 2017. "*Top Chef* Is Delivering a Satisfying Season Right on Time." NPR, February 23. Accessed May 31, 2017. www.npr.org/sections/monkeysee/2017/02/23/516824213/top-chef-is-delivering-a-satisfying-season-right-on-time?scrlybrkr=ef910d1a.

———. 2017. "*Missing Richard Simmons* and the Nature of Being Known." NPR, March 21. Accessed May 31, 2017. www.npr.org/sections/monkeysee/2017/03/21/520943717/missing-richard-simmons-and-the-nature-of-being-known?scrlybrkr=ef910d1a.

———. 2017. "*Veep* Reinvents Itself in the Shape of a New Humiliation." NPR, April 17. Accessed May 31, 2017. www.npr.org/sections/monkeysee/2017/04/17/524333817/veep-reinvents-itself-in-the-shape-of-a-new-humiliation?scrlybrkr=ef910d1a.

———. 2017. "Hey You, Prestige Television Fan: Here's Why You Should See a New Play." NPR, April 18. Accessed May 31, 2017. www.npr.org/sections/monkeysee/2017/04/18/523930863/hey-you-prestige-television-fan-heres-why-you-should-see-a-new-play?scrlybrkr=ef910d1a.

———. 2017. "The Good and Goofy *Great News* Comes to NBC." NPR, April 25. Accessed May 31, 2017. www.npr.org/sections/monkeysee/2017/04/25/525536592/the-good-and-goofy-great-news-comes-to-nbc?scrlybrkr=ef910d1a.

Hughes, William. 2015. "You'll Have to Fight *Xenoblade Chronicles X* to Get to the Fun It's Hiding." *A.V. Club*, December 3. Accessed June 1, 2017. www.avclub.com/review/youll-have-fight-xenoblade-chronicles-x-get-fun-it-229086?scrlybrkr=5d68ca22.

———. 2016. "*Oxenfree* Tells a Great Horror Story by Taking Its Teenage Heroes Seriously." *A.V. Club*, January 19. Accessed June 1, 2017. www.avclub.com/review/oxenfree-tells-great-horror-story-taking-its-teena-230764?scrlybrkr=5d68ca22.

Ihnat, Gwen. 2017. "Why Are There So Many Shows About Time Travel Right Now?" *A.V. Club*. March 2. www.tv.avclub.com/why-are-there-so-many-shows-about-time-travel-right-1798258622.

Jackson, Panama. 2017. "Do You Watch *Greenleaf*? You Might Should Watch *Greenleaf*." *VSB*, April 28. Accessed May 31, 2017. http://verysmartbrothas.com/watch-greenleaf/.

James, Peter. 2016. "If Shakespeare Was Writing Today, He'd Be a Crime Writer." *Guardian*, April 23. Accessed June 1, 2017. www.theguardian.com/books/2016/apr/23/shakespeare-crime-writer-today-roy-grace-peter-james.

Jenkins, Craig. 2016. "Red Hot Chili Peppers' *The Getaway* Is Their Best in Years." *Vulture*, June 20. Accessed June 1, 2017. www.vulture.com/2016/06/album-review-red-hot-chili-peppers-the-getaway.html?scrlybrkr=b97276da.

Johnson, Jenna, and Abigail Hauslohner. 2017. "'I Think Islam Hates Us': A Timeline of Trump's Comments about Islam and Muslims." *Washington Post*, May 20. Accessed May 31, 2017. www.washingtonpost.com/news/post-politics/wp/2017/05/20/i-think-islam-hates-us-a-timeline-of-trumps-comments-about-islam-and-muslims/?utm_term=.0797765277c6.

Jordison, Sam. 2015. "How Reading Joseph Conrad Has Changed with the Times." *Guardian*, October 13. Accessed June 1, 2017. www.theguardian.com/books/booksblog/2015/oct/13/joseph-conrad-changing-faces-victory.

Kakutani, Michiko. 2016. "In Harper Lee's Novels, a Loss of Innocence as Children and Again as Adults." *New York Times*, February 19. Accessed June 1, 2017. www.nytimes.com/2016/02/20/books/in-harper-lees-novels-a-loss-of-innocence-as-children-and-again-as-adults.html.

———. 2016. "Curtis Sittenfeld's *Eligible* Updates Austen's *Pride and Prejudice*." *New York Times*, April 11. Accessed May 31, 2017. www.nytimes.com/2016/04/12/books/-2016-04-12-books-eligible-curtis-sittenfeld-review.html.

Kelly, Gwyneth. 2016. "Beverly Cleary Is 100. Ramona Quimby Is Timeless." *New Republic*, April 12. Accessed June 1, 2017. https://newrepublic.com/article/132599/beverly-cleary-100-ramona -quimby-timeless.

Kermode, Mark. 2015. "*Steve Jobs* Review: Decoding a Complex Character." *Guardian*: November 15. Accessed May 31, 2017. www.theguardian.com/film/2015/nov/15/steve-jobs-film-review -aaron-sorkin-danny-boyle-michael-fassbender.

Kirsch, Adam. 2016. "The Patron Saint of Inner Lives." *The Atlantic*, April. Accessed June 1, 2017. www.theatlantic.com/magazine/archive/2016/04/the-patron-saint-of-inner-lives/471468/?utm _source=SFTwitter.

Kittle, Penny. 2008. *Write Beside Them*. Portsmouth: Heinemann.

Lake, Thomas. "The Book of Tebow." *Sports Illustrated*. Accessed June 1, 2017. www.si.com /longform/tebow/index.html#asection-1.

Larrington, Carolyne. 2016. "How to Win the Game of Thrones." *1843*, June 22. Accessed May 31, 2017. www.1843magazine.com/culture/the-daily/how-to-win-the-game-of-thrones.

Leclair, Catherine. 2017. "Carhartt Is the Uniform of Both the Right and the Left." *Racked*, April 17. Accessed May 31, 2017. www.racked.com/2017/4/17/15226134/carhartt-wip-right-left -america-workwear.

Lee, Patrick. 2016. "*Amplitude* Presents Music Not Just as a Reason to Live but as Life Itself." *A.V. Club*, January 7. Accessed June 1, 2017. www.avclub.com/review/amplitude-presents-music-not -just-reason-live-life-230204?scrlybrkr=5d68ca22.

———. 2016. "*Layers of Fear* Aims for Arty Horror, But Its Strength Is Simple Scares." *A.V. Club*, March 1. Accessed June 1, 2017. www.avclub.com/review/layers-fear-aims-arty-horror-its -strength-simple-s-232977?scrlybrkr=5d68ca22.

Lehman, Christopher, and Kate Roberts. 2014. *Falling in Love with Close Reading: Lessons for Analyzing Texts—and Life*. Portsmouth: Heinemann.

Liming, Sheila. 2016. "The Puerility of *Purity*: How Franzen's Latest Novel Rewrites an Edith Wharton Novel You've Probably Never Heard Of." *L.A. Review of Books*, March 11. Accessed June 1, 2017. https://lareviewofbooks.org/article/the-puerility-of-purity-how-franzens-latest-novel -rewrites-an-edith-wharton-novel-youve-probably-never-heard-of.

Livingstone, Josephine. 2017. "The Passion of Rei Kawakubo." *New Republic*, May 3. Accessed May 31, 2017. https://newrepublic.com/article/142457/passion-rei-kawakubo.

Longenbach, James. 2016. "Less Is Moore." *The Nation*, March 31. Accessed May 31, 2017. www .thenation.com/article/less-is-moore/.

Lord, Jo. 2016. "Restaurant Review: East Coast Provisions Reimagined, Rebranded, and (Mostly) Remarkable." *Richmond Times-Dispatch*, December 14. Accessed May 31, 2017. www.richmond .com/food-drink/restaurant-reviews/restaurant-review-east-coast-provisions-reimagined -rebranded-and-mostly-remarkable/article_90c0a3ae-55d4-59b1-8638-275b6cad5126.html.

Malla, Pasha. 2016. "How the Jumpshot Brought Individualism to Basketball." *New Yorker*, March 14. Accessed June 1, 2017. www.newyorker.com/news/sporting-scene/how-the-jump -shot-brought-individualism-to-basketball?scrlybrkr=f59cd3c9.

Marshall, Sarah. 2016. "Bedtime Stories About Jail." *New Republic*, April 19. Accessed June 1, 2017. https://newrepublic.com/article/132808/bedtime-stories-jail.

Marzorati, Gerald. 2016. "The Twilight of Nadal." *New Yorker*, March 7. Accessed June 1, 2017. www.newyorker.com/news/sporting-scene/the-twilight-of-nadal?scrlybrkr=f59cd3c9.

McCaffrey, Ryan. 2016. "*Firewatch* Review." *IGN*, February 8. Accessed June 1, 2017. www.ign
.com/articles/2016/02/08/firewatch-review?watch&scrlybrkr=c2c63e1c.

Miller, Laura. 2016. "I Want to Read Everything." *Slate*, April 25. Accessed June 1, 2017. www
.slate.com/articles/arts/books/2016/04/helen_oyeyemi_s_short_story_collection_what_is
_not_yours_is_not_yours_reviewed.html?scrlybrkr=7027ae7e.

Moffett, James. 1994. "Coming Out Right." In *Taking Stock: The Writing Process Movement in the
'90s*. Edited by Thomas Newkirk and Lad Tobin. Portsmouth: Heinemann, 1994.

Molanphy, Chris. 2017. "Bruno Mars' New No. 1 Proves He's the Canniest Hit-Maker of the
Decade." *Slate,* May 5. Accessed May 31, 2017. www.slate.com/blogs/browbeat/2017/05/05
/why_bruno_mars_that_s_what_i_like_is_no_1_on_the_hot_100.html?scrlybrkr=7027ae7e.

Murray, Donald. 1968. "Give Your Students the Writer's Five Experiences." In *Learning by
Teaching*. Portsmouth: Heinemann, 1982.

———. 1973. "What Can You Say Besides Awk?" In *Learning by Teaching*. Portsmouth:
Heinemann, 1982.

———. 1974. "'What, No Assignments?'" In *Learning by Teaching*. Portsmouth: Heinemann, 1982.

———. 1977. "Our Students Will Write—If We Will Let Them." In *Learning by Teaching*.
Portsmouth: Heinemann, 1982.

———. 1985. *A Writer Teaches Writing*. Boston: Houghton Mifflin Harcourt.

Neary, Lynn. 2008. "Jo March: Everyone's Favorite Little Woman." NPR, June 8. Accessed May 31,
2017. www.npr.org/templates/story/story.php?storyId=91245378&scrlybrkr=ef910d1a.

Neri, G. 2016. "*The Girl in the Well Is Me* by Karen Rivers." *New York Times*, March 11. Accessed
June 1, 2017. www.nytimes.com/2016/03/13/books/review/the-girl-in-the-well-is-me-by-karen
-rivers.html?rref=collection%2Fcolumn%2Fchildrensbooks&action=click&contentCollection
=review&region=stream&module=stream_unit&version=latest&contentPlacement=5&pgtype
=collection&_r=0.

Newkirk, Thomas. 2005. *The School Essay Manifesto*. Shoreham: Discover Writing.

Newman, Judith. 2017. "Dear Book Club: It's You, Not Me." *New York Times*, May 11. Accessed May
31, 2017. www.nytimes.com/2017/05/11/books/dear-book-club-its-you-not-me.html.

New York Press Room. 2016. "Craig Jenkins and Jen Chaney Join Vulture." *New York Magazine*,
May 24. www.nymag.com/press/2016/05/craig-jenkins-and-jen-chaney-join-vulture.html.

Nichols, John. 2016. "David Bowie, the 'Apolitical' Insurrectionist Who Taught Us How to Rebel."
The Nation, January 11. Accessed June 1, 2017. www.thenation.com/article/david-bowie-the
-apolitical-insurrectionist-who-taught-us-how-to-rebel/.

North, Anna. 2015. "Writing Is the Process of Abandoning the Familiar." *The Atlantic*, May 19.
Accessed May 30, 2017. www.theatlantic.com/entertainment/archive/2015/05/by-heart
-writing-means-wandering-into-the-unknown/393602/.

NPR Staff. 2016. "11 Very Different Opinions About the New Radiohead Album." NPR, May 10.
Accessed June 1, 2017. www.npr.org/sections/therecord/2016/05/10/477441132/11-very
-different-opinions-about-the-new-radiohead-album?scrlybrkr=ef910d1a.

Nussbaum, Emily. 2016. "Not-Guilty Pleasure." *New Yorker*: February 8 and 15. Accessed May
31, 2017. www.newyorker.com/magazine/2016/02/08/not-guilty-pleasure?scrlybrkr=f59cd3c9.

———. 2017. "Archie's and Veronica's Misconceived Return to *Riverdale*." *New Yorker*, April 3. Accessed May 31, 2017. www.newyorker.com/magazine/2017/04/03/archies-and-veronicas -misconceived-return-to-riverdale?scrlybrkr=f59cd3c9.

———. 2017. "Goodbye *Girls*: A Fittingly Imperfect Finale." *The New Yorker*, April 18. Accessed May 31, 2017. www.newyorker.com/culture/cultural-comment/goodbye-girls-a-fittingly -imperfect-finale?scrlybrkr=f59cd3c9.

O'Brien, Lucy. 2016. "*That Dragon, Cancer* Review." *IGN*, January 15. Accessed May 31, 2017. www.ign.com/articles/2016/01/15/that-dragon-cancer-review?scrlybrkr=c2c63e1c.

"Occupational Employment and Wages, May 2015: Education, Training, and Library Occupations." *Bureau of Labor and Statistics*. Accessed July 29, 2016. www.bls.gov/oes/current /oes250000.htm.

Oliver, Lauren. 2014. "*I'll Give You the Sun* by Jandy Nelson." *The New York Times*, November 6. Accessed May 31, 2017. www.nytimes.com/2014/11/09/books/review/ill-give-you-the-sun-by -jandy-nelson.html.

Paine, Neil. 2014. "Advanced Stats Love Jackie Robinson." *FiveThirtyEight*, April 16. Accessed June 1, 2017. https://fivethirtyeight.com/datalab/advanced-stats-love-jackie-robinson/.

———. 2016. "Kobe Haters Are Stuck in 2008." *FiveThirtyEight*, April 14. Accessed June 1, 2017. https://fivethirtyeight.com/features/kobe-haters-are-stuck-in-2008/.

Paine, Neil and Carl Bialik. 2016. "How Losing to the Celtics Changes the Warriors' Odds of 73 Wins." *FiveThirtyEight*, April 2. Accessed June 1, 2017. https://fivethirtyeight.com/features/how -losing-to-the-celtics-changes-the-warriors-odds-of-73-wins/.

Paskin, Willa. 2017. "The Other Side of Anne of Green Gables." *New York Times*, April 27. Accessed May 31, 2017. www.nytimes.com/2017/04/27/magazine/the-other-side-of-anne-of -green-gables.html.

Plagge, Kallie. 2016. "*Undertale* Review." *IGN*, January 12. Accessed May 31, 2017. www.ign.com /articles/2016/01/13/undertale-review?scrlybrkr=c2c63e1c.

Plaschke, Bill. 2016. "As Hero or Villain, Kobe Bryant Never Took the Middle Ground." *L.A. Times*, April 17. Accessed June 1, 2017. http://www.latimes.com/sports/lakers/la-sp-kobe -plaschke-20160417-column.html?scrlybrkr=93dd3f06.

Pols, Mary. 2016. "Tracy Chevalier's *At the Edge of the Orchard* and Jane Hamilton's *The Excellent Lombards*." *New York Times,* April 21. Accessed June 1, 2017. www.nytimes.com/2016/04/24 /books/review/tracy-chevaliers-at-the-edge-of-the-orchard-and-jane-hamiltons-the-excellent -lombards.html?rref=collection%2Fsectioncollection%2Fbook-review&action=click&content Collection=review&region=stream&module=stream_unit&version=latest&contentPlacement =9&pgtype=sectionfront&_r=0.

Poniewozik, James. 2016. "Review: *Fuller House* Is a Forced March Down Memory Lane." *New York Times*, February 26. Accessed May 31, 2017. www.nytimes.com/2016/02/27/arts/television /fuller-house-netflix-review.html.

Purdy, Jedediah. 2015. "Maybe Connect." *L.A. Review of Books*, October 4. Accessed June 1, 2017. https://lareviewofbooks.org/article/maybe-connect.

Rabinowitz, Abigail. 2016. "Donald Trump and Freshman Essays." *Guernica*. September 13. Accessed September 13, 2016. www.guernicamag.com/donald-trump-and-freshman-essays/.

Rad, Chloi. 2016. "*The Witness* Review." *IGN*, January 25. Accessed June 1, 2017. www.ign.com /articles/2016/01/25/the-witness-review?scrlybrkr=c2c63e1c.

———. 2016. "*Layers of Fear* Review." *IGN*, February 14. Accessed June 1, 2017. www.ign.com /articles/2016/02/14/layers-of-fear-review?scrlybrkr=c2c63e1c.

———. 2016. "*Devil Daggers* Review." *IGN*, February 26. Accessed June 1, 2017. www.ign.com /articles/2016/02/27/devil-daggers-review?scrlybrkr=c2c63e1c.

Read, Bridget. 2016. "Charlotte Bronte May Have Started the Fire, but Jean Rhys Burned Down the House." *LitHub*, April 21. Accessed June 1, 2017. http://lithub.com/charlotte-bronte-may -have-started-the-fire-but-jean-rhys-burned-down-the-house/.

Redmond, Shana L. 2016. "Faith Under Fire: Jay Z's 'Spiritual' Is a Modern Song of Sorrow." NPR, July 13. Accessed June 1, 2017. www.npr.org/sections/therecord/2016/07/13/485743005/faith -under-fire-jay-zs-spiritual-is-a-modern-song-of-sorrow?scrlybrkr=ef910d1a.

Roark, Caley. 2017. "*MLB the Show 17* Review." *IGN*, March 27. Accessed June 1,2017. www.ign .com/articles/2017/03/27/mlb-the-show-17-review?watch&scrlybrkr=c2c63e1c.

Robinson, Tasha. 2017. "*And We're Off* Proves Brevity's Not Always the Soul of Wit." NPR, May 7. Accessed May 31, 2017. www.npr.org/2017/05/07/525769373/and-were-off-proves-brevitys-not -always-the-soul-of-wit?scrlybrkr=ef910d1a.

Romeo, Nick. 2017. "Cormac McCarthy Explains the Unconscious." *New Yorker*, April 22. Accessed May 31, 2017. www.newyorker.com/books/page-turner/cormac-mccarthy-explains -the-unconscious?scrlybrkr=f59cd3c9.

Romm, Jake. 2016. "Why Trump's *Time* Cover Is a Subversive Work of Political Art." *Forward*, December 8. Accessed May 31, 2017. http://forward.com/culture/356537/why-times-trump -cover-is-a-subversive-work-of-political-art/.

Rumens, Carol. 2016. "Poem of the Week: 'Jasper' by Tony Conran." *Guardian*, April 25. Accessed June 1, 2017. www.theguardian.com/books/booksblog/2016/apr/25/poem-of-the-week-jasper -by-tony-conran.

Sanskrit, Derrick. 2016. "*Firewatch* Sees Relationships Rise from the Ashes of Loss." *A.V. Club*, February 8. Accessed May 31, 2017. www.avclub.com/article/firewatch-sees-relationships-rise -ashes-loss-231876?scrlybrkr=5d68ca22.

Scott, A. O. 2016. "*Moonlight*: Is This the Year's Best Movie?" *The New York Times*, October 20. Accessed May 31, 2017. www.nytimes.com/2016/10/21/movies/moonlight-review.html.

———. 2016. "Review: *Hidden Figures* Honors Three Black Women Who Helped NASA Soar." *New York Times*, December 22. Accessed May 31, 2017. www.nytimes.com/2016/12/22/movies /hidden-figures-review.html.

Seabrook, Andrea. 2008. "Hester Prynne: Sinner, Victim, Object, Winner." NPR, March 2. Accessed May 31, 2017. www.npr.org/2008/03/02/87805369/hester-prynne-sinner-victim -object-winner?scrlybrkr=ef910d1.

Serrano, Shea. 2017. "The Mixed Blessings of the NBA Playoffs." *The Ringer*, April 26. Accessed May 31, 2017. https://theringer.com/2017-nba-playoffs-nbshea-spurs-kawhi-leonard-warriors -kevin-durant-33fd66416b44.

———. 2017. "The Spurs Need LeMarcus Aldridge to Rejoin the Living." *The Ringer*, May 3. Accessed May 31, 2017. https://theringer.com/2017-nba-playoffs-lamarcus-aldridge-san-antonio -spurs-132c69008a4e.

———. 2017. "The James Harden Pick-and-Roll Is Nightmare Fuel for Defenders." *The Ringer*, May 5. Accessed May 31, 2017. https://theringer.com/2017-nba-playoffs-terror-moves-james -harden-isaiah-thomas-john-wall-e894a87cbb9b.

Sheehan, Jason. 2016. "Reading the Game: *No Man's Sky*." NPR, December 11. Accessed May 31, 2017. www.npr.org/sections/alltechconsidered/2016/12/11/504876059/reading-the-game-no -mans-sky?scrlybrkr=ef910d1a.

———. 2016. "Reading the Game: *The Last of Us*." NPR, December 31. Accessed May 31, 2017. www .npr.org/sections/alltechconsidered/2016/12/31/505592646/reading-the-game-the-last-of-us ?scrlybrkr=ef910d1a.

———. 2017. "Reading the Game: *Shadow of Mordor*." NPR, February 27. Accessed May 31, 2017. www.npr.org/sections/alltechconsidered/2017/02/24/515685000/reading-the-game-shadow -of-mordor?scrlybrkr=ef910d1a.

———. 2017. "Reading the Game: *Stardew Valley*." NPR, April 27. Accessed May 31, 2017. www .npr.org/sections/alltechconsidered/2017/04/29/523940086/reading-the-game-stardew-valley ?scrlybrkr=ef910d1a.

Sheffield, Rob. 2016. "Review: Lady Gaga's *Joanne* Is Her Best in Years." *Rolling Stone*, October 21. Accessed June 1, 2017. www.rollingstone.com/music/albumreviews/review-lady-gagas-joanne -w446032?scrlybrkr=9d803542.

Sherman, Rodger. 2017. "Gonzaga Made the Foul of the Year to Secure a Trip to the Championship." *The Ringer*, April 3. https://theringer.com/2017-ncaa-tournament-gonzaga-south -carolina-4b8633df5d5d.

Shulevitz, Judith. 2016. "*Grit* by Angela Duckworth." *New York Times*, May 4. Accessed June 1, 2017. https://mobile.nytimes.com/2016/05/08/books/review/grit-by-angela-duckworth.html ?smid=fb-nytimes&smtyp=cur&referer=http://m.facebook.com.

Simmons, Bill. 2016. "LeBron Is Still Painting His Masterpiece." *The Ringer*, October 25. Accessed May 31, 2017. https://theringer.com/lebron-is-still-painting-his-masterpiece-bdad85037eb0.

———. 2017. "The Greatest, Best, and Most Historic NBA MVP Column Ever." *The Ringer*, April 14. Accessed May 31, 2017. https://theringer.com/bill-simmons-2017-nba-mvp-james-harden -russell-westbrook-kawhi-leonard-4f617e8d5df5.

Sindu, S. J. 2016. "Sanctuary: Jeanette Winterson Saved My Life." *L.A. Review of Books*, April 20. Accessed June 1, 2017. http://lareviewofbooks.org/article/sanctuary-jeanette-winterson -saved-life/.

Skrebels, Joe. 2017. "*Little Nightmares* Review." *IGN*, April 26. Accessed May 31, 2017. www.ign .com/articles/2017/04/26/little-nightmares-review?scrlybrkr=c2c63e1c.

Smith, Ryan. 2014. "*Titanfall* Supplants Its Ancestors with Speed and Scale." *A.V. Club*, March 18. Accessed June 1, 2017. www.avclub.com/article/titanfall-supplants-its-ancestors-speed-and -scale-202272?scrlybrkr=5d68ca22.

SPIN staff. 2016. "The 100 Greatest David Bowie Moments." *SPIN*, January 16. Accessed June 1, 2017. www.spin.com/2016/01/100-greatest-david-bowie-moments/.

Stockman, Angela. 2015. *Make Writing: 5 Teaching Strategies That Turn Writer's Workshop into a Maker Space*. Hack Learning Series. Cleveland: Times 10 Publications.

Strauss, Valerie. 2017. "We Are Teaching Kids How to Write All Wrong—and No, Mr. Miyagi's Rote Lessons Won't Help a Bit." *Washington Post*, May 8. Accessed May 8, 2017. www.washington post.com/news/answer-sheet/wp/2017/05/08/we-are-teaching-kids-how-to-write-all-wrong-and-no-mr-miyagis-rote-lessons-wont-help-a-bit/?utm_term=.7b2dafb90514.

Stuever, Hank. 2016. "You Already Know *Fuller House* Is Bad. But Are You Adult Enough to Resist It?" *Washington Post*, February 26. Accessed May 31, 2017. www.washingtonpost.com /entertainment/tv/you-already-know-fuller-house-is-bad-but-are-you-adult-enough-to-resist -it/2016/02/24/b2116982-d994-11e5-925f-1d10062cc82d_story.html?utm_term=.a3acbb36c127.

Temple, Emily. 2017. "Who Will Win the Literary Kentucky Derby?" *LitHub*, May 5. Accessed May 31, 2017. http://lithub.com/who-will-win-the-literary-kentucky-derby/.

Thompson, Wright. 2016. "The Secret Life of Tiger Woods." *ESPN*, April 21. Accessed June 1, 2017. www.espn.com/espn/feature/story/_/id/15278522/how-tiger-woods-life-unraveled-years -father-earl-woods-death?scrlybrkr=39c45192.

Threadgould, Michelle. 2017. "The Cult of Selena and the Fiesta de la Flor Festival." *Racked*, April 18. Accessed May 31, 2017. www.racked.com/2017/4/18/15245272/selena-image-fiesta-de-la-flor -festival.

Tolentino, Jia. 2017. "Ivanka Trump Wrote a Painfully Oblivious Book for Basically No One." *New Yorker*, May 4. Accessed May 31, 2017. www.newyorker.com/books/page-turner/ivanka-trump -wrote-a-painfully-oblivious-book-for-basically-no-one?scrlybrkr=f59cd3c9#.

Tucker, Ken. 2017. "Kendrick Lamar Extends His Vocal and Emotional Range on *DAMN*." NPR, April 27. Accessed May 31, 2017. www.npr.org/2017/04/27/525879802/kendrick-lamar-extends -his-vocal-and-emotional-range-on-damn?scrlybrkr=ef910d1a.

Travers, Peter. 2015. "The Revenant." *Rolling Stone*, December 22. Accessed May 31, 2017. www .rollingstone.com/movies/reviews/the-revenant-20151222?scrlybrkr=9d803542.

Vanderhoof, Erin. 2016. "Beyoncé with the Good Art." *The Nation*, May 9. Accessed June 1, 2017. www.thenation.com/article/beyonce-with-the-good-music-lemonade-review/.

Vinton, Vicki. 2017. *Dynamic Teaching for Deeper Reading*. Portsmouth: Heinemann.

Viruet, Pilot. 2017. "*Dear White People* Is Hilarious, Real, and Necessary." *Vice*, April 27. Accessed May 31, 2017. www.vice.com/en_us/article/dear-white-people-is-hilarious-real-and-necessary.

Vishnevetsky, Ignatiy. 2016. "The Coens Swipe at Religion, Counterculture, and Hollywood in *Hail, Ceasar!*" *A.V. Club*, February 23. Accessed June 1, 2017. www.avclub.com/review/coens -swipe-religion-counterculture-and-hollywood--231650?scrlybrkr=5d68ca22.

Vulture editors. 2016. "7 Best New Songs of the Week." *Vulture*, July 12. Accessed June 1, 2017. www.vulture.com/2016/07/this-weeks-best-new-music-jay-z-schoolboy-q.html?scrlybrkr =b97276da.

Vulture staff. 2017. "Mac DeMarco's *This Old Dog* and 8 Other Albums to Listen to Right Now." *Vulture*, May 5. Accessed May 31, 2017. www.vulture.com/2017/05/albums-this-week-mac -demarco-slowdive-pond-and-more.html?scrlybrkr=b97276da.

Waldman, Katy. 2016. "The Borrowed Light of the Real." *Slate*, March 18. Accessed June 1, 2017. www.slate.com/articles/arts/books/2016/03/joyce_maynard_s_under_the_influence _reviewed.html?scrlybrkr=7027ae7e.

———. 2016. "Licked by Fire." *The Atlantic*, April 8. Accessed June 1, 2017. www.slate.com /articles/arts/books/2016/04/sallie_tisdale_s_violation_reviewed.html?scrlybrkr=7027ae7e.

———. 2017. "Spectacle and Imposter." *Slate*, April 20. Accessed May 31, 2017. www.slate.com /articles/arts/books/2017/04/double_bind_women_on_ambition_reviewed.html?scrlybrkr =7027ae7e.

Walker, Kara. 2015. "Toni Morrison's *God Help the Child*." *New York Times*, April 13. Accessed May 31, 2017. www.nytimes.com/2015/04/19/books/review/toni-morrisons-god-help-the-child .html?_r=1#.

Wang, Esther. 2016. "Moving Beyond 'Crazy Rich Asians' in the Stories We Tell About China." *Buzzfeed*, April 19. Accessed June 1, 2017. www.buzzfeed.com/estherwang/chinese-encounters -in-novels?scrlybrkr=92f51312&utm_term=.olN1RNl3R#.dvJdjN69j

Weidenfeld, Lisa. 2016. "*House of Cards* Is as Frustrating and Enjoyable as Ever." *A.V. Club*, March 2. Accessed May 31, 2017. www.avclub.com/review/house-cards-frustrating-and-enjoyable -ever-232749?scrlybrkr=5d68ca22.

Weldon, Glen. 2015. "French, English, Comics: Proust on Memory, in Any Language." NPR, July 12. Accessed June 1, 2017. www.npr.org/sections/monkeysee/2015/07/12/421156566/french -english-comics-proust-on-memory-in-any-language?scrlybrkr=ef910d1a.

———. 2017. "*The Lego Batman Movie* Drags The Caped Crusader." NPR, February 8. Accessed June 15, 2017. www.npr.org/sections/monkeysee/2017/02/08/513979164/the-lego-batman -movie-drags-the-caped-crusader-out-of-the-shadows-again.

———. 2017. "A Guide to Free Comic Book Day 2017: The Don't-Misses and the Near-Misses." NPR, May 5. Accessed May 31, 2017. www.npr.org/sections/monkeysee/2017/05/05/525707610 /a-guide-to-free-comic-book-day-2017-the-dont-misses-and-the-near-misses?scrlybrkr =ef910d1a.

Wilkinson, Alissa. 2017. "The Summer Movie Sequels and Reboots to Watch and the Ones Nobody Needed." *Vox*, May 2. Accessed May 31, 2017. www.vox.com/summer-movies/2017/5/2 /15331304/summer-movies-sequels-reboots-Ranked.

———. 2017. "Why Silly Summer Movies Matter." *Vox,* May 26. Accessed May 31, 2017. www.vox .com/summer-movies/2017/5/5/15506482/summer-movies-matter-sexy-robots.

Zaleski, Annie. 2016. "Fleetwood Mac's *Mirage* Is a Well-Crafted Diamond in the Rough." *A.V. Club*, July 25. Accessed June 1, 2017. www.avclub.com/article/fleetwood-macs-mirage-well -crafted-diamond-rough-239731?scrlybrkr=5d68ca22.

Zoladz, Lindsay. 2016. "With Her New Solo Album (and Her New Relationship) Gwen Stefani Proves the Value of Public Insecurity." *Vulture*, March 6. Accessed June 1, 2017. www.vulture .com/2016/03/gwen-stefani-this-is-what-the-truth-feels-like.html?scrlybrkr=b97276da.

———. 2017. "Drake, Chance the Rapper, and the Millennial Divide." *The Ringer,* June 14. Accessed June 1, 2017. https://theringer.com/drake-chance-the-rapper-millenials-a3d59f1c3477.

ALSO AVAILABLE
from Allison Marchetti and Rebekah O'Dell

grades 9–12

ALLISON MARCHETTI • REBEKAH O'DELL

writing with mentors

HOW TO REACH EVERY
WRITER IN THE ROOM
USING CURRENT, ENGAGING
MENTOR TEXTS

FOREWORD BY PENNY KITTLE

Heinemann
DEDICATED TO TEACHERS™

Grades 9-12 • 978-0-325-07450-4
2015 • 224pp • $25.50

In *Writing with Mentors*, Allison and Rebekah prove that the key to cultivating writers who can see value and purpose for writing beyond school is using dynamic, hot-off-the-press mentor texts. In this practical guide, they provide strategies for:

- finding and storing fresh mentor texts from trusted traditional sources to the social mediums of the day

- grouping mentor texts in clusters that show a diverse range of topics, styles, and approaches

- teaching with lessons that demonstrate the enormous potential of mentor texts a every stage of the writing process.

READ A SAMPLE AT Heinemann.com